PETER
SCHMEICHEL
ONE

MY AUTOBIOGRAPHY

with Jonathan Northcroft

HODDER

First published in Great Britain in 2021 by Hodder & Stoughton
An Hachette UK company

This paperback edition published in 2022

2

A CIP catalogue record for this title is available from the British Library

Paperback ISBN 978 1 529 35412 6
eBook ISBN 978 1 529 35414 0

Typeset in Minion Pro by Hewer Text UK Ltd, Edinburgh
Printed and bound in Great Britain by Clays Ltd, Elcograf S.p.A.

Hodder & Stoughton policy is to use papers that are natural, renewable
and recyclable products and made from wood grown in sustainable
forests. The logging and manufacturing processes are expected to
conform to the environmental regulations of the country of origin.

Hodder & Stoughton Ltd
Carmelite House
50 Victoria Embankment
London EC4Y 0DZ

www.hodder.co.uk

To my mother and father. The original risk mode team. If they hadn't gone to all that trouble, none of this would have happened.

CONTENTS

FOREWORD
by Eric Cantona

We had just won the FA Cup final against Liverpool in 1996. After the match the club organised a big dinner at a hotel to celebrate the victory. We had a few beers, which were well deserved after winning the Double again. There was a band – with a pianist and a trumpet player – providing music for the event. Peter can play the piano very well, and I had started learning the trumpet during my suspension for the famous kung fu kick. So we asked if we could play with them. They agreed, no doubt curious to see how we were going to do.

Peter sat down at the piano and I picked up the trumpet. The drummer accompanied us, and the 100 people in our audience (players, families and friends) dutifully listened (they were very polite). I remember Peter playing very well, but I also remember that I did too. That must have been the effect of the alcohol – like when you're drunk and you feel you can speak good Russian in Russia – because in reality I am as bad as Peter is accomplished. But there is something that strikes me about that moment: is it better to remember yourself as being good when you were bad, or as being bad when you were good? My overriding memory is of feeling very free – and that's more than enough for me.

Peter was a great companion – not just in that musical moment, but throughout my years at Manchester United. When we played away from home the team would leave the day before and spend the night in a hotel. Peter and I would share. People tell me that nowadays players have their own rooms with a massive bed. How times have changed. Back then, it was the two of us in one room: the giant that is Peter (6 ft 4 in) and me (6 ft 2 in) in two narrow single beds. It was a bit cramped, but we still managed to move mountains together with our friends for United.

Peter is a born leader. He has the gift of being able to put everyone at ease and a natural authority that makes him respected on and off the field. On the pitch, as a goalkeeper, he was the last line of defence. In front he had ten team-mates to protect him and I can tell you that if one of them wasn't putting the effort in, Peter was there, standing over him, yelling in his face – and more often than not the team-mate in question would remember his message for months and years to come. I was on the receiving end once, so I know what I'm talking about, and I couldn't say anything back because Peter was right a thousand times over. That is how you win the respect of others. Screaming and shouting, yes – but only when it is necessary, when it is for the right cause and the right reasons.

Peter was also the first goalkeeper to come out of his goal and confront an opponent the way a handball goalkeeper does. Without diving, standing tall, stretching out his arms and legs to spread himself as much as possible. Today all goalkeepers do that, but Peter was the first. Just as Antonín Panenka has a penalty named after him, we should call this move a 'Peter Schmeichel'.

A bientôt, mon ami.

PREFACE

When you love something, give your life to something, it has to have some kind of meaning. Because if not, then what? I guess this is a book about the why, and so much of what I want to say was shown to the world at Parken Stadium, Copenhagen, on 17 June 2021.

Denmark were playing Belgium in Group B at Euro 2020, five days after Christian Eriksen's cardiac arrest in their opening game of the tournament, against Finland. Those moments when Christian lay lifeless on the grass, as doctors worked on his chest and the Danish team formed a protective circle round him, were my hardest experience in football.

My son was in that circle. His friend was the body on the grass. I was at the Parken, working for Denmark's state broadcaster, DR, and I couldn't help but look at Kasper and think of my boy, of what he was going through. What if it had happened to him?

I was also full of thoughts about Christian, his partner, Sabrina, and his family. How could the fittest of players, the guy who always ran the most in the side, have suffered this?

Why?

The feelings were still overwhelming – I think for all Danes – when our team returned to Parken Stadium to face the Belgians. So many windows in Copenhagen displayed Danish flags carrying the words 'Eriksen 10' and, driving to the game, the sight was beautiful. The national anthem was raw and charged with power, and energy surged through Denmark from the first whistle. Yussuf Poulsen scored in the second minute and the celebrations – I cannot remember emotion like that ever. Nothing close. And I include the Nou Camp, 1999.

There were only 25,000 people in the Parken, but there I was, looking at the players, seeing the fans, hearing the noise and letting the same feelings pour out from inside myself. It was this incredible release of everything that had accumulated over all the days and hours since Christian's collapse. And from that moment football was important to everyone again.

Denmark lost to Belgium, but that didn't matter. Our players continued playing with energy and passion and quality and so much strength deep inside. And kept doing so, all the way to the last second of extra time when losing in the semi-finals to England. At Wembley in that game, Kasper gave one of the great goalkeeping performances in a tournament. My son and his team, our Denmark team, showed the world at Euro 2020 that it is okay for football to mean something, in fact that it has to be meaningful – otherwise why love it, why watch it, why risk your life doing it like their mate Christian did?

They played with meaning, and if life is like a long, free piano piece, that's how it should be played – with meaning. In mine, I have always started with the *why*. I tend to run on instinct, passion. When I do something there has to be a reason. I need the fuel of meaning.

I found meaning at Manchester United. The club was always more than a workplace to me. It was my childhood dream, the one I loved from afar growing up as a football-mad kid in a far-off country – and from the moment I got there, I was in an environment where I felt at home.

The playing traditions of United and the boldness of Sir Alex Ferguson fitted the footballer I wanted to be – an attacking goalkeeper – and at United I found myself surrounded by people with mindsets the same as my own. Part of the mental make-up we shared was living in the now and giving everything in the moment. The attitude at United was that you moved on. On to the next game, the next challenge, the next trophy, the next season.

We would move on during games: concede a goal and blank it out of our minds, focus on our next attack. The manager would move on. Despite the myths, Fergie was never one for inquests in the dressing room. Yes, his hairdryer could blow a gale, but the gusts never lasted. After a match he said what needed saying, then sent us off for our bath and hardly spoke about the game again. It was all about moving on to the next match.

Move on. It is a character trait of mine, an impulse engraved in my personality. It was me at twenty-seven when, laden with luggage, I just went straight from Manchester Airport to the Cliff for my first United training session in 1991. It was me at seven, when I was a restless kid haring around a concrete housing estate on the edge of Copenhagen in 1970. It is me at fifty-seven, in 2021: Peter Schmeichel, ex-footballer but still seeking out challenges and reasons to keep on the go.

So, why write this book?

Why would a person who likes moving on want to look back?

Retracing my life for these pages in your hand did not always feel natural but it did feel necessary, for it is thirty years since I signed for United and changed my life by doing so, and it was time to take stock. In middle age you reflect. Why me? Why did I end up doing what I did, becoming who I am? In my specific case, I ask, 'How could I have had all those dreams of United when I was that restless Copenhagen kid, and end up lifting the European Cup as United's captain?' I wanted to take that journey back into myself, to try and understand.

There is another reason. This is not my first autobiography. I published one in 1999 but I have lived so much life since then and it was one of those cheap and cheerful footballer books that players of my era knocked out quickly, without giving it any great detail or depth.

I understand, now, that your life story is a big thing. It is one of the few things on this earth that are truly precious and yours. And so this time I wanted to do it properly, I wanted this to be the one. This book. *One*.

And you know what? All the looking back wasn't so bad. I learned that sometimes nostalgia can be okay. While writing this, I re-watched old games, read accounts of old seasons, even reconnected with some old team-mates and friends, and found the experience, overall, enriching.

This is my family's story too. It felt important to tell it, and once you read the second chapter you should get my meaning. So, I'm going to take you to the pitch, to Old Trafford, to the Nou Camp, to Wembley, to the Stadio delle Alpi. But I am also going to take you to a restaurant in Tivoli Gardens where a father tinkled a piano to please the diners with some jazz while his son, fresh from football practice, waited in the corner for his lift home. Dad – and me.

Sometimes nostalgia is okay. Sometimes looking back can even help you move on. Life can only be understood backwards, Søren Kierkegaard said, but it must be lived forwards.

Peter Schmeichel

Copenhagen, July 2021

1
RISK MODE

For national service, I was a fireman for the Danish land army, so I know about emergency drills. And we were right in the middle of ours: Manchester United, at the Nou Camp, 1999, with eleven minutes and ten seconds to go.

We had switched. Without panic or instruction from the manager, we had flipped to what I always thought of as our 'risk mode'. To a mentality like the educated gambler who goes all-in. We would invest everything to get back in this game.

In risk mode you take all the normal game elements away. You stop caring about formation and tactical convention. You do not worry what it looks like; you ignore the chance the opposition might score again and embarrass you. You shut out negatives; every pass, movement, action is a positive one. You put strikers on, you throw defenders forward. Sometimes goalkeepers too. There is nothing you won't put on the line.

Risk mode became our routine in 1999. Against Arsenal, Liverpool, Charlton, Juventus and Inter Milan we scored late, broke hearts, won from the brink. There was a method we followed when we were chasing games, although with precisely eleven minutes and ten seconds to go at the Nou Camp, things did not look so good. In that moment, the football was floating over my head and into the open goal behind me – it seemed.

It was chipped by Bayern Munich's substitute, Mehmet Scholl, a player with top quality. As I jumped, left arm fully stretched, white glove reaching high, I knew he had struck the perfect up-and-down; his effort had the correct weight for the ball to drop under the crossbar. I twisted in mid-air to land facing my goal and watched.

Bayern were hard enough to crack when protecting the one-goal lead they had held from the sixth minute. If they went 2–0 up, this Champions League final was theirs. And down the ball dropped, towards my goal.

Now, I could make this dramatic. I could pretend there were all sorts of thoughts and feelings inside. My situation: *Peter Schmeichel. Last game for Manchester United. Captain on the night. Champions League final, playing for a trophy that had become my obsession.*

Playing for the club I had loved since being a little Danish boy with Lou Macari and Gordon Hill on the wall of his bedroom in a block of flats on the edge of 1970s Copenhagen.

Thirty-five years old. No clue where the career was heading after this match. No club to go to and no firm plan, just a removal lorry booked to take all the Schmeichel family stuff back from a house in Bramhall to wherever.

Two kids, Kasper and Cecilie, both sitting somewhere among the 90,000 people in this stadium's steep, curved tribunes. Manager, Alex Ferguson, who at half-time gave one of the great team-talk lines: 'At the end of this game the European Cup will be six feet away, and you'll not even be able to touch it if we lose.'

I could say all this was going through my head, but the truth is none of it was. Nothing was. I never allowed myself to have sentimental feelings; not in my football career. How could they help with winning? And, letting *any* other factors enter your thinking – that is not how risk mode works. It's about investing *everything* into the comeback, mentally, physically, positionally, decisions-wise, and the second you go off track you lose. So, you don't think. You do.

Now, Scholl's chip is over me and I am watching the ball come down. I know it could go wide, hit the post or creep in, but I do not prepare for this last possibility. Watch the footage; you will see, as the ball drops, I am actually half-turned, ready to get it upfield and start another attack – when it bounces off the post, into the ground and up into my gloves.

The moment I catch the ball Jaap Stam is turning to face upfield and Ryan Giggs, Dwight Yorke and Teddy Sheringham are already on the move, expecting me to find them with a kick or throw. They are in risk mode too. All of us have been in this mindset most of the second half. Six minutes after Scholl's chip, Carsten Jancker crashed an overhead kick against my bar and this might sound silly, even arrogant, but I was not in the slightest bit rattled. I knew it was not going in. All my experience told me it wasn't.

That's risk mode. That's the mentality. *Nothing can hurt me.*

Risk mode had started long before the 1999 team came together. Giggsy, Denis Irwin and me, we had been around long enough to remember coming back to beat Sheffield Wednesday in 1993, when Steve Bruce, with his grin and his head, scored in the eighty-sixth and ninety-sixth minutes to give birth to the phrase 'Fergie Time'. Over the following years the risk mindset grew. Fergie was a risk-taker; I really liked that aspect about him. He would take defenders off, put an extra striker in, stick Giggs at left back, throw Brucey and Gary Pallister up top. It would create an electric wave through the team, an awakening: *Now we have to do this.* We were comfortable in taking all those chances and gambles because we knew it came from him.

In the Nou Camp we began taking risks quite early. There was a moment, around sixty-five minutes, when Jaap Stam intercepted the ball deep in our half, laid it off to David Beckham and just kept running, over the halfway line and deep into Bayern territory. A minute later, Teddy came on for Jesper Blomqvist, giving us not only a third striker but a magnificent header of the ball, who we could start playing up to. Then our gambling increased. Dwight Yorke went close with a header, Andy Cole tried scoring with an overhead kick, Denis and Gary Neville began pushing right up high, and I was sprinting to take goal kicks and bowling the ball out from hand as fast as I could. You could feel the dynamics of the game shifting. Those Bayern chances meant nothing because we accepted that giving chances away was the price to pay for the chances we were taking ourselves.

The first little crack in Bayern was Lothar Matthäus's substitution. Matthäus will forever be criticised for coming off in that final, but he was thirty-eight and he was tired; you could see that on the pitch. We had exhausted him. But he was Bayern's most vocal presence, the one who organised their defence, especially at set pieces. Removing him added to the chaos we created.

Ole Gunnar Solskjær came on for us, seriously annoyed. He was narked by the manager putting Teddy on first. Ole had

thought, *Twenty minutes to go and he's making a substitution . . .*
those are my *twenty minutes*. Still, what I saw when I watched
Ole run on to the field looked good for us. You could see
purpose, a certain sharpness in his stride.

Ole worked Oliver Kahn with his very first touch, a header.
Then Teddy could not quite wrap his foot around the shot when
Ole set him up with a back heel. Yorkey had a couple of near
misses, one after a pass from Gary Neville who, like Denis, was
now more winger than full back, advanced impossibly high.

We understood precisely the risks and rewards of what we
were doing. Get up there, get the ball flying around their area,
and we had Yorkey, Ryan, Teddy and now Ole, with his incredible nose for being in the right place. If they headed it out, we
had midfielders on the edge of their area who could fire the ball
back towards their goal. The more we pushed up, the more they
would be pushed back – meaning we could defend with fewer
men and push up even further, a vicious circle for them. There
was a psychological element. We knew we had created a reputation for late goals and that when we pushed at an opponent this
would play on their minds. If they had a breakaway, fine. *Come
and shoot*, I would think, *because you'll just be giving us back the
ball*. Does that sound crazy? I don't know. But in risk mode, you
can only allow yourself to think about positive outcomes.

Like us, Bayern came into the game trying to win a Treble. Their
coach, Ottmar Hitzfeld, had outmanoeuvred us with Borussia
Dortmund back in 1997. This time, Bayern were the only team
we had faced all season and been unable to beat – drawing with

them twice in the group stage. They were awkward to play against: good structure, well led. You looked at them in the tunnel: Matthäus, Stefan Effenberg, Mario Basler, Oli Kahn. Fantastic players. Then they lined up and it was in a way that was going to make things difficult for us: five in defence, four in midfield and only Carsten Jancker up front – a clever move by Hitzfeld, this back five and the midfield protection limiting space for Coley and Yorkey.

In the build-up, Fergie had kept things light. Our training session at the Nou Camp the previous evening was probably the most relaxed one we ever had. We did his favourite exercise, a possession game he called 'boxes', and he even took part himself, full of joking. The entire preparation was about keeping people happy and relaxed; we did very little tactical work and his team talk, made at the hotel in Sitges before we left for the stadium, was short. It was fifteen minutes of reinforcing our own strengths, telling us how proud he was, telling us this is the best trophy to win: go and win it.

Yet when you played for Fergie for a few years, you got to know all his little giveaways. I knew he was nowhere near as relaxed as he seemed. When he went around whistling and humming, in an apparently easy mood, that often meant he was nervous and covering it up. You almost preferred hearing him coming round the corner making his other sounds, the coughing and clearing his throat. Those were a sure sign he was agitated – but at least you knew where you stood.

There was a lot of whistling and humming and faked easiness around the hotel in Sitges. Watching him closely, I could see that, going into that final, he was probably more nervous than he had ever been for a game of football. The half-time speech about almost touching the trophy – that was about him as much as it was about us. He was in his thirteenth year at Manchester United, his twenty-fifth as a manager, and his ultimate ambition was to win the Champions League. With forty-five minutes to go, but 1–0 down, he had never been closer and yet further away.

Two questions were on our minds going into the game. The first concerned the pitch. It was the talk of the bus on the way back from practice at the Nou Camp. The surface was incredibly firm, gym-hall hard, the kind where you have to take extra care with your touches. How would it affect the game? The other question was: how would we play in midfield? With Roy Keane and Paul Scholes suspended, the manager had lined up with David Beckham and Nicky Butt in the middle in training, so you could guess what the plan might be. Ryan was disappointed. He was right to be.

When Fergie revealed the starting XI, it was indeed with a central midfield of Becks and Butty. Jesper Blomqvist was on the left and Ryan would have to play on the right. There are a couple of ways in which Fergie got a bit lucky in the final, and team selection is one. Ryan would have been better in the middle and David in his normal spot on the right. Although David played well in the centre, keeping going with that incredible work rate of his, Ryan would have done just as well there, and the biggest single problem we had in the match was that we had to do without David's crosses.

Yorkey has called David the most underrated player, which given David's fame might sound odd, but I know exactly what

Dwight means. The quality of David's delivery cannot be over-stated. It was just remarkable. The game has never seen crossing like that, before or since. Anyone who regards David as just the pretty boy does not know their football.

Coley and Yorkey lived off David's delivery and without it, plus the fact Ryan could not provide many crosses because he kept having to come inside, there was nothing for the strikers. Clever side that Bayern were, they kept forcing us through the middle, where they had packed the pitch. At set pieces and corners, initially they organised us off the park. They even incorporated the surface into their thinking: knowing back passes would bobble on the hard ground, they had Jancker following the ball in every time it came back to me. From the first whistle we seemed nervous and insecure everywhere, and then came their goal. Jancker bought a free kick and what happened next is the kind of thing you get blamed for by people who know nothing about goalkeeping. Most people, in other words.

The UEFA Pro Licence involves independent study on a topic of choice which you present to the group. I did my licence at St George's Park and my topic was direct free kicks. There is a Danish system used for ball-tracking in golf called TrackMan which is moving into football and accumulating data on free kicks. I used that data for my study and found something fasci-nating, which is that, statistically speaking, the perfect free kick travels for precisely one second, no matter from where or with which technique it is struck. What does that mean for the goal-keeper? They have one second to do three things – react, move, save – and the bigger they can make their reaction time, the better they will be able to execute the other two. So, if you are taking a free kick, your principal thought should be 'How do I limit their keeper's reaction time? How do I stop them seeing the ball until late?'

I finished my Pro Licence presentation with the goal scored against me at the Nou Camp. Basler, from the edge of my box, and to the right of my goal, curled it low round the wall into the left corner of my net as I stood, flat-footed. I looked the fool – but I only looked the fool in old-school thinking. *A goalkeeper can't be beaten like that, blah blah.* Ron Atkinson babbled on about it in the ITV commentary.

But what did Bayern do? This was before the rule change that now prevents the attacking team attaching players to the defensive wall. As Basler lined up his kick, Jancker strolled over to our wall, tailed by Jaap, and Markus Babbel shoved himself onto the end of the wall, shrugging off Butty's attempts to jostle him away. From having the four-man wall I had asked for and carefully organised, suddenly there were four extra players around its edges, all affecting my view of the ball. Babbel blocked my sightline completely and I had to crouch and step to my right to see the ball. As I did so, Babbel spun and ducked, and Basler curled the ball exactly where I had originally stood. I did look silly, but it was a clever, coordinated free-kick routine – and that's goalkeeping. So much is not about the big stuff like eye-catching saves, but about the little details like positioning or having your weight on the right foot. You accept certain things that come with the territory: such as, when you look bad you can look *very* bad. To the uneducated eye, at least.

Did Basler's goal play on my mind? Not even for a second. Goals never did, nor mistakes – not during games. Analysing

9

was for afterwards. In the moment, I was good at putting stuff out of my mind, and it's a bit like my approach to living: what's the point of dwelling on the past? Life must be lived moving forward – Kierkegaard had the right mindset for goalkeeping.

Long before half-time I was thinking, *Let's get this to the break and regroup.* Bayern were shutting us out. Every part of our game was a struggle. It was clear we would have to change something, and at half-time, for the first time all week, Fergie bared his teeth. His speech about the beautiful trophy, the one we had strived our whole lives for, that we should take a good look at on our way back out because, the way we were playing, we weren't going to get anywhere near touching – it hit home. Yet he did not make the tactical changes we needed and when his first substitution involved sending on Teddy not Ole, it seemed weird. Why *wouldn't* you put on Ole in the situation we faced?

Whatever was in his mind, he got those substitutions right. One way of telling the story of the game would be that Fergie chose the wrong midfield, then changed everything, a little by accident, with his substitutions. But who cares what his intentions were? I don't. If he had picked the perfect team and put on a tactical masterclass to beat Bayern 3–0, we wouldn't have won the Treble the unforgettable way we did. And isn't the way it worked for us a mirror of life: that nothing's perfect, but by trial and error you can work it out?

How did we crack Bayern, then?

Everyone knows that it was Teddy who equalised, thirty-four seconds into stoppage time. But who won the corner, do you remember? We won a corner kick on the left thanks to one of our players overlapping and playing a left-footed cross from a left-winger's position: who?

Nope.

Still no.

I'll tell you. Gary Neville.

Our right full back, maybe our most obedient, least free-spirited player, *Gary Neville – yes, Gary Neville –* won a corner by popping up on the byeline, on the left wing. *That* is risk mode. It may be the only time in his whole career that Gary found himself with the ball by the left corner flag, but in risk mode you go where the game leads you. Gary had sprinted over to the left to launch one of his throw-ins into their box, then stayed out on the flank in case Bayern cleared and possession was recycled his way.

All Gary was thinking about was the positives. If Bayern had counterattacked and scored because he was so chronically out of position, it would have been game over and he would have been forever blamed. But risk mode involved not worrying about the chance of humiliation, and that is why, as David placed the ball on the corner-kick spot, I came charging all the way from my penalty box into theirs. I had a thing going with Fergie's No 2s – first Brian Kidd, then Steve McClaren – where I would shout to the bench and they would indicate when ninety minutes were gone. I knew we were in stoppage time because Steve had already made the crossed-wrists sign. I knew it was now or never.

My final moments as a Manchester United player might easily have involved embarrassment. Imagine Bayern had cleared David's corner, gone up our end and scored into an empty goal, with me stranded upfield. I would be the guy whose last act for United was conceding a comedy goal. But when I went up for that corner I had no consideration for anything except getting into their box and creating havoc – just havoc and confusion. Throughout, Bayern had been so well organised that even in those few situations where we could benefit from one of David's deliveries – free kicks and corners – they had us under control, marked to a T. I wanted to break up that organisation. *You've dealt with everything, but let's see if you can deal with me.*

Not 'deal with me' in the sense that I was likely to score. I mean, I did end my career with one of the better scoring records for a goalkeeper. I managed eleven goals for club and country. That is only one fewer than the career totals of Gary Neville and Jamie Carragher combined. In my very first year as a senior player with Gladsaxe-Hero I scored a goal, a header at a free kick, that made the difference in us avoiding relegation at the end of the season. I scored twice in one game in Denmark – both penalties – and had scored in Europe for Manchester United, versus Rótor Volgograd. But how often had it happened? Not very. Not compared to the number of times I went into the opposition box.

I did not go into Bayern's box with the idea of scoring or being the hero. I was just trying to throw something different into the mix for Bayern to cope with. David was even waiting for me; he knew I was coming up, the whole team did. Trying my luck in the opposition area, late on as we chased a goal, was simply part of my game, part of *our* game. It was just another risk-mode ploy, an extra button to press, a different play to enter into the equation.

When the corner came in, I made for the area where David was always most likely to land it. I am not the greatest header of the ball, my instinctive timing is to arrive underneath it so I can reach my hands up and claim it. Pretty much every header I ever connected with, I mistimed. And so it was at that corner. Play the video and you will see I made a wonderful leap ... wonderful if the requirement had been to catch the ball. I got completely under it, making faint contact with the top of my head, but that did not matter. What mattered was the chaos I created.

Three Bayern players tried to challenge me: Babbel, Jens Jeremies and Thomas Linke. All their orderly and disciplined marking went out of the window as three Germans were sucked towards the big, blond, green-shirted figure who, so illogically, was invading their box. Three men challenging me meant three of our players would be left free and one was Yorkey. He mistimed an attempt to play the ball back across the goalmouth and Michael Tarnat cleared but, off balance, he made a skewed connection. From the edge of the box Ryan miscued his shot. It pinballed to Teddy – another who Bayern left unmarked – and Teddy scuffed it in.

So, what we had was one good corner kick, one mistimed goalie's header, Yorkey off balance, Tarnat off balance, a crappy shot, then a scruffy finish. Add all that up and it amounts to one thing: chaos. Chaos is what risk mode is about creating. Bayern were devasted. You saw it all over their faces. I remember Becks, after his red card in the 1998 World Cup, saying to the press, 'It's only football; it's not the most important thing in life.' Well, David was a young man then and I think he was very wrong.

Because if you are any kind of winner, when you are in the thick of competing for something, football *is* the most important thing in your life; it has to be, you have to make it that way. In Fergie's post-match interview at the Nou Camp he says that claiming the trophy is the greatest moment of his life. Fergie, who has three sons and several grandchildren. When things go the other way, therefore, it is the opposite – you feel it is the worst moment of your life and there is nothing, absolutely nothing, to comfort you. That is what Bayern were suddenly facing, the possibility that, having been in control the whole final, having hit the post and bar, they might suddenly throw it all away. We saw men in a daze.

Once in risk mode, you do not hit the off button. You stay with it until the job is done. You could liken us to hunters: when we got the smell of blood, we just moved on and on and on and on until we killed. There was no thought of sitting back and waiting for extra time. Ole won another corner and trotted into their box. David delivered again and the chaos we created for the first goal still had Bayern gripped. They were all over the place. Tarnat was on the post but standing up, leaning on it, like a man waiting for a bus – what was that about? They allowed Teddy a clean header and Ole's golden leg did the rest. Kahn did not even react to the ball going into his net. He looked still in shock from the first goal.

My first instinct was to charge upfield again and join the celebrations, but I stopped myself. If I ran all the way there, I would have to sprint all the way back and suddenly we were only seconds away from winning the Champions League. Manchester United did not need their goalkeeper with his pulse going at 180 if there was one last attack to defend. Instead, following a random impulse, I did a flip-flop, famously caught on TV when, through a miracle of good judgement, the broadcast director cut to me, but as soon as that was over my stomach was in knots.

From the moment I got back to my box after Teddy equalised, I had been more nervous than ever in my life. I was thinking, *It's extra time, golden goal. I cannot be the one to make a mistake and give it away.* I had been taking deep breaths and still trying to compose myself when Ole scored. Nerves, in matches, were very unusual for me, but this was terrifying. And now, at 2–1, with a few seconds still to play as Bayern prepared to take their kick-off, I had all these nasty thoughts: *Don't shoot, Christ don't shoot, I'm in no state to save the ball.* Those few seconds felt like hours. Then Pierluigi Collina blew. Bloody hell. What had just happened?

What just happened?

Then came a second feeling. *Yeah . . . but what did people expect? We are Manchester United. Coming back when all seems lost: this is who we are, this is what we do.*

We had arrived in Barcelona on an unbeaten run that stretched back to December, bouncing from challenge to challenge and overcoming it, a game every 4.6 days. We had been doing this stuff since that Sheffield Wednesday match in '93.

'They never give in. That's what won it,' said the manager in his flash interview, following his immortal line of 'Football, bloody hell!'

The other thing he said was in response to ITV's reporter, Gary Newbon, who praised him for throwing me forward for the corner where we equalised. 'I didn't send him. He went up on his own. But anyway . . .' Fergie replied.

What happened at the Nou Camp, of course, was beyond scriptable. Yet when it did happen, it felt so fitting: the perfect way to win, given our journey to that point. In the run-up to the final there had been this thought I could not shake out of my head, that we would be playing on 26 May, on what would have been Sir Matt Busby's ninetieth birthday. Before he died in 1994, I got to know the great man and understand how much living to see Manchester United reclaim the English title meant to him. Reconquering Europe, against a team from Munich, on Sir Matt's ninetieth birthday, felt so perfectly fitting too.

Me? The last bit of handling I did as Manchester United's goalkeeper involved receiving the European Cup from Lennart Johansson and – with Fergie holding the other ear – raising that big, old, beautiful trophy to the sky. Roy's suspension meant that ever since the semi-final against Juventus five weeks earlier, I had known I would be captain and that triumphal moment was a possibility. But never once had I tried to imagine it. Building up to the game, I had not allowed myself a single thought along the lines of *My last United game, how will the journey finish? What will this final involve for me?*

That is not how our minds worked in that remarkable team. What happened after Collina's whistle? What was touching the trophy actually like? What was in my mind when I sprinted over to jump on Teddy, when I lifted Raimond van der Gouw in the air, as we goofed about before the presentation? Honestly – I have no idea.

I am blank. Sometimes elite sport is described as like being in a pressure cooker – well, you know what happens when you take the lid off a pressure cooker, all the steam escapes. There is nothing left. My memories of what happened after full time are not my own; all of them are recreated from other people's photographs and stories, from the TV footage, the newspaper articles and well-known anecdotes. Even the victory party in the Hotel Arts Barcelona that night is something of which I only have vague, vague memories. Except for one thing: Fergie and Martin Edwards scrambling to get me to sign a new contract and stay.

That is a story for later.

There is one thing I do have clear recall of from the period in between the full-time whistle and leaving the Nou Camp, disbelieving and elated, on the team bus. And that is my son, Kasper, and Teddy's son, Charlie, just materialising in our dressing room.

Kasper was supposed to leave the stadium with his sister and mother on one of the official buses. That is how they do things at big UEFA and FIFA games: details like transport for those with special tickets, like players' family members, are organised with military precision. You arrive and depart on a specific bus, where you have a specific seat allocated to you, which leaves at a specific time, from a specific place and goes to a specific destination. This was the era just before mobile phones became commonplace and so while having our boys turn up and join the dressing-room celebrations was absolutely special, unexpected and unforgettable for me and Teddy, it was also a bit of a worry.

These boys were not on their bus: did their mothers know where they were? How could we even contact them to say they were safe?

We grabbed some club officials, who relayed the message on and on and on until word finally got to their mums. We sorted a lift for the boys to get back to their hotel. Only later did we ask the biggest question of all: how on earth did they even get to the dressing room in the first place?

This was a stadium of 90,000. There was pandemonium. There were also very strict UEFA rules which meant that different parts of the Nou Camp were considered different 'zones' and to get into each specific zone you needed specific accreditation. Kasper didn't speak Spanish and nor did Charlie. They had no money. Yet the lads blagged their way through checkpoint after checkpoint after checkpoint – until they reached the dressing room.

They could have been two boys from anywhere, but then again maybe not. Because have you ever seen them? Apparently, with every security guard they met, they simply pointed to their faces and said, 'Look, my father is Teddy Sheringham, look, look, my father is Peter Schmeichel.'

2
TOLEK THE SPY

The resemblance between me and my father is also strong, although height: that was something I got from my mother. When I ask the *why* – why me, why did a little boy from Gladsaxe grow up to do something extraordinary? – maybe I should start with a dad who was far from ordinary himself.

While other children on our estate had standard Danish parents, with standard nine-to-five jobs, my father was Polish and his shifts as a musician started when the restaurants at the Tivoli Gardens opened at seven in the evening and finished when Copenhagen's bars emptied at five in the morning. More than that, he had another line of work – though it was not something anyone in the family knew about until much later. You see, my father was a spy.

To be precise, a double agent.

His name was Antoni. Antoni Aleksander Schmeichel, though my mum called him Tolek and that was also how he was known on stage. Poles like nicknames and boys christened Antoni usually grow up being known as Tolek or Antek. Tolek means 'gift from God'.

Not that Dad was religious. Despite growing up in a Catholic environment in Pomerania, north central Poland, he became an atheist and would often remark, 'If there was a God and he was as good as they claim he is, I would not have had to endure what I had from such an early age!' Could you blame him? His childhood was ripped away at an age when children are just starting school. My dad had demons because of what he suffered.

He was born in the late summer of 1933 in Wąbrzeźno, a town of 10,000 traditionally known for farming and brewing, which was part of the German Empire until being handed back to Poland after the First World War. We are not sure where the name Schmeichel comes from, but it does sound Germanic. Dad had two sisters, Malgorzata, who was older, and Helena, who was younger, and a brother, Julian, the youngest of the kids. My father's father, Julian Maks, was a musician and his mother, Anna, was a homemaker – well, until the war.

When the Nazis invaded Poland, the first thing they did was attack the Free City of Danzig, now Gdańsk. This was on 1 September 1939. Anna was heavily pregnant with my uncle, Julian, and Julian Maks found himself on the frontline, having been among the thousands of Poles to enlist in their national army as tensions with Germany rose. He was an ordinary soldier, serving in Danzig, and a bomb from a Nazi battleship landed on his barracks, leaving him very badly injured. The next day, when the family tried to see him in hospital, it had been emptied. There was nobody there. No doctors, no nurses, no patients.

They never saw his body. There was never a funeral and no official confirmation ever came that he was dead, although his wounds had been so severe, there seemed little doubt. So, that was my grandfather: killed by the first shots of the Second

World War. My dad's sixth birthday was in the same week he died.

Nothing could be the same. Anna joined a Polish resistance movement formed by young Christians called Sword and Plough. In December, Julian was born. Pomerania was occupied by the Nazis and the arrests and deportations – to concentration camps – of Poles and Jews began.

For my father, the end of the war proved as traumatic as the start. In January 1945, the Red Army rolled in to 'liberate' Poland – but really to take it over. The Russians rounded up masses of Poles, those considered a threat to their rule, and these included anybody who had worked for the resistance. In front of my father, his brother and his sisters, Anna was dragged from their house and bundled away by soldiers. Dad never saw her again. He was eleven.

What exactly happened to his parents, especially his mum, was one of the big questions of my father's life; a heavy backpack of hurt that he always carried around. He made many attempts to trace Anna and, over the years, many theories became taken as facts. Initially, and for a very long time, the family assumed Anna had been deported to Siberia, but when my older sister, Kathrine, was in college she read a study about the Katyn massacre which suggested new evidence connected to mass graves discovered in a forest in western Russia during the 1940s.

Thousands of bodies had been found there, thought to belong to Polish army officers, but this study, called the 'Katyn Mystery', suggested that the remains of many ordinary Polish civilians were dumped there too. The theory was that these included the normal men and women who the Russians branded 'traitors' and made disappear in 1945 – among them former members of the Polish resistance. My dad began believing that this is where Anna lay.

It was only much later – when he was an old man, nearing the end of his own time on this earth – that Dad learned the truth about what had become of his mother. Only then was he able to start forgiving her. He had always felt that, by helping the resistance, however brave that was, she had placed not just her own life but her children's lives at risk and paid the consequences. Another thing my dad carried around with him was anger. It never took much for it to erupt. What happened with his mother, I think, was at the root.

After her disappearance, he and his siblings went to live in nearby Chełmża with his mother's parents and he adored them, especially his grandfather, Boleslaw – my middle name. Boleslaw had served as a chaplain in the Polish cavalry before civilian life, in which he had two occupations. One was as a janitor for a social insurance company. The other was as a musician.

Boleslaw played in a brass band and was also a talented violinist who made a bit of money on the side playing at parties and events. My dad absolutely idolised him; his grandad became his companion and inspiration. Before long he would join Boleslaw in performances, the pair of them walking the streets of Chełmża and country roads around the little town – sometimes five, six, seven, eight miles at a time – to get to their performances. Dad, a boy of eleven or twelve, was accompanist, playing the accordion.

He liked sport and boxed, rode speedway and ran the 3000 metres for a local sports club called LZS Ostaszów. He tried football too, playing in the backyard, but was never any good. Music was his true passion and as soon as he was old enough he enrolled in the state music school in the nearby city of Toruń. The French horn was his main instrument, but he got in a fight – I'm sure it was over a girl – and he was kicked in the mouth, losing most of his teeth and the embouchure needed to play brass and woodwind. He switched to piano and channelled his talent there. Back in Chełmża he formed a successful band, the White Cats.

Then came a gig that changed his life and made mine possible. He took a job in a circus orchestra and ended up in Sopot, a seaside resort on the Baltic sandwiched between Gdańsk and Gdynia. It has the longest wooden pier in Europe and was a famous Polish entertainment spot. In the late 1950s, when he arrived, there was a big bohemian scene which he threw himself into, playing in jazz ensembles and hanging out with actors, directors and musicians at Spatif, a nightspot of local legend.

He played in orchestras at the Bim-Bom Student Theatre and Coastal Theatre, and in the summer of 1959 a sensation came to the latter, a production of a new play called *A Taste of Honey*, written by a young Englishwoman called Shelagh Delaney. Tickets were gold dust and one day my father was standing at the stage door, with a couple in his hand, waiting to give them out to some friends he had arranged to meet. A pretty girl approached and asked if she could buy one, because the box office was sold out. This girl was taller than him and spoke in

German but turned out to be a Dane. She was a ship's nurse: my mother, of course. Inger Stovring was her name.

My mum is a trouper and as remarkable as my father, in her way. When she was seventeen, her own mother died giving birth to my youngest aunt. Her father, a carpenter, married their housekeeper.

This brought a whole lot of religion into the equation. My mum's stepmother was a God-fearing woman who wanted a strict Christian upbringing for her stepdaughters, but Mum was not having that. She rebelled. As soon as she was able to, she left the family home in Thisted, which is on a fjord right up in the north-west of Denmark, and moved to Copenhagen, where she had been born. She qualified as a nurse and made it her career.

A job came up on an ocean liner. She has always been an adventurous sort. The ship was called MS *Batory* and sailed the Gdynia–America line, on which Copenhagen was a stop-off on voyages from Poland to Montreal. Copenhagen was where she embarked and disembarked.

Mainly, her role involved being a nanny for children of the passengers, most of whom were either emigrating or emigrants returning from North America to Poland. She was also used as an interpreter, for as well as Danish, she spoke good German and English.

She worked on the *Batory* for a year or so and became very curious about what Poland was like. At the end of one crossing she asked if, instead of getting off at Copenhagen, she could stay on board until Gdynia, but these were Cold War times and without the right permissions and paperwork it was impossible, she was told. When the boat reached Denmark she disembarked and returned to her apartment.

Why she changed her mind, she never knew, but an instinct made her have second thoughts and go back to the docks. The *Batory* was still there and she sneaked aboard, returning to her usual cabin. She was only discovered halfway through the crossing to Gdynia and her presence caused an almighty stir. With no visa, she would be risking trouble in Poland, but she didn't care.

In Thisted, a quiet, sometimes boring town, what had kept her going were the arts. The headmaster at her school started a choir which became her passion. She loved music, performance and the theatre. So it was natural that when she stepped off the boat at Gdynia, she headed straight to nearby Sopot, with its famous scene. There, she learned *A Taste of Honey* was the must-see show, but she just could not score a ticket. That was, until she spied a good-looking young musician, at the stage door, with tickets in his hand.

My dad was part of the ensemble playing musical accompaniment to the production. Apparently the first thing my mum asked him, after persuading him to part with a ticket, was if she could see backstage. She had always been curious about what went on behind the scenes at a play. He said he would show her some time and they agreed to meet up when he next had a break between performances. Their rendezvous was at the Golden Street Café, the most well-known restaurant in town. That was their first date, and for a few days they hung out, enjoying each other's company. Falling in love. Soon it was time for my mum to return to Denmark, but a few months later she came back to see him – and on her second visit to Poland, they decided to get married.

The wedding was on 16 February 1961, in Sopot, in a small ceremony attended by a dozen or so people, mostly his theatre mates. He was twenty-seven, she was twenty-six. Being a foreigner, my mother could only remain in Poland for a short while every visit. Her longest stay was for six months, until a temporary visa ran out. After returning to Copenhagen that time, she decided she no longer fancied going back and forth to Poland. There was a baby on the way – Kathrine – and Denmark was where Mum wanted to raise her family.

Something I take from her is a tendency towards firm decisions and she made one then: my dad would just have to get himself to her country, though she had no real idea how hard that was going to be, nor how much pressure he was already coming under from the Polish authorities. The secret police knew all about his relationship with a Westerner, of course, and one of its operatives had been paying him menacing visits. Major Groszek – my dad never forgot his name.

Once, this guy had given him a piece of paper to sign. It was effectively a contract that would commit my dad to becoming a police informer. He refused, but the visits, the questions, the pressure on him kept coming. Out of nowhere, he received a call saying he was going to be conscripted to join the army – even though he was beyond conscription age. Still, despite the squeeze on him, he refused to spy.

He thought my mum might be able to get him to Denmark on the *Batory* but realised the secret police were keeping tabs on him and abandoned the idea. In the end it became inevitable. His only way out of the country was by cooperating with Polish intelligence. They sent him to Warsaw for training courses in spying, which included techniques for how to operate undercover in a foreign environment. They gave him a list of contacts and finally deemed him ready. You can go to Copenhagen, they said, but you must spy on the Danes.

He took a train to Copenhagen via Berlin. It was his first time outside of Poland and he had to cross Berlin to change trains. Walking to his next station he felt paranoid, like he was being watched. He passed by a section of the Berlin Wall being built. Seeing it made him scared and brought home the realities of the Cold War. On his train to Denmark he made a decision – whatever the consequences, there was no way he was going to become an agent in the West.

In Copenhagen, he asked directions to the nearest police station and turned himself in. The Danish police had no idea what to do with him, except throw him in the cells. This was 5 September 1961, his twenty-eighth birthday. After a few days there was a visitor, someone from Danish intelligence, and the deal was this: he could join his wife, but would have to become a double agent. He protested but, in the end, had no choice. Anyway, what, really, was there to report? Poland spying on Denmark? Denmark spying on Poland? Whatever 'intelligence' there was to gather – or pretend to gather – would be very low-level stuff.

There are a lot of things I will never know. As kids, none of us had any idea about our dad's double life, and though my mother was aware of what he was up to, she was not privy to the details. I do remember, as time went on, my father beginning to make visits to the Polish embassy and I now know it was to report whatever insignificant things he reported.

But as much as he could, he stayed away from anything to do with his homeland. He went off the radar for Poland. Poland could not exist for him, when I was growing up. It is the reason that neither I nor my three sisters can speak Polish – which is a great shame – and why none of us really have a relationship with Poland. We were raised very much to be Danes. That is how it had to be.

Occasionally, Polish visitors stayed with us, including my uncle Julian, who was an incredible worker. He would come over to Denmark for the summer circus season. His talent was putting up marquees and nobody could work as long or as quickly as him. But the Poles in our midst seemed aliens to us kids: they were noisy, we couldn't understand their language, they liked to drink. Dad did not make too great an effort to connect us with them. And even in later life, when my father started going back to his homeland and grew to love it again, he remained very reluctant to put anything down on paper or even tell stories about his past.

In January 1962, Kathrine arrived. I followed, born in Copenhagen on 18 November 1963. Margrethe, my middle sister, came along in September 1965. What none of us knew was that we were not Danish. Our official citizenship was Polish and it took until November 1971 for my father to successfully complete the long process of having our status changed. I have the paperwork and it includes a certificate from the Polish embassy, dated three days before my eighth birthday, which states that Piotrowi Boleslawowi Schmeichel is no longer a Pole but now a Dane. We joke with our youngest sister, Hanne, born in August 1972, that she is the only one of us who is 100 per cent Dane.

Home until I was seven was Buddinge, a suburb in the north-west of Copenhagen. When my dad came to Denmark he had to learn the language (he and my mother communicated in German initially) and he never lost his way of speaking Danish with a heavy accent. Mum was a senior nurse at the State University Hospital, seven days on, seven days off, her shifts running from 4 p.m. until midnight, when she was in charge of four wards. My father found work as a pianist and played at a fine-dining restaurant in Tivoli Gardens in the centre of Copenhagen called Nimb.

He would start on the piano while diners were eating their meals and then, when it was time for dancing, switch to the organ. He played a beautiful Hammond B3. The season at Tivoli began on 1 May and continued until 15 September and he spent seventeen summers entertaining people there, tinkling the keys every evening from seven until eleven, without a single day off. Usually, after my football training, I went to my mother's ward for a lift home after her shift, but sometimes I took the bus to Tivoli and sat in the corner at Nimb, watching him play. At eleven he would take me home. That stopped when he took a second job, as pianist at a nightclub called Altoria. Then, he would have to rush from Nimb across town to the club and perform until five in the morning. It was a tough life for him. He played at Altoria six nights a week and Nimb seven evenings a week. His daytimes were for catching up on sleep.

There were other gigs. In 1970 we moved to Høje-Gladsaxe, a new high-rise development on the edge of the city. The estate had two shopping centres, one housing a pub with function rooms and a nightclub which was open every night. The Danish state broadcaster was based nearby and the club was frequented by all these guys who were heavy drinkers. My father played there. He also had stints playing in the shopping-centre concourses and in other communal areas in the development, which were soulless gigs for a quality pianist but made him a local mini-celebrity. My overriding memory is simply that he always seemed to be working, grafting, and he was often tired and sometimes irritable as a result. The hours he kept meant I could go days without really seeing him. My mum's work was exhausting too and her shift patterns meant that some weeks I saw very little of her.

Reflection happens when you get older. You look at your kids and consider in which ways you have influenced them. Then you look back at what you got from your own parents, the traits and values. One thing that seems obvious is the sheer effort my mum and dad put in to make ends meet with four children. Their sacrifices seem scarcely believable. I have always been a grafter myself; hard work allowed my talent to fly. Another thing I maybe take from them is being unconventional. Living ordinarily? I never have. I think back to Saturdays as a kid. Just as my friends were settling down with their parents for an evening of family television, we only had our mother for company every second weekend, and I cannot remember a single Saturday when my dad was there. One Saturday in two, when my mum was on hospital shifts, we sat alone, three little kids, Kathrine in charge.

That wasn't as bad as it sounds – and we were happy. We received the same love and care our friends did – it is just that we had to grow up with a little more independence than them. Home always felt a safe environment and there was always music in the house. Dad wanted us to play instruments, though he lacked the patience to be a good teacher. He was a little too forceful, too unforgiving, and his painstaking approach to practice did not suit an instinctive, impatient son like me. Nevertheless, today I play the piano, guitar, drums and sing. Music is a pillar of my life: my father's gift to me.

I knew he was quite good. More than quite good. Jazz was his true passion and not long before the illness he suffered at the end of his life, I took him to a jazz house in Copenhagen to see Lee Konitz, his favourite saxophonist. It was awful – so I thought. But Dad, oh my God, he enjoyed it so much. For his seventy-fifth birthday I gave him his own private jazz concert and hired a guy, recommended by my sister, who became a friend – the pianist and drummer Carsten Dahl. Carsten, who turned out to be a massive Brøndby fan, put together a trio and their playing was sensational, my dad was so happy. Then after six songs Carsten stood up and said, 'Hey, Tolek, the piano is yours.' No, no, said Dad. 'Oh, go on.'

And so my father sat down on the stool and started playing 'Autumn Leaves', the Joseph Kosma jazz standard. *The falling*

leaves drift by my window/The autumn leaves of red and gold.
Carsten looked at me and I looked at him with expressions that
said, 'Wow.' I could not believe how well my dad played. He had
not practised for so long. There was only one other time I saw
him play in public with others and it was just as precious. In
1986, we were out celebrating my parents' silver wedding anniversary at Nezer's piano bar in Copenhagen and Dad was once
more encouraged to get up on stage and perform. Once again,
he was so, so good. I was incredibly proud that he could play
like that.

He could be a funny guy. When the *Manchester Evening
News* interviewed my mother before the 1999 Champions
League final, he hopped on the piano and played a comic
rendition of 'Rule Britannia' in the background as she talked
to the journalist by phone. Dad loved his football and claimed
Manchester United was always his team – he loved my
bedroom wall – but his grip on the mechanics of the sport was
not always strong.

My Gladsaxe-Hero youth team once played a big cup semi-
final against a club called KB (which became FC Copenhagen),
who had this brilliant kid called Michael Laudrup playing up
front for them. The game was at KB's ground and at half-time
we were sitting on the pitch, receiving our instructions from the
coach, when my father strolled over with a bottle of Coca-Cola
and interrupted the team talk. Just talked over our coach. 'Boys,
would any of you like a Coke?' He spoke in his thick accent,
which of course was comical to some of the boys. It was just
naivety, but my team-mates took the mickey out of me for a
good while afterwards and even now, forty-plus years later,

when I get together with old Gladsaxe-Hero friends, they refer to That Time With Your Dad and the Coke.

The real story of his life spilled out of my dad, quite suddenly and unexpectedly, when we were taking a stroll in 2009. I was with him in Berlin on a cold October day. We were there because I was hosting Danish television coverage of the opening bout of the Super Six World Boxing Classic: Arthur Abraham versus Jermain Taylor. The promoter, Kalle Sauerland, a friend of mine, knew Dad was a boxing fan and gave me two front-row seats so I could bring him along.

Dad and I had a few days in Berlin and our walk that day took us near the central railway station. Dad said, out of the blue, 'All this has changed . . .' It was then that he started telling me the whole story of his flight from Poland, of stepping off the train full of worry, his spying assignment, seeing the wall being built, his arrival in Denmark. We had never talked so openly. It was an unforgettable moment of bonding between father and son.

Even on that day, almost fifty years after his journey out of Poland, he was still paranoid that somebody might be watching him. That fear, created by his early years and by the pressure the Polish authorities put on him after meeting my mother, remained ingrained. His process of reconnecting with Poland began in the 1980s when Lech Wałęsa and the Solidarity movement signalled the country was changing, and once communism ended, his journeys home to visit his brother, sisters and other family became regular.

There were two or three such trips a year and he made sure everyone in the neighbourhood knew when one was coming up. Everything people didn't need – old bikes, old prams, nappies, even Zimmer frames – he would load in his VW van and he'd set off for Toruń or Gdańsk. In his later years, his visits were more mini-breaks with my mother. He loved the Polish markets, scouring them for old musical instruments, becoming a collector. When he died, he left us with more than thirty old violins, one from the 17th century, and a couple of double basses. My mum, sisters and I are not quite sure what to do with them.

He passed away on 7 May 2019, aged almost eighty-six, and I think he was at peace. Before his death, he had put the mystery of what happened to his mother more or less to bed. The strangest thing happened. On a visit to Toruń, my father was in a bakery and bumped into a man who recognised him. 'Were you Anna Schmeichel's son?' he asked. He went on to tell my father that a relative had survived a concentration camp outside Moscow and had written the family a letter, describing incarceration there.

The letter mentioned Anna. My grandmother had died of illness in the camp, but not before she had become a heroine among fellow prisoners. She had spent her time helping other inmates out, carrying things for the sick and the weak and fighting for better conditions, treatment and food. The author of the letter was from the same area as Anna, and had written about her at length. Finding out that she had been so heroic softened my father's hurt. The betrayal he felt melted away. He saw his mother in a different light.

The traumas of his life in Poland left a mark. My dad was an alcoholic. A working life that involved long, late nights where drink was all around did not help, but I think the drinking was mostly because he was in pain. From Denmark, he made repeated attempts to trace his mother. I have his printouts from all the Google searches in hope of locating her. I have his correspondence with the Red Cross when – in vain – he tried using its international tracing service to discover her fate.

Dad stopped drinking in 2000. We nearly lost him. I will get to the story, but getting him to go sober almost destroyed my relationship with him. Happily it went the other way and in the last two decades of his life we became best friends. The bond between him, Kasper and Cecilie was also strong. My mother – still a trouper – lives in the apartment in Copenhagen where they spent their final years, and I guess we all reflect that, when you think of everything in his life, it was no wonder that Tolek Schmeichel was a bit weird and short-tempered sometimes. Also, a bit thirsty.

His grave is 200 yards from my house, out near the shore, and I go to see him often, usually with fresh flowers to lay. Do I feel a bit Polish? Not really. But I am proud of my unusual roots and my middle name, Boleslaw. Thanks to my career and then Kasper's, my father even gained a little profile in Poland in his later years and on a couple of occasions sat down with Polish newspapers and TV reporters to give interviews. In one of these he described his life this way: 'It was a beautiful dance on roses, but I also stepped on spikes and bled heavily.'

The meeting in the bakery shows the power of . . . what is it . . . fate, coincidence? And here is another example.

A Taste of Honey, the play my mum scored a ticket from my dad for, in a far corner of Poland, in 1959. She quite enjoyed it, but didn't understand the Polish dialogue, despite returning to the theatre in Sopot to watch it a second and third time. When it came to Copenhagen, she saw it again and could finally appreciate it fully. Anyway, do you know any details about the play?

Well.

It is set in Salford, Manchester. Its main male character is Peter.

3
OLD TRAFFORD AT LAST

The two football clubs in my blood had father figures and you could say both were the type of parent who likes to be in control.

They had different personalities and ways of getting what they wanted, but what they created was similar: clubs that felt like families, with them very much at the head. They were successful men who wrote new history; they could be a little ruthless sometimes, as well. They were Sir Alex Ferguson and Per Bjerregaard.

The story of my transfer to Manchester United in 1991 brought them together. Bjerregaard was my chairman at Brøndby, a qualified medical doctor and former player who turned Brøndby into pioneers, the first fully professional club in Denmark and its dominant team. He brought the Laudrups – Finn, the father, Michael and Brian, the boys – to the club and signed players like me, Lars Olsen, Kent Nielsen and Kim Vilfort, while appointing winning managers like Morten Olsen and Ebbe Skovdahl. Fergie? You have probably heard of him.

I first met Fergie in the front room of an ordinary home on the outskirts of Copenhagen. It belonged to Finn Willy Sørensen. Finn Willy was a former player and coach who lived near Brøndby's training ground and early one morning in

September 1990, before I left my house for practice, I got a phone call from him. He said after training can you come round? I trained and then drove over, and in Finn Willy's house was Alex Ferguson.

Fergie introduced himself and said, 'Peter, like you I am disappointed we haven't been able to sign you yet, but I have seen enough to know that you are the guy I want. I am going to wait for you. So, work hard, play well, keep progressing and I will see you next summer.' He got up, shook my hand and left to go back to the airport. I was dumbstruck. I had hardly said a word. I turned to Finn Willy: wow, what the hell happened there?

That surprise visit was a boost I needed, because by then I was in a long struggle with Bjerregaard over my desire to make my dream of moving to Old Trafford happen. Manchester United had made their first bid to sign me four months previously, in May, but at the time it seemed to me that Bjerregaard was playing games. It was as if me, my future, my ambitions and my contract were just another set of pieces for him to keep in play.

The story starts in the middle of 1989. I was in my third season with Brøndby, on my way to a third successive Danish title, and had cemented myself as No 1 for the national team. I was twenty-five and my progression from Gladsaxe-Hero in the Danish third division was going pretty well. Out of the blue, Finn Willy contacted me.

He knew my then father-in-law, Svend Aage Hansen, who had been my coach at Gladsaxe-Hero. Finn Willy said he was working with a football agent called Rune Hauge and Rune would like a word with me. In those days players seldom had agents. There was this one guy who would sniff around any player in the spotlight at Brøndby and say, 'Hey, I've got you a club,' but he never did. In terms of proper agents, agents in the modern sense – reps you signed and worked closely with – nobody on the small scene in Denmark had one of those.

But Rune and I set up a meeting. Rune is from Voss in Norway and talks in a Bergen dialect, which made things . . . interesting. There are enough similarities in our languages for a Dane to understand 90 per cent of what a Norwegian says when speaking in their own tongue, and vice versa. In normal circumstances, anyway. The exception involves people who speak Bergensk. We do not understand them well at all. Talking with Rune, my comprehension was down to about 60 per cent. I'd get one of his sentences and then the next would confuse me, but the gist was clear: he had been keeping an eye on me and thought he could help my career.

Already, he was working with Bjerregaard to help Brøndby sign players, he said, but then he posed a question: did I want to stay at Brøndby for ever? No. Then what do you want? Rune asked. I said to play well, develop my career and reach a bigger club. What club exactly? I said Manchester United. Until this point, it was in the back of my mind that maybe here was another chancer, another time-waster, just one more guy hoping to leech a little money from players. But Rune looked me in the eye and said, 'I can work with that.'

These were the days before mobile phones, so every Friday night he would call on my house telephone. We would catch up about my situation. I understood so very little of what he was saying but understood the most important message, that he conveyed every time, which was that we were moving in the right direction. He had begun to strike up a relationship with Alex Ferguson. Be patient, Rune would say, keep playing well.

It turned out I had already caught Manchester United's attention. Later, Alan Hodgkinson, who became my coach for Monday-morning goalkeeping sessions at the club's old training ground, the Cliff, revealed Fergie had sent him to scout me thirteen or fourteen times. Alan liked to say, proudly, 'I only had to watch you once to phone Fergie and say you have to sign this guy.' The first time Fergie saw me himself he was peering through leaves.

That was in Marbella, where ahead of the 1990 campaign in Denmark, Brøndby held a training camp. Morten Olsen, our new manager, was obsessive about improving fitness and we would be woken early, meet at 8 a.m. and go for a half-hour run around the golf course to loosen up, then return to the hotel, change into our gear, eat breakfast and go out for a training session at 10.30 a.m. Training might last two hours and, afterwards, we had lunch, rested and would then head back out for another session. Every day. The winter sun on the Costa del Sol gave Olsen far more scope to work us than the rain and snow back home.

This was late January and during a period when the pressure on Fergie was at a peak. This was the season – 1989–90 – when it could have gone either way for him. He had not won in the league since the middle of November and Manchester United were seventeenth in the old English First Division, with a tricky FA Cup fourth-round tie away at Hereford United coming up.

In the Stretford End at Old Trafford you had that silly banner that became infamous: 'TA RA FERGIE'. The English papers were full of speculation that Fergie could be sacked.

To prepare for the tie, Manchester United flew in for a couple of warm-weather training days, using the same complex as us in Marbella. They even stayed in the same hotel. For me it was like Disneyland – *Wow, there's Steve Bruce, look there's Bryan Robson, ooh it's Mark Hughes*. I sneaked a shy hello to some of them, but I was too exhausted from all the running Morten had us doing to actually go out and watch them train.

Being Manchester United, their training took priority. The complex had only one pitch, so we had to let United do their session first before we could get on the grass. The pitch was about 200 yards from the hotel and, to reach it, you walked down a path through a little wood. One day, after United's practice, Fergie stayed back and hid in the trees to watch me. According to him, he was looking at this crazy guy flying left, right and centre, saving everything, controlling everything, yelling like a madman, and thought here was something he had never seen before. He decided to keep an eye on me.

Forward planning, when it came to team-building, was one of Fergie's greatest strengths, and in hindsight I love the fact that even in his dark hour, with his own future on the line, he was trying to plot Manchester United's future by finding a new, young goalkeeper. And he beat Hereford, survived and went all the way to the FA Cup final. Wembley is the setting for the next part of my story.

On 15 May 1990, Denmark played England under the famous old twin towers. We had the Laudrups, Vilfort, John Sivebæk and Flemming Povlsen, but England were not bad either, with players such as Gary Lineker, Paul Gascoigne, Terry Butcher and Chris Waddle – who won his fiftieth cap. I could not wait for the game. For the first time, I was going to play at what, for me, was the most important ground in the world. Yet when we trained at Wembley on the eve of the match, I discovered that the stadium (this was before its revamp) was an old dump. It was still Wembley, though, still better than any stadium I had ever seen. The pitch was just, wow.

I left, excited, promising myself that tomorrow I would play better than I had ever played, because this was the game of my dreams. And there was further motivation. From Rune, I knew that the rumblings of interest from clubs in England were becoming stronger. On the day of the game, after lunch and just as I was set for an afternoon kip, he called me in my room at the Royal Garden Hotel in Kensington.

'Okay,' Rune began, 'it's official: we have three bids for you. We've got West Ham . . .'

I thought, *Hmm, West Ham*.

'We've got Liverpool.'

Okay . . . Liverpool.

'And then we've got . . . Manchester United.'

What?

'Yes, they have put in an official bid.'

Whoah!

Rune asked what I wanted and I told him that he knew the answer very well. 'There is only one thing to do and it is to go with United. That's what I want.'

'Okay,' said Rune. 'Play well.'

I did play well. I was flying. England won 1–0 but the head-lines the next day were about me. I almost felt separated from the real world. My lifetime's ambition was coming true. I did not tell any of my team-mates about Manchester United. I did not want to jinx anything.

The next day, as soon as I arrived back at my house in Copenhagen, Bjerregaard rang. He said he had had some inter-esting calls and went on to confirm what I already knew. He asked what I wanted. I said, 'Manchester United.'

This was where I met my first disappointment with Bjerregaard – it would not be my last. I had joined Brøndby from Hvidovre in 1987 on a two-year contract, but it quickly became clear I was an asset and Bjerregaard wanted to tie me down. This was just a year into Brøndby being fully professional and all the players at the club were on the same wages. However, he offered me a new contract in which, thanks to some extra sponsorship, I could be paid a little more. Officially it would be a four-year deal, but I would be allowed to leave after two years: Brøndby just needed to announce four years because that would help the club commercially. Bjerregaard and I shook hands on it, a gentleman's agreement.

Now, two years were up and I was clear about my wishes. 'Let me go to Manchester United,' I said, and 'Fine,' Per replied. I thought that was that.

And I never heard from him on the matter again. Not a word. We finished the season, had a short break and came back ready for a UEFA Cup campaign in the autumn, and there was still nothing from Bjerregaard, absolutely nothing. What he did not know was that, thanks to Rune, I knew what was happening behind the scenes, which was that he had asked for far too much money – a transfer fee of £1.2m, which was crazy, because the world-record fee for a goalkeeper was only a little more than that – £1.7m. But Bjerregaard would not budge. Rune was doing his best, yet there did not even seem scope for negotiation.

In hindsight, Morten Olsen might have had something to do with it. He was a new coach, had just won the league and was preparing to tackle Europe. He had been building and improving a new Brøndby team and I was not a player he wanted to lose. That was fair enough, but Bjerregaard's behaviour was odd. Normally so personable and charming, he suddenly became very cold. Okay, I thought, if you want to play hardball, I can play hardball, and perhaps it was petty, but we began completely ignoring each other around the club.

It was around this time that Fergie, as if by magic, appeared in Finn Willy Sørensen's front room. After his visit I asked Finn Willy what I should I do. Finn Willy said, 'Well, Peter, he is still scouting you, he knows what he wants and now you know Manchester United will come back for you. So, what you have to do is get your head down, work really hard, play really well and put this move beyond doubt. Your target for this season should be Player of the Year. That's how good you need to be.'

Okay, I thought. I can do that. And I got my head down. Worked really hard. Played really well. Became Player of the Year – I was Denmark's PFA Player of the Year, Brøndby Player of the Year, Player of the Year in every newspaper. I felt I wanted to show the world, be so good that so many clubs would come in for me that Bjerregaard could not avoid selling me. I was in incredible form during a UEFA Cup run in which Brøndby became the first Danish team to reach a European semi-final.

In May 1991, with seven rounds to go of the Danish Superliga season, we flew to Jutland, to play Ikast, a team which later merged to form FC Midtjylland. In the airport there was an exhibition stand showing off a gleaming new car; a BMW, I think. Bjerregaard sidled up behind me. 'You like this car? I can give you one of those,' he said.

Up to that point I had been ignoring him, making sure I had nothing to do with him. I had even gone out of my way to avoid him at the Brøndby Christmas party. I felt cheated, manipulated; that I couldn't trust him or anything he had to say. Most of all, I did not want to play his games any more – but now here he was, laying on the charm.

I can give you one of those shiny cars . . .

I stared at him. He said, 'Peter, I have something I'd like to talk to you about. I think I have an offer you cannot refuse.' He concluded by asking if we could have a meeting. I said yes. What he didn't know was I'd been working with a lawyer to explore how to get out of my situation, a guy Rune had used before, who was the Danish equivalent of a QC. He was called Jan Gronlund and he looked the part. His moustache was waxed and curled at the edges, he had a full beard, he was always elegantly dressed. He looked like he could represent royalty. When you met him, you felt a little in awe.

We beat Ikast and returned to Copenhagen, where Per approached me again at training. He said he really wanted that meeting and I suggested Friday after practice – exactly as Jan had advised me to do. Bjerregaard was on the back foot. He clearly wanted the meeting straight away. With him, everything was a game, a play. An example is that when he started up Brøndby's professional department he went to the most notorious agent in Europe and offered to pay him a full daily rate if he could teach him all the biggest tricks in the football trade. So, he agreed to Friday, but I could see his mind was ticking over.

We said one o'clock. Then I asked if we could make it two, just to be awkward and keep him on the back foot. On Friday, Jan was running late and so I called Per and said, 'We won't be able to make it until two thirty.' It went quiet on the other end of the line.

'*We?*'

'Yes,' I said, 'me and my lawyer.'

'Oh, oh, urrrr,' said Per, 'we can find another date.' I said no to that and insisted on half two. Jan had predicted this would happen, that if Bjerregaard knew I was bringing assistance he would want to prepare himself in another way, want time to work out a play. Well, we were not going to give him time.

We arrived at half past two and went to the office of Brøndby's CEO, Finn Andersen. Nice guy. Nice, nice guy. Somebody who would never double-cross you. It was another deliberate move, to get Per out of his office and on neutral ground. He and Andersen sat on one side of the desk, me and Jan on the other.

Jan had a pinstriped suit on. A white shirt, the curled moustache, gold-rimmed glasses. He shook hands with the other two and took out his business cards, laying one in front of each. He said, 'My name is Jan Gronlund and I am authorised by the highest court in the country. So, how much does Peter cost to release in the summer?'

This completely bamboozled them, hit them right between the eyes. They were scrambling. And Jan became relentless: bang, bang, bang, hitting them with questions and statements of our intentions. We got to a point where they didn't know which leg to stand on and where it was agreed – I could be released.

'Okay,' said Jan. 'So, it is clear. Peter will leave this summer and there is no doubt this time. *Is* there? Good, good . . . so what was it you wanted to talk about?'

Bjerregaard stammered something about a plan he had dreamed up that would enable Brøndby to pay me more money without breaking their wage structure and persuade me to stay.

'No,' Jan said, 'we're not doing that.' And he stood up to leave.

I had to drive him back to his office in central Copenhagen, a fair journey. For a while, I sat in silence. I thought my life was over, that this meeting had been an absolute car crash, that it would come back to haunt me. Those guys held my contract, after all, and I'd just let them be bulldozed by this pinstriped, moustachioed heavy. I was sure there was going to be a price to pay. Jan turned to me.

'That went *fantastic*,' he said, beaming, 'that was good. Now you can be released. Nice, eh?'

I was, like, *Christ, what happened there?* But he was so happy and he said, 'Hey, this guy, Bjerregaard – who does he think he is? He can't do it.'

He sat there, absolutely ridiculing the man who was used to having every Brøndby player in the palm of his hand. Jan knew his stuff, of course: via Rune he was aware of the fee Manchester

United were willing to pay and he understood better than I did that now the deal would have to go ahead.

I have read somewhere that it takes three seconds to make your mind up about somebody you meet and three years to change those first impressions. I am a person who works on gut instinct and I think I have been right about people 95 per cent of the time.

Martin Edwards was trustworthy. I discovered that if he gave you his word about something, that was it. He would follow through. My very first encounter with him gave me that sense – which is how I came to 'sign' for Manchester United and yet not sign for them. Not initially. You see, my first four games for the club were played without a contract.

My transfer, for a fee of £505,000, was agreed in the closing weeks of the Superliga season. On 9 June 1991, a Sunday, Brøndby won a Copenhagen derby against BK Frem to climb above Lyngby and go top with two rounds of fixtures remaining. Three days later, Denmark were to face Italy in Malmö and I used the short window before my international game to fly to England to agree terms with United, accompanied by Rune. We were picked up at Manchester Airport, driven to Old Trafford and taken straight to Edwards's office.

My assumption was that he would want to finalise and sign the contract as quickly as possible. Instead, Martin greeted us with a smile, looked at me and said, 'Come.' He led me round the stadium to the Manchester United museum, and on the way we passed the Munich Memorial Clock, on which time stands still at four minutes past three on 6 February 1958, the moment of the Munich air disaster.

Martin began talking about Munich and the Busby Babes and, during a tour of the museum, continued telling me the history of the club. He wanted to make sure I understood precisely what the responsibility of playing for Manchester United involved; that at this football club they treasured their own and had a past they would always carry in their hearts. This told me everything about Martin and his priorities. We returned to his office and agreed terms easily. Then came the catch. There was no contract for me to sign. Manchester United were about to float on the stock market and because of this could not sign players until after 1 August. After explaining this, Martin offered me his hand. This is as good as a contract, he said. I believed him, and shook.

Back in Copenhagen, I went to the ferry port to catch the boat to Malmö and found the media waiting for me. I was taken aback. How had news of my trip to Manchester leaked out? Not that I cared, particularly, because I felt incredible. In the Italy game, I was flying. It felt like an out-of-body experience. I was in the clouds. I'd been dreaming of Manchester United since I was eight or nine and as a boy had a little nightly ritual where, last thing before I went to sleep, I would imagine playing in goal for Manchester United, with my best friend as the right back, and in my little scenario we were the heroes. Now, in one month, I would be putting on that United goalie kit for real. I was almost there.

It was a busy few weeks. I returned from international duty to help Brøndby win the Superliga. My last game was at Lyngby, where a 1–1 draw secured us the title. Then I tied the knot. Kasper was four and my daughter, Cecilie, was still a baby, and I thought it would be easier for us to travel to a new country as a family if Bente and I were married.

I started pre-season with Manchester United, still minus any official paperwork. I was paid and looked after, however. It turned out I was right about Martin Edwards – a handshake *is* as good as a contract with him. In Manchester United's entire existence, Martin might be the person who has been given the worst deal. Supporters see him as a villain, but while he did upset them at times and make a lot of money when he sold his shareholding, I think he was also one of the most important people in the club's history. He always wanted the best for it and made some hard choices for United's benefit. Floating the club was one of those. Although unpopular, it left United better prepared than rivals for the commercial oppor- tunities of the Premier League. Martin was also the man who appointed Fergie, then stuck with him, believing in his project in spite of poor results in the first few years. And, most of all, he was one of the club's culture-bearers, as he showed at our first meeting.

Pre-season training began at Littleton Road. We then went to Norway, to play four friendlies, the first against a Japanese team called Mazda. It was the first time Fergie had ever seen me play in the flesh. It could have gone better. One of their players scored from about 50 yards out, just hit it and it flew into the top corner, completely ridiculous, just one of those miracle strikes. Everyone was laughing, but in a good way, because I had been saving everything in training. So that was me, beaten almost from the halfway line in my first United game. Was the goal my fault? Nah. Never is . . .

The other friendlies went much better. We won them all and I played particularly well in a victory over Viking Stavanger. On the coach afterwards, the legendary David Meek of the *Manchester Evening News* sat down with me and said, 'Where did you come from, again?' I had forty-two Denmark caps, had played in a European semi-final and won four Danish titles by then, but I tried not to be offended.

We returned to England on 2 August. The flotation was complete and now the club could sign players, but the squad was leaving straight away for a short Scottish tour, before flying off again to Vienna for a friendly with Austria Memphis. We were not scheduled to have a full day in Manchester until 9 August – but that was after the window closed for international registrations. The only way to get my contract signed was for me to head straight to Old Trafford with Rune after arriving back from Norway, and we only had a few hours to play with because the squad was leaving for Scotland that afternoon.

Another snag. When we sat down in Martin Edwards's office we found him apologising again. The flotation had changed Manchester United's accounting practices and now there was a problem. But Martin's word is Martin's word and he said the way to fix things was for me to sign for an extra year, allowing him to spread the signing-on bonuses he had agreed to, while keeping me within the wage structure. Another year at Manchester United? Inside, I was thinking . . . *yeah*. I felt like I had won the lottery. But, for the sake of negotiating, we said, 'Oh, that's disappointing, that's such a shame.' I mentioned that

I had been looking at houses. Martin smiled. No problem. He would provide the money to buy me one. I bounced out of that room.

My first game at Old Trafford was on 11 August, Manchester United versus a Republic of Ireland XI in Sir Matt Busby's testimonial. Sir Matt was still a presence around the club and it was thrilling to be involved in a match for him. My league debut was against Notts County, at home, the following week. We won 2–0 and my first four competitive appearances brought four clean sheets. I made a mistake versus Leeds to concede my first goal but went on to post eight clean sheets in my first eleven games. I have to bring this up because you know what annoys me? When David de Gea was struggling early in his Manchester United career this narrative appeared that 'Oh, Peter Schmeichel had a difficult start as well.' No, I didn't. I came flying in. Propaganda, that one: a little white lie to help De Gea, which might have originated in the manager's office.

I did have a few issues, logistical and comical ones, on my first day of practice, however. This was just before we left for Norway. I was picked up from Manchester Airport by Norman Davies, the kit man, in the manager's car and driven straight to the Cliff training ground. I had six or seven suitcases and bin bags with me, full of all sorts of gear, having imagined that prior to practice I would be able to dump them at the hotel where I was staying.

Our drive to the Cliff was pretty awkward because Norman didn't know who I was and I didn't know who he was, and when we reached the training ground the bags had to come out, because this was Fergie's car. So, Norman, a lovely, lovely man, helpfully carried them all into the dressing room, piling them where I would be sitting. The dressing room was tiny and these bags filled up half the space. I was early, probably half an hour before everyone else, and had absolutely no idea what to do.

You know that feeling you experience when you find yourself in a new place, an office, a school, whatever, and you simply don't know the norms of that environment? It is awkward. And, let me tell you, it is *very* awkward when that place is a football dressing room and you're sitting alone, waiting for everyone to arrive, your belongings piled around you like some tourist who has missed their train.

I was feeling cramped and weird, but then, one by one, the players walked in – and maybe this was my first real taste of how warm a workplace Manchester United would prove to be. When I had come over from Denmark in July, the club put me up in the Amblehurst Hotel in Sale, a place popular with players, staff and their families, and I was having a drink at the bar when I noticed this guy looking at me. I knew him from somewhere. Half an hour later he came over. 'Are you that goalkeeper Manchester United are signing?' he said. He gave me his hand. It was Clayton Blackmore. We chatted and his friendliness blew me away.

Luckily, on this first day at training, me sitting amid my towers of bags, Clayton was one of the first to arrive and this gave me somebody I knew. Then Mark Hughes walked in. Mark Hughes! He was a hero to me. But he came over and humbly shook my hand. They all did that, one by one, and last to arrive was Bryan Robson. To me, Bryan Robson was God; to any

Manchester United fan he was. And Bryan came and sat down next to me and put out his hand. 'Hey, Pete,' he said.

You know Robbo has this unmistakeable deep voice? 'HEY, PEEETE.' He smiled. 'We will look after you,' he said. Feeling less of a weirdo, I began looking forward to training. That day, as became the routine, we went across to the club's other pitches on Littleton Road for the first session and, though it was pre-season for the others, I had just finished the Danish campaign and felt in the best shape of my life. Let the running commence. Brian Kidd had just taken over as Fergie's assistant and was in charge. 'Okay, easy start,' he said. 'We'll do boxes. Peter, you can go with Walshy [Gary Walsh] and Jim [Leighton] and do some half-volleys.'

'No,' I said, 'I'm in the boxes.'

Everyone started laughing. But I repeated myself. 'I'm in the boxes. I need to be in the same training as everyone else.' I followed a principle, instilled by my goalkeeping mentor since my Hvidovre days, Jørgen Henriksen, that went against normal conventions and it was that a goalkeeper should train with the outfield players and leave the specialist goal-keeping drills for extra, individual sessions. Clearly, at Manchester United, they had never heard this one before. People were still laughing when I repeated myself again: 'I'm in the boxes.'

Kiddo had divided the outfielders into two groups, older and younger ones. Without saying another word I just went over and stood in the older group. Everyone was still looking at me. Kiddo eventually said, 'Okay, Peter.' And that was my first training.

I was glad to have stood up for myself. It takes three seconds to make your mind up about people, remember, and it was important that the first impressions I made on the group included the fact I had character. I was the new guy with all the bin bags who they were laughing at before I touched a ball – but also someone who would clearly do things his own way.

Quite quickly, they realised I was an okay goalkeeper as well.

4
MR HECTIC

This is not a book of regrets, but maybe it is one of doing my accounts. Of reconciling the good and not-so-good that I see when looking back at younger years in the attempt to answer that question I ask myself now: *why me?* How come I could say, at eight years of age, 'I want to play for Denmark and Manchester United and win the FA Cup at Wembley,' and make it happen?

And, if we are adding things up, how did the guy on the pitch tally with the person I felt inside?

When I peer in the rear-view mirror at Peter Schmeichel, new Manchester United signing, twenty-seven years old, I see somebody who was probably a bit too hectic to be around. English is my second language, but I think 'hectic' is the word: someone a little frenetic, a bit full-on. A radio with the volume turned up and an off switch that did not always work.

I came into the club this ambitious guy, pumped up, and it was because I was so serious about succeeding. I took everything about my job extremely seriously. I shouted throughout games; I yelled in training, even at the young players. I never compromised. Never backed down. I look back and, frankly, can see this guy who could be incredibly annoying to be around.

I am not the same person now, but I don't sit wishing that the younger Peter Schmeichel had been different. I set out to reach a distant goal and made the best use of my abilities and knowledge at the time. I accept who I was. And I only have to look at the honours board to know I did something right.

Let me try and explain where Mr Hectic came from.

I told you about my need to take part in the same training as the outfield players. That included all the conditioning work. A midfielder might run 11 kilometres in a match and a goalkeeper 5 kilometres, but I wanted to be just as fit as David Beckham or Roy Keane, yet I'm a big fella – 6 foot 4 and 16 stone when I was playing – so when we did running exercises I was never going to be the fastest.

My attitude, however, was to want to be the best. On a longer run I would always go out right at the front, knowing that at some point I would have to let go, because we had some incredible athletes, but that when I dropped back, I'd still end up in the top third thanks to having been so far ahead to start with. I pushed my big body onwards via pure will, by using phrases like 'If I give up now, I'm a failure', 'If I stop, I will never become a Manchester United goalkeeper'. I had these words ringing in my head all the time.

At Brøndby we had a run on Tuesday afternoons called '15, 15, 15'. You ran round the pitch with cones placed near the corner flags. This meant you had to run the bends sharp. You ran the first round of five laps in fifty-five seconds per lap, with a minute's rest between each one. Then you did the next set of five in fifty-two seconds. Finally, five in fifty seconds.

When I came to the corner, I never cut it. Some did, but I made it my mantra: 'I will never cut corners – cut a corner and I will fail.' That's great, but now encounter that mentality as one of my team-mates. I despised anyone who cheated in their standards – and let them know.

You will hear all these stories about me erupting at training, about all the guys taking great pleasure in chipping me on the practice field. They knew I got angry. But *why* did I get angry? It is because what you do in training manifests itself in games.

My mentality was, when practising, I would do my utmost to save that next shot, knowing that would make me better equipped if I faced a similar situation in a match. Then some comedian finds it funny to chip me. Would you try that chip in a match? No chance. Try a chip for Manchester United and you had better score with it. So why not practise the things that you are actually going to do in a game?

That was my attitude but, when you are fifty-seven not twenty-seven, when you have come away from playing, you see things with different eyes. The pressure of the job, the pressure to win, the pressure of being a Manchester United player – that was constant, for everyone. In those circumstances, sometimes it is okay to let off steam and have fun. That is all the other guys were doing.

Back then, I tried to put everything into every training session and every game, thinking I always clicked a switch and returned to being a human being at the end of it. But, looking back, probably I was not as good at that as I imagined. All these years on, I think, *It would be nice if my attitude had been a little better – not so angry. Maybe I could have toned it down a bit.*

Then again, it could be wishful thinking. Maybe I am just doing what old fellas do –looking at a young man and thinking where does all this *energy* come from?

I do know, for example, that my biggest strengths included concentration and alertness. I was always ready. In most games Manchester United dominated, but – especially because we played with risk – there would always be one or two moments when I suddenly had to be at my highest level of focus and physical preparedness. All that yelling and behaviour of mine – it was designed to keep me in the game. Being on full war footing in every moment may have led to the odd time I looked silly, but I don't care about that. I was never isolated from the game and always able, at any instant, to jump to action and compete.

Sometimes I find myself wishing that I had celebrated really good saves with my team-mates. Then I think: the goalkeeper who does that – how do they look if they then make a mistake? Often, I find myself between two stools.

Littleton Road summed up what a homely club Manchester United was in 1991. You changed at the Cliff, hopped in your vehicle and made the three- or four-minute journey there. Every day it was the same players driving because certain lads did not want dirty kit in their car. The youth players went in minivans.

There was a much bigger field at Littleton Road than at the main training ground, with five or six pitches, but it was by no means as secluded. There was a gate and a fence, but when Manchester United weren't training, people would come walking their massive bulldogs, letting them poo all over the place. Before we arrived in the morning the ground staff had to remove all the turds. All around were terraced houses and there was a path that ran along the side of the fields leading to a little footbridge. This was Salford and we saw all sorts: intruders who we had to throw out, police chases. The locals knew that at the end of the path there were bollards which meant a police car couldn't follow, and of course when there was a chase everyone paused training and watched as the poor, flustered officers had to slam on the brakes and stop. We would have a little smirk and the gaffer would growl, 'Right, back to work.'

My first lodgings were homely too: the Amblehurst Hotel, 44 Washway Road, Sale. Three stars. The owners were Mike and Inga Prophet, who lived there with their four children and became family to me. Mike is a big Manchester City fan but also a good friend of Bryan Robson's, and the Prophets really looked after the Schmeichels while we got used to England and searched for a home.

We stayed at the Amblehurst for three months. Andrei Kanchelskis, another new signing, stayed there too. As did Jim Ryan and Pop Robson, who had just joined the club's coaching staff. The Amblehurst was a kind of safe space for Manchester United people, and after games, especially victories (and there were plenty of those), 80 per cent of the squad would make their way there, with friends and family, to have a drink. In the evenings players often stopped by and on Sundays brought their kids for lunch.

One day at training, Steve Bruce asked how the house-hunting was going. The answer was not too well. I did not have enough time, didn't know the area well enough. He said the house next to his was empty and had been on the market for some time, so why didn't I come round? I did. Steve and Janet, his wife, gave me dinner and that was the beginning of a beautiful friendship between our families which continues to this day. Kasper is still great pals with Alex Bruce, and Kasper's daughter, Isabella, is in the same class as the daughter of Amy Bruce (Steve's daughter and Alex's sister).

The house? Oh, it was perfect, right at the end of a cul-de-sac, with close neighbours, yet not so close that you were overlooking one other. We lived in it for the rest of my Manchester United career.

Once or twice a week, the Schmeichels and Bruces went out for a Chinese meal together. It was an important factor in the relationship I built with Steve on the pitch. Without it, given all my screaming and shouting – often directed at my defenders – I think we might have fallen out.

My sense is that Steve understood me, understood there was a bit more to me as a person than the pumped-up jock; indeed, that it was just part of who I was when I played. Gary Pallister, so laid-back by nature, was comfortable with it too, likewise Denis Irwin. Each one of them understood that a vocal and demanding keeper behind them was much better than having somebody quiet. Fergie hand-picked personalities who could handle confrontation, who were strong enough to stand up to opponents or anyone else. They didn't have to be dominant types like me, but they did have to have backbone. Gary Neville was a big player because of his mentality more than his ability. He made it because he could hack it.

I learned from Steve. As soon as training and matches were over, he became so warm and relaxed. I took lessons from that and calmed down over time. In my external life I let my guard down a little. You could stroll over to Brucey's house, knock on the door and it would be 'Hey come in, have a cup of tea.' Or 'Hey, I'm watching the cricket, come in, do you want a glass of wine?' A lot of things can weigh you down as a player at one of the high-pressure clubs, and Steve showed me a way of putting football aside sometimes and just living life. His warmth makes him a special person. Our other neighbours, Phil and Janice, were lovely people whose children, Simon and James, played with Kasper and Cecilie. You would have a beer with them and just be normal, not a footballer. That was a new thing for me in many ways.

After eighteen games in the 1991–92 English First Division I had eleven clean sheets and after twenty-one – the halfway stage – we were top of the table, two points ahead of Leeds United, with two games in hand. We were the leading scorers, had the best defence. Brucey, Pally and I gelled quickly, and I brought something new to the team – a dominant goalkeeper, who came for crosses and pushed the defenders out of his box. There were some tough forwards in the division, big guys like Iain Dowie, Niall Quinn, Lee Chapman, Brian Deane, but I was going from game to game loving the battle. I felt like I was on one big adventure, visiting all these English grounds, facing all these famous teams I had dreamed about. It was a special time in my life. The kids were lovely ages – Kasper was turning six, Cecilie was a cute toddler – and friends were always coming over from Denmark to stay. I was so happy. Everything was good.

Except on the pitch. The second half of that season: how bad were we? It started with an unbelievable game, on 1 January, against Queens Park Rangers at Old Trafford. They were fifteenth and Fergie's fiftieth birthday was the day before. He took us all to the Midland Hotel, a departure, because we never stayed in hotels before home games.

When your preparations are disrupted, even slightly, you're never 100 per cent. And when you find yourself trying to get some sleep in a hotel in central Manchester . . . on New Year's Eve . . . then let me tell you, you're *disrupted*. There was so much noise. Many of us had a restless night. Bleary-eyed, we played and this guy Bailey – Dennis Bailey, we had hardly heard of him – scored a hat-trick. Fergie never had us hotelling before a home game again.

From there, we struggled. The goals began drying up. In a stretch of twenty games there were only three where we scored more than once. We went goalless for three consecutive matches, against Nottingham Forest, Wimbledon and QPR, and got to mid-April facing a backlog of fixtures and a schedule that asked us to play five times in ten days. We played on 16 April, 18 April, 20 April, 22 April and 26 April – crazy.

On 18 April we drew with Luton – they got relegated. On 20 April we lost to Forest and on 22 April we lost to West Ham – they got relegated too. Their goal was a fluke, coming when the ball hit Gary Pallister and flew in. Nothing seemed to be going our way. It felt like Leeds, on the other hand, were getting the breaks. On 26 April they kicked off before us and we watched part of the game as they held on for a lucky 3–2 win at Sheffield United. Then we went out and lost again – at, of all places,

Anfield. This defeat meant Leeds were champions, whereas Manchester United passed the grim milestone of twenty-five years without an English title.

Tiredness, injuries, the pile-up of games, the terrible pitch (and it was terrible) at Old Trafford: we could make excuses, but when it came down to it, at the crunch point of the season we took two points from four games, two of those against sides who went down. We ran out of gas. Just gave it away. The media were saying 'same old United' and a lot of people, at the time, felt it came down to psychology – but looking from a distance it was simpler than that. We weren't quite good enough. The thing that always comes to me when I compare the 1991–92 side with our later teams is that it wasn't really there – just not quite up to champion level.

Paul Ince aside, our midfield was not strong or settled enough. It had Darren Ferguson, technically very good but slow, and Mal Donaghy, Mick Phelan. Neil Webb got injured playing for England and never truly recovered. Knocks also kept Robbo out a lot. One thing which came out of that season was a realisation in Fergie that it wasn't enough to just take Incey and stick him with A. N. Other in the middle. He converted Brian McClair to a midfield player and McClair–Ince became a really strong unit, a platform for our success the following season.

We needed to evolve in other ways too. This was Ryan Giggs's first season as a regular and he was fantastic, but very young. It was natural there were games where he was up and games where he was down. With that experience under his belt, he was incredible the next year, Andrei the same. Fergie learned that a couple of the squad would have to leave for the club to kick on and I look back at that 1991–92 season as one of evolution, of making an investment that paid off in the campaigns that followed.

I was to have the summer of my life, with Denmark at Euro 92, but when I left for Copenhagen in May I didn't want to know about football. I just wanted to get away from it all. I had been told, upon joining, that I was going to be the last piece of the jigsaw for Fergie, the factor that took Manchester United over the line, and to discover I was not was a little blow to the pride. Most of all, I was just not used to coming second. With Brøndby, the routine was winning stuff.

In Europe, United won the Super Cup but exited the Cup Winners' Cup to Atlético Madrid. We lost the first leg 3–0 in the Vicente Calderón and there was an incident in the game that illustrates how my habit of asserting myself made me hard to be around sometimes. Atlético went ahead when Paulo Futre came in from the right and dummied me. I thought he was going to square the ball and had moved to cover the pass when he stopped, turned his foot and stroked it home. I could see it all happening and was convinced I would be able to adjust and still save the ball, but when I tried to change direction my foot slipped.

This was four months into my time in England. I spoke English pretty well, but there was still a slight language barrier. I wasn't quick enough with my vocabulary to say exactly the right thing at the right time: in the heat of the moment, things could come out wrong. In the dressing room at half-time in Madrid, Fergie crucified me and I defended myself but sounded silly. It was a mistake, a big goalkeeping mistake, I knew that

– but I came across like I was refusing to take responsibility. What I was trying to say was that I had gambled on a cross and that slipping had stopped me from recovering the situation – not that slipping meant it wasn't my fault. Not quite being precise in how I expressed myself could make me sound worse in confrontations.

Another unwanted memory: back then, Fergie allowed us one glass of wine the night before games, but I never indulged – until that trip. For some reason I decided I fancied a glass. It probably had zero to do with my error, but I never did it again.

The highlight of the season was winning the Rumbelows Cup and that felt incredible. Think about this eight-year-old kid, from a concrete village in a country far from England, dreaming about Wembley finals. Our 1–0 win over Nottingham Forest was a little taste of that. The game itself was forgettable, but I do remember walking round the stadium with the trophy, seeing all the United scarves in the air, with the glow of knowing my whole family was in the crowd.

One other game sticks in my mind and it was our sixth of the season, against Wimbledon at Selhurst Park. I want to tell the story to help you understand how that brash, confrontational, sometimes even obnoxious guy you will see if you look at old footage and pictures was – and wasn't – me. I was him, some of the time, in training, and I was him, most of the time, in games. And being that guy was a deliberate act, a useful match tactic.

On the pitch I was arrogant – consciously. I wanted to annoy the opposition, I wanted to be in their heads – especially those of their strikers. I needed them to understand it was me they were up against. Not any old goalkeeper. *Me*.

I had a coach, in my early days, who said when you catch the ball always bring it into your body. Clutch it to your chest. Show the world 'This ball belongs with me.' Players would come up close and I would deliberately look through them, or past them, holding that ball, never even acknowledging their presence.

So, 3 September 1991, we go to Wimbledon. Since my league debut in a 2–0 win against Notts County, I had been flying. I was good in training, four clean sheets in the first four games. My team-mates decided to wind me up. 'Just wait 'til you play Fash,' they began saying. 'Oh, Fash will find you out.' All these little comments. Fash this, Fash that.

I have to admit, he got in my head – not through his own doing but because of our dressing-room banter. I started thinking, what is it about this Fash? Who is this guy? *Wimbledon: John Fashanu. Okay.* I developed this attitude that I was not going to be beaten by Fash. *I don't care how tough the guy is. I will not acknowledge him on the pitch. In fact, when the game comes, I will do everything I can to annoy 'Fash'.* I wanted to communicate to him that he meant nothing to me, and we had a few early moments of contact where I challenged hard and just stared right through him. It was all going well until he scored from a cross I came for and never got to. We won 2–1, but I learned a lot from that mistake.

On the pitch, Fashanu was this guy who could be really nice and polite to everyone. 'How are you, are you okay? Oh I'm sorry.' But when the chance came, he would be a downright, absolute bastard. They were all like that, Wimbledon: ninety minutes of brutal, merciless football and afterwards the nicest people in the world.

I knew, with Fash, my moment would come. You get opportunities in games and at that time refereeing was a bit different – you could 'defend' yourself, I guess. Fast-forward to February 1994, we are at Selhurst Park facing Wimbledon in the fifth round of the FA Cup. A ball comes over the defence and Fash is chasing in while I come out and it becomes clear it is going to be a 70–30 in my favour.

So, as I catch the ball just before my 18-yard line, I keep my leg out, braced and straight. Old Fash run right into it and for the first time I speak to him. 'Oh, John. Are you okay? I had to protect myself, John. Oh dear, I'm so sorry.' It is a painful one but he's Big John Fashanu, so he says, 'I'm. F-ine.' And he jumps up – but I can see he is in absolute agony.

Soon after that, there is another ball and this time it is in his favour. I come out, knowing that it is crunch time. Have I won my battle? No way can I back down and pull out, but this time he can really hurt me. And . . . he jumps over me. He never came near me again.

It was in such moments that the arrogance I adopted helped. There were a lot of strikers with whom I had relationships similar to my one with Fash. I am sure they hated me. But the arrogance was something I left on the field. Off it, I hope – I believe – I was a different person. When you are younger, you don't always understand the contradictions in your life, or personality, and it took the years passing, a lot of reflection, a divorce and for me to meet a soulmate, my wife, Laura, to make sense of everything.

To digest why I had to be a different guy on the pitch from the guy I saw in the mirror. To understand the person that I am really supposed to be.

I cannot escape the fact that Mr Hectic was me. But at twenty-seven I faced a completely different set of challenges and decisions from those I face at fifty-seven. I could not approach them in as relaxed and content a way as I approach life now. Yes, I looked bad at times. But yes, very much yes, I got to where I wanted to get to, and my way of acting fuelled stages of the journey. It took a certain personality to be part of Alex Ferguson's Manchester United, and a certain hardness of character to help the club get back to the top of English football after twenty-six years.

When I look at my team-mates and my manager they were similar to me. Fergie was a lot more light-hearted than his public image, but if people believed him to be a hairdryer-wielding tough guy all the time, then fine. He didn't care. Eric Cantona never cared how the public perceived him. Mark Hughes never cared, Brian McClair never cared, Incey never cared. Pally? He didn't give two flying hoots what people thought. And how good was Pally, by the way?

Life is understood backwards: I reckon it is simply part of middle age to look back, shake your head at your younger self and think with a smile, *What were you doing?* When you're younger you are consumed by what you want to achieve. You clear away the obstacles and plough onwards. When you are older, you realise that life is as much about enjoying yourself and showing kindness and love, but the riddle is: if you had thought that way in your earlier years, would you have ever got ahead the way you did?

I think about it a lot. Look at things this way. From, let's say, the age of two to the age of twelve or thirteen you have your carefree years. Then, you can fool around, but after that you need to start working towards something, figuring out what you want to be, applying yourself at school. By twenty-two, twenty-three, you need to know your path in life. So everything is packed into those ten years, the task of turning yourself from a kid into a grown-up with a career – all while you're travelling through adolescence into early adulthood and physically developing; when you're naive, idealistic, you fall in love every minute, your emotions are everywhere.

Then it is just the long drag, when dinner with friends is the highlight of your month, and little changes. It is only when you experience a real life change, like a divorce, that you have to dig deep, assess everything, think about the implications for your kids, truly examine who you are.

My gift is not only what I have found with Laura – someone who has gone through similar things, someone who is relaxed about this world – but it is having Kasper, a son who is pursuing the same career that I undertook. I can take no credit for the brilliant goalkeeper he is in any technical sense – all that is down to work he put in himself. People say did you train him in the back garden? No, I had no time or energy for that. When I came home from training it was the last thing I wanted to do, I was too tired. And whatever kind of dad you think that makes me, that's how it was.

But the one thing I can say I have helped with is making sure he doesn't step on the same traps I did myself, and one of these involves how he projects himself. Playing the games, being the No 1 goalkeeper, succeeding on the pitch in England and beyond – I found that the simplest part of the whole thing. The hard part was coming across as the person that I, at least, believe I am.

With the advent of the Premier League, suddenly TV asked for more time with us. You had to be a more popular person, more active in the media, and I didn't know how to do that comfortably. I wish I'd communicated more and communicated better. I tended to avoid interviews and then when I did say something, I was way too honest. And honesty can very easily get you into trouble. I try and help Kasper be a bit more measured when he is getting his messages out.

When he feels he wants to say something strong, in an interview or social media post, he likes to run it past me and often my advice will be to sleep on it and consider what he will really gain by speaking out. Will the public understand him properly, or will his words be twisted? Will they provide an excuse for certain outlets to produce a sensationalised story? Often, upon reflection, Kasper will let things lie – or get his message out in a subtler way.

I wish good counsel had been available when I was playing, but only a few footballers – like Ryan Giggs, with Harry Swales and Fergie – had advisers who protected them and their image. It was an era when agents were generally there just to do deals. If I was to advise my younger self it would be to seriously work on your media training.

What else? I would find other ways to channel the amount of energy I had. I would say, 'Come on, Pete, dial it down a bit . . .' Recently, I watched one of our games versus Arsenal and was struck by how much David Seaman was the opposite to me. I love David. He was one of my favourite goalkeepers; I hugely admired how calm he was. Yet I could not have been like that. If I was as chilled as him, I'd fall asleep. For me, I had to maintain a certain energy level on the pitch. So, I couldn't be David – but I wonder if I might have at least attempted to become something in between David and me.

Finally, I'd try and just be a little less, yeah . . . hectic . . . to be around. Even though, inside, I always understood perfectly that I was merely one player of eleven and that I needed the other ten guys to fulfil my ambitions, I did not always show that. I would advise the young Peter Schmeichel to try being more open and show his appreciation to those team-mates more.

Would I have been just as successful with all that on board? I think I would. But who knows? The only thing I can be certain of is that an eight-year-old boy from far away grew up and made it all happen and, in that, I would not change a thing.

5
CHAMPIONS

On the awful day at Anfield when our title hopes died in 1991–92, Fergie admitted to the press that 'losing has had a numbing effect on us'. But when he talked to us in the dressing room he was already looking for ways to move past our pain. He spoke about disappointment and about dealing with such a feeling. But then he began speaking about how well we had played throughout the season, how our progress had been fantastic. And so, from that moment, from the very bottom of that low, he was building us back up. He was nearly always a brilliant manager in defeat. That day, his tone, his message were perfect: he could have gone absolutely berserk, but that would not have helped us at all.

With one more game to play, against Tottenham, we had one more week together when we might have stewed in disappointment, but Fergie would not let that happen. He continued to talk about how well we had done and how we had to put the experience gained to good use the next season. He sent us away for the summer with as much positivity as he could and while the hurt of losing remained, there was a sense of closure. The big talk had been done. When we came back it would be a fresh start.

The fact that 1992–93 was the first season of the Premier League was good for us. There were adverts for the new competition, razzmatazz. You got a name on your shirt and a squad number, and this was the talk of the dressing room – who would get which number? All of that helped us; it felt like drawing a line under the past, and a new beginning. In pre-season Fergie kept returning to his themes: 1991–92 was something to put down to experience, something we could use, it would be the final piece in our jigsaw. He was comforting. He kept telling us how far we had come, how good we were.

I reported for the new season two weeks late and ten feet tall, because of Denmark's success at Euro 92, and walked back into a squad that was in an excellent mood: looking forward, positive, all trace of the trauma of April gone and in exactly the right frame of mind for the challenge ahead. One great strength of Fergie's was recruitment. He never looked just at ability; he looked at mentality, the sturdiness of the player's character. He signed players who could deal with adversity, guys who on a Tuesday night of stinging rain at Charlton in January would perform like it was a May day at Wembley. Men who handled things.

So, in some senses, the work of rebuilding us was already done before he started it – because he knew that, as people, we would find our own ways of bouncing back. Nonetheless, the way he played things in the wake of 1991–92 was masterful. He was a genius at never burdening players with the big picture: that, he would keep to himself and the coaching staff. Us, he kept focused on whatever was in front of us.

I'll give you an example. When preparing for a game, he would hardly mention the opposition or specifics of the match until the last moment. During the week, there might be a comment like 'We can only do forty-five minutes' training today, I want you fresh on Saturday,' but it was rare that he would say the name of who we were playing. It was all about protecting us. Like most teams in that era, we had an established playing style and first-choice XI and very little changed, tactics or selection-wise, from week to week. Everything was geared to staying grooved and concentrating on our own tasks. After matches there were seldom detailed debriefs; the mindset was 'move on'. In the dressing room at the end of a game Fergie would just say a couple of things and was very brief. It would be 'Blah blah blah,' then 'Go and get your bath, see you Monday,' and that was the end of that.

The one time it was different was when the following game was Liverpool. Then, he would go, 'Blah blah blah, it's *******
Liverpool next. Get your bath and see you Monday. Be ******* ready.' I don't think there is anyone who disliked Liverpool more than the manager, and those were the weeks when the routine changed. In those weeks it was *very* clear who we were playing next and Fergie was right on his toes, making sure everyone was fit and ready.

The way we went into 1992–93 not dwelling at all on 1991–92 fitted our culture. Denmark's Euro 92 miracle had restored my appetite and confidence to levels higher than ever. What was really cool was that when I arrived back in Manchester, the guys threw a little party to celebrate me winning the Euros, organised by Robbo and Brucey. They were proper captains. Seven or eight players came to my house and it felt amazing. To see their genuine pride in my achievement – what a feeling.

Fergie only made one signing, recruiting Dion Dublin from Cambridge United for £1m and went into our first game, away to Sheffield United, with a starting XI that featured ten players who had also started our final game of 1991–92. Dion was on the bench. Five minutes in, we conceded the first ever Premier League goal when Brian Deane scored a header from a flick on following a long throw. He beat me again, from the penalty spot, after fifty minutes and we lost 2–1.

Our second game, we lost 3–0 to Everton, who scored three breakaway goals even though we dominated possession, and in the first Premier League table ever published – newspapers waited until two rounds of matches were complete – you will find Manchester United right at the bottom, in twenty-second place. We drew our third game, with Ipswich, at Old Trafford. The Stretford End had been demolished for rebuilding and we found ourselves in this weird stadium with scaffolding and rubble behind one of the goals.

To the outside world, Manchester United looked in crisis. We had been the title favourites, but after taking one point from three games everyone was saying same old United again. But I wasn't panicking. Our performances were way better than our results and this is how it was from my viewpoint on the pitch. I looked in front of me and saw Brucey and Pally: yeah, those are my guys. I looked right and saw Paul Parker: yep, you don't get many better right backs. I looked left and saw Denis Irwin: Denis! Complete class, superb professional. I could begin to feel very comfortable.

I looked into midfield and there was Ince and McClair: well, *that* is all right. I looked to the wings: Giggsy, Lee Sharpe and Kanchelskis, *wow*. Up front I saw Mark Hughes and Dion: not bad, *not bad at all*. I knew we were in decent shape – we all knew we were in decent shape. The manager remained confident; he showed not the slightest sign of doubt or panic.

Dion made his first start when we travelled to Southampton and decided it with a late, poacher's goal. We went from twentieth place to third place with five wins and five clean sheets on the bounce, including a 2–0 victory over Leeds. The sadness involved Dion breaking his leg in a nasty tackle against Crystal Palace. It ended his season.

Then, suddenly, we struggled again. We drew five in a row, lost to Wimbledon at home, to Aston Villa away. We stopped scoring. Apart from two outstanding strikes from Sparky in a 2–2 draw with Liverpool, during a run of six league games our only goal came from the spot, and we weren't scoring in knockout competition either, going out of the UEFA Cup on penalties to Torpedo Moscow after two 0–0 draws, and out of the League Cup 1–0 to Villa.

I don't remember it, but I gave an interview in which I said we wouldn't win anything unless we bought a striker, and after losing in the league to Villa, Fergie conceded, 'Maybe we don't have a lot of natural goalscorers in the team.' The international break came at just the right time. We returned with a 3–0 victory over Oldham, and a few days later Fergie stumbled across precisely the piece of the puzzle we were missing – he signed Eric Cantona.

Eric was instrumental. Eric was that little bit of something else. Eric was . . . Eric. The transfer happened so quickly that rumours he might be joining lasted only a day, but in that short time I remember thinking, 'Let this happen, please let this happen.' Because I thought he was incredible. I liked him from the very first time I saw him on *Match of the Day*. I hated that he was playing for Leeds, of course, but from the moment he arrived in England I loved his differentness. The Charity Shield sealed the deal for me, watching him score three fantastic goals versus Liverpool. *Wow, this guy is magnificent.*

We already had someone a bit different in the dressing room – Andrei. He didn't speak the language and had an interpreter in the dressing room, this at a time when, apart from a few of us English-speaking Scandinavians, there were very few foreigners in the English game. But Eric was *different*-different. You know how rumours go around football? There was talk about how Eric was this proper weird guy, and we had heard it all. Silly stuff. Then there was the fact Leeds were offloading him, despite how superb he had been for them on the pitch, and that chequered history, which everyone knew about, of him having six different clubs in France and often being in trouble there. Mystique surrounded him. *Who is this guy?* And then suddenly, boom, there he was at the Cliff.

His first day was unforgettable.

Eric walked in . . . and you expected something else. You expected someone else. A dominant character, maybe. Somebody flamboyant. But what came in through that dressing-room door was a very shy person, very shy. Someone who couldn't look people in the eye, who felt so uncomfortable in his new surroundings that he quickly got changed and went out through the door to the pitch.

Nobody had ever gone to the pitch thirty minutes before training. At the Cliff, behind one of the goals, was the wall of the indoor arena and, without anyone to train with, Eric went there and started kicking a ball against the wall. He popped it up in the air, chested it down. Left foot, right foot, volleys, first-time touches. Boom, boom, boom – in perfect control of the ball.

The canteen at the Cliff had windows onto the pitch. So did the manager's office. And the coaches' office and the treatment room. Everyone gathered to watch: *What is he doing?* He had people mesmerised.

Among them were the kids. Scholes, Butty, Beckham, the Nevilles. They were still in the younger group, who had a separate dressing room, and that first day they just watched Eric and said nothing. Then the next day – it was a bit like when the cat does something and then the kittens, slowly, slowly, sneak in and do the same thing – before you knew it, the young kids were out before training too, kicking balls against the wall and chesting it down.

One of Eric's biggest contributions was demonstrating an awareness of what the job of a footballer should be. He infused a culture that you can actually improve your skills without having a coach there helping you. This evolved over the years and soon you had Gary Neville practising throw-ins and crosses on the run, Beckham practising corners and free kicks, and eventually everyone staying out after training to do some specialist work.

I felt an instant bond with Eric because I had the same attitude to practice too: as I mentioned, thanks to Jørgen Henriksen, in training I joined in everything the outfield players were doing. All my specialist work, my goalkeeping drills, were done in my own time. For my first year, there had not been the opportunity to do that extra practice as part of my daily routine at the Cliff, but thanks to Eric suddenly individual training became the culture. I applauded him.

He also brought difference on the pitch, this catalogue of extra options in any game. Whenever I got the ball, my first instinct was to look for a throw-out that would set up a quick counterattack and I already had wingers who could outrun anybody to release – Andrei, Sharpe and Ryan – or I could hit Sparky, who was exceptional at taking the ball down and keeping it for the team.

But now I had Eric as well. Eric – he had the strength and technique to take *any* ball down, left foot, right foot, head, chest, but he was also brilliant at finding the pocket of space where no defender would follow him. So very often, when I looked for a throw, he was free. And that was just me. Imagine the options he suddenly gave to our midfielders. When he received possession, he could always do something unexpected, and once Ryan and Andrei and the full backs caught on, it was incredible – we were penetrating the opposition all over the place, with Eric's passes finding their runs.

I've played with one other magician like that: Michael Laudrup. Oh my God, what a footballing genius Michael Laudrup was. Towards the end of our careers we played for this fun team that nobody knew about, called the Show Stars. It played one game every summer somewhere in Denmark and contained actors, musicians and footballers. After we had played, we would record a song and have a massive party. I liked playing up front in this game and once said to Michael, 'You pass the ball, I'm ready to run.' And Michael said, 'No . . . you run, *then* I'll pass it. I'll find you.' It was like turning football on its head.

Next time we got the ball I ran and, boom, the ball was there, right at my feet, in front of the goal and in my natural step. I only had to touch it into the net. That was Michael. Eric was the only other team-mate I had who was comparable.

People always ask: what was it about Ferguson? Was it the hairdryer? They think about the almost negative things. But I'll tell you. What Fergie was really good at – and he did it again in the summer of 1993 when he recruited Roy Keane – was understanding exactly what a team needed and finding not just the right player but the right type: someone independent, strong-minded, who could stand up for themselves whatever the circumstances. They didn't have to be loud but they did have to have character, and the hairdryer was only used rarely – in general, Fergie encouraged players to be who they were and didn't seek to dominate.

He looked at Eric's background as a strength not a weakness. Six clubs in France? He got kicked out of them because he had a desire and strength of character that others couldn't handle. And someone who gets into so much trouble and gets dumped so many times yet *still* wants to play – well, that guy must have an *unbelievable* love for football. That is what Fergie saw. He encouraged the individuality in Eric and made no excuses to the rest of the squad about treating him differently. However, all the stories about Eric getting leeway when it came to things like dress code – they are true, but the significance gets overblown. Because Fergie treated every player differently to an extent. Everyone was managed and dealt with according to their personality and what they needed, personally, to go out and fulfil their individual potential.

We won two games in twelve in the lead-up to Eric's arrival; afterwards we lost only three in twenty-nine. Yet the mind plays tricks. My recollection is that we just took charge of the Premier League and began running things, but looking at the old results and tables it's interesting to see that, apart from very brief spells when we were first, we weren't really in charge until the last seven games, when we went top again and never let the spot go. My false memory, I think, is because of the calmness I remember in the camp once we got our teeth into that season and realised Eric had completed us as a team. And Fergie was right. The experience of 1991–92 did help. We knew just to stay on track and not look at what rivals were doing. I don't want to sound arrogant, but we knew we were the best side in the league, and being top, that was just how it should be.

Villa and Norwich played good football, in front of great home crowds, and did their best to push us. In fact, both still sat above us going into April. But maybe our biggest obstacle was the surface at Old Trafford, which did not suit our skilful players and quick, fluent game. There were no Desso pitches then. The Manchester weather left our playing surface bare and muddy and it had to be piled with sand to prevent it disintegrating completely. It sloped up in the middle too, so much that if you were sitting in the first row of the South Stand, you couldn't see the front row of the North Stand. We all hated that pitch and in 1992–93 it got worse than ever. We basically played our home games on a sandpit.

This was also the era before the Premier League had a ball sponsorship. Clubs chose their own balls and we tried different options, hoping to find one that was good for playing on sand. The key game of the whole season was Sheffield Wednesday at home, on 10 April 1993, and for that we chose a ball that was coated with a bit more plastic than standard, because of the sand. It was like a rock. We just couldn't play our football and for an hour the game was dreadful, nothing happening in it, until the referee, Mike Peck, pulled up with a hamstring injury. One of his assistants, John Hilditch, took over.

This was the game that coined the phrase 'Fergie Time', but the idea that Manchester United simply got to play on until we scored – I'm sorry, it's a myth. The time required for the change of refs plus other stoppages probably added up to more than the nine minutes which were added to the game. As for the officials 'wanting United to win' in that match – almost the first thing the new ref did was give Wednesday a penalty, which John Sheridan converted. We just could not find an equaliser no matter how much we pushed but then, in the eighty-sixth minute, from a corner, Brucey powered this fantastic header home for 1–1 and suddenly we were pouring forward at them.

We had six men in their box when, from one of Ryan's crosses, we won another corner. Ryan delivered it, Wednesday cleared and Pally chased down and sent the ball back into their box. From a deflection, it looped towards Brucey, who planted his head through the ball again for the winner. Manchester United 2 (Bruce 86, 90+6) Sheffield Wednesday 1 (Sheridan 65 pen). A little side story is that Wednesday's keeper was one of Steve's closest mates in the game – Chris Woods.

The best celebrations, *ever*, in football were by Fergie and Brian Kidd in that moment. Fergie loses it. He's on the pitch and I think he's about to do somersaults or something, but then he remembers he is the manager of Manchester United and more or less collects himself. But Kiddo doesn't have any inhibitions. He is on his knees. He is kissing the ground and looking into the sky. The clip has been replayed countless times, but I still have to laugh out loud when I see the footage again.

That game was not just a turning point of 1992–93, it was key to our entire development. The turnaround we produced in those final minutes that day built something we came to believe in and rely upon over the years to come, which Fergie teams adopted long after most of us had gone. It was an ethos of playing until the referee said you could play no more, of always investing, of committing men, energy, emotion – everything you had – in pursuit of late equalisers and winning goals. Of risk mode. Of never giving in.

Without '93, there might have been no '99.

The win over Wednesday sent us top and we were champions by ten points in the end. At the Cliff, despite what was at stake, the atmosphere was so good. Fergie's confident demeanour set the tone but Kiddo was unbelievable too.

He was the one who took practice and was out there on the grass with us all the time. And his training was inspirational. He is a northerner first of all and has a northerner's mentality, which is to be light-hearted and try and look on the bright side of every situation – yet to retain a certain toughness behind the banter and smile. He was always looking to make training a happy event and would come in and say, 'Guys, we have to do a bit of this . . . but I promise it is only going to be fifteen minutes.' We went out with a positive mindset, no matter how hard the work was going to be.

His drills tended to be imaginative, his possession games were fun, he was always telling us how good we were and making us feel relaxed and reassured. We especially enjoyed stuff like finishing, but this meant him having to come up with ways to fool the manager. Fergie didn't like finishing training, he thought it risked injuries – so Kiddo was always sneaking it in.

We became Manchester United's first league champions since 1967 on 2 May. It was a Sunday and at the precise moment Villa lost at home to Oldham, meaning we were champions with two games still to go, everything changed for us. It changed in terms of our profile, our status, I guess in terms of us being stars. It was almost a physical thing – you felt like something shifted internally.

On the day itself we trained in the morning in preparation for playing Blackburn on the Monday night and there was no real talk about the title, just a bit of casual chat like 'Oh, yeah, Villa are playing Oldham, are you watching the game?' Oldham were fighting relegation and I guess none of us expected them to win at Villa Park, but our lack of interest was mostly because we were focused on Blackburn, knowing the title was ours if we won that game.

My routine was to have lunch at the club then go home, do whatever and have an afternoon kip around four o'clock. I was not going to waver from that. Villa kicked off at four but I didn't even think about their game. I had my sleep and woke around half five, a bit tired, and thought, *Oh yeah they're playing.* So I put Sky on and looked at the little score caption on the screen. Aston Villa 0 Oldham 1, ten minutes to go. *Bloody hell.* I immediately turned the TV off and did not know what to do. I followed my only instinct – which, I'm not kidding, was to scamper behind my sofa and hide. So there I was, a grown man of twenty-eight, crouched behind my settee, terrified to look at the TV.

Eventually, I managed to turn it on again: 1–0, five minutes to go. I turned it straight back off. I stayed behind the sofa. I hit the remote. Injury time. 'Off' button.

I was lying on the carpet, in the middle of trying to hit 'On', when people I had never seen in my life came running into my street, celebrating, whooping, yelling, 'Champions!' Aston Villa 0 Oldham Athletic 1, FT. Within half an hour, our little cul-de-sac in Bramhall became like Deansgate on a Friday night. It was known that Brucey and I lived there, and car after car came down the road, horns beeping, flags trailing from the windows. And before the hour was out, the whole team was in Brucey's house beginning the most incredible party.

We phoned the manager. 'Congratulations, boys, well done,' he said. 'No drinking – we're playing tomorrow.' Everyone laughed at that one. We were not short of alcohol and car after car kept arriving. I got to bed in the middle of the night. Except for one other occasion, it was the only time in my whole career that I drank the day before a game and, fantastic as the party was, I am not entirely comfortable when I reflect upon it. The excuse in the back of my mind was *We are not playing until 8 p.m. tomorrow, it'll be all right*, but I was still cutting corners. I never cut corners.

The next day I helped Brucey clear up and cannot tell you how many empty bottles of wine there were, strewn all over his house. Our families had been at the party too. For home games, we had a routine where Brucey and I travelled in one car together while our wives and kids went together in another car, and we followed this routine, picking up Incey – who also lived in Bramhall – en route. We drove to Old Trafford talking about the night, the party, all the funny stuff that had happened. We barely spoke about having just become English champions.

But when we neared the stadium there was no escaping that fact. We drew up on the stadium forecourt off Stretford Road, to park outside what is now the Treble Reception. Normally, three hours before kick-off, you could just drive down the road, but this time it was absolutely jam-packed with people and every one of them seemed to be waving a 'Champions' flag. To a noise that was incredible, through this ocean of flags and supporters, we crawled to our parking spot.

At the pre-match meal, everyone was a little tired, quiet. We went downstairs for the team talk and the manager didn't start it with 'congratulations' or anything. He just got straight to business. 'We're playing Blackburn, we have to win this, no letting up,' and then he read out the team. The stadium was already packed when I went out for my warm-up, an hour before kick-off, but when we started the game we were terrible.

The night before was still in our system and we were a goal behind before we knew it. This was embarrassing. We couldn't be champions and play like that, not when so many people had come to celebrate – and something happened. Unspoken, we just clicked into game mode. After that we played our best hour of football of the whole season, with Ryan scoring an incredible goal into the top corner, Incey bursting through to make it 2–1 and then with nearly the last touch Pally, our only regular who hadn't scored all season, slotted home a cheeky free kick.

Flags are like balloons. There is something about them that just makes people happy. Fans with flags become more vocal, and as our supporters waved their banners, songs were sung with the force of twenty-six years of hurt being released – it was one of the experiences of my life.

Afterwards, everyone went to the Amblehurst and stayed overnight, following another epic party. I woke the next morning very, very tired and in desperate need of rest, but Robbo announced, 'Right, send your wives and families home, we're going to the races.' So, we went to Chester races and stayed in the champagne enclosure. I remember Denis Irwin saying later, 'We went to the races and the only horse I saw was a police horse,' and that summed up our priorities for the day.

I came home extremely tired and possibly very drunk and woke up at 11 a.m. the next day. *Urgh. Uh oh. Why is the phone ringing? No!*

Robbo again.

'PEEETE,' he said. 'Bring the family. Barbecue at my house. NOW.'

So, with the families we had a barbecue, with a few more beers, at his house in Hale.

Finally, we eased up. There was one more game to play, Wimbledon away, and it was time to start preparing. On a difficult pitch, against a difficult team, we gave another great performance and won 2–1. The best thing about Wimbledon away is that, for Manchester United, it was always like playing a home game – because Wimbledon's following was so small it meant the rest of the ground filled up with London Reds. Selhurst was like a mini-version of our own stadium that day.

It was not the worst setting for us to finish and when the final whistle went there was a pitch invasion. The referee happened to blow when I had the ball in my hands – and that ball, decorated with everyone's signatures, is in the Manchester United museum. As all the fans poured onto the pitch, I just stuffed it under my shirt and started running. I cannot remember what happened after that.

6

DOUBLE, THEN ZERO

Recruitment, as I have said, was one of Fergie's great strengths, and finding players with the right skills and character for our team was only part of his knack. He was also a master of timing. He had an incredible sense for when we needed a change of personnel.

The most famous example is when Mark Hughes, Incey and Andrei moved on at the end of the 1994–95 season. The departure of three players who were so important and popular was painful to the rest of us in the squad, and a shock to the press and fans, but it proved necessary so that he could bring the Class of '92 into our side. That was Fergie: always looking at what he had in the pipeline, always scheming about who he could buy to bring improvement, always tracking which young players were coming through and thinking how to create space and opportunity for new faces. He always had two brains, one focused on the present and one that looked ahead. One day, after I retired, I got an insight into the extent of his planning when I visited him at Carrington.

It was at a time when Manchester United were in a slump of form and Christmas was approaching. The team had just struggled versus Everton. I went to the training ground – it is one of the things you do as a former player, as a little show of support. You cannot change anything but maybe you can cheer up a few people in the building.

I found Fergie out on the training pitch, in high spirits. He was always like that when times were tough on the pitch: joking and full of banter, whistling tunes. He saw me. 'Oh, Pete, Pete – come over!' We were chatting away, with him in this great (outward) mood, and he said, 'Come with me.'

I knew what we were about to do. I had witnessed the routine for years. When the first team was at work, he liked to go around all the pitches, have a little chat with the reserve coach while casting an eye over their players, and do the same with all the youth teams. That is what we did and we eventually arrived where one of the younger squads was practising. We stood watching this one particular kid. Fergie said, 'See him, not next season but the season after . . . he'll play half of our first League Cup game.' He had it all mapped out, the opportunity he was going to give this boy – eighteen months into the future. That was him, even during difficult times, forever plotting where the next talent was coming from and how he was going to use it.

We took our game to another level in the 1993–94 season and the difference was him signing Roy Keane. At the time, I didn't understand Fergie's logic. Why did we need another midfielder? But when I look back, his thinking was very clear. After winning a title and releasing a whole lot of tension and emotion in the way we did, if you just stick with exactly the same personnel you might go flat. Without change you stagnate.

As a manager, you sometimes have to take a winning team and throw a spanner in the works; do something that puts players on edge and makes them work even harder. Roy was a big, big signing, a British transfer record, and the best young midfield talent in the country. Adding him put everybody on the front foot again. Players want to play with other good players, and as soon as he arrived you wanted a piece of the action, to be on the field with him.

In my time, the one summer when Fergie did not make a major change was 1994 – he only added David May, a back-up defender – and we won nothing in the season that followed. In 1993, Roy was exactly the player to kick us on. His abilities aside, his education had been at Nottingham Forest under Brian Clough who, like Fergie, developed his players to be strong personalities.

It meant Roy was able to step straight into our environment without batting an eyelid. I am convinced there was another element at the back of Fergie's mind. I think he was already planning to move Incey on and Roy's arrival was the beginning of the process. There were certain things about Incey that the manager just did not like. He enjoyed Incey's banter and upbeat mood and everything he did on the pitch was good, but Fergie had a negative view of his influence on the younger group. Paul called himself 'Guvnor', and it didn't say 'No 8' on his boots, it said 'Guv'. Fergie didn't like that. Some have suggested he was concerned about Paul leading Ryan astray, but I disagree: their friendship made Ryan, a boy in the squad, feel safe and secure. I think the issue was how Paul's example might affect other, less gifted young players. Fergie did not want a set of mini-Guvnors emerging from our reserves, thinking it was all about swagger and not the team.

Ryan blossomed in 1993–94, scoring seventeen times, and Lee Sharpe had his best season, contributing some very important goals. Eric was masterful. Some of the things he did – my God. The Wimbledon goal. The Southampton goal. *The Arsenal goal*. Incredible. Then there was Mark Hughes, who did have lulls, but who would then pop up with the right timing and do crazy things on the pitch like volleying a ball first time into the top corner. He scored wonder goals regularly. Mark's later career in management may have made people forget Mark the player – and just how good he was.

Then there was Denis. He is also underestimated. As a goal-keeper, what you want most of all from your defenders is consistency, to know they are going to do the same right thing every time a dangerous situation occurs. Denis was more dependable than any other footballer I played with. He could play left back and right back to the same world-class level. I've never seen a right-footed full back able to cross from the left as well as he did. He is one of the best players Manchester United ever had and every now and then, when I meet up with Fergie, we talk about Denis and desperately try to recall mistakes he made: we can never come up with any. Then you add in Denis's personality: he is a witty lad but a quiet lad, very genuine and very kind, the type who is the bedrock of a good dressing room.

In the league we were 14 points clear by the end of November and in such form that before a draw with Norwich on 4 December, we had taken 65 points from a possible 72, including results at the end of 1992–93. Pep Guardiola gets credited with introducing the full-team possession game to England, but we played that way. I was a keeper who started attacks. I could throw the ball fast, far and accurately, and as soon as it was with me, Ryan, Sharpe or Andrei would sprint forward on the flanks looking to be released. I found it easier to distribute to Ryan because, as a right-hander throwing to the left, I could release the ball with a slinging action and make it curve naturally from out to in. Distributing to the right, I needed to arc the ball the other way, which meant getting it over the opposition full-back's head but not with such curl that the ball would run out of play. But when I did land the ball in one of those wingers' paths our speed on the break was unstoppable.

Andrei was an incredible talent. He never used a word of English in all the time he played for us, then as soon as he went to Rangers, after spells at Everton and Fiorentina, he revealed he spoke it perfectly well. Because of their culture, a lot of Russian and Eastern Bloc teams would play football in a very technical but indecisive way, with nobody taking individual responsibility – but Andrei wasn't like that. He would shoot from any angle and in training I didn't like his shot because, on top of being fast in his execution – he is probably the quickest player I played with – he had this very short backlift and power-ful strike that came at you, almost knuckleball style, without side spin, and could sting if you weren't positioned right. I understood how he scored so many goals for us. Keepers were a little frightened of him.

Incey was a brilliant player, a ball-winner who went box-to-box in midfield in a traditional English way, whereas Roy was a little less conventional. He liked attacking down the right channel and could be hard for opponents to pick up. He had energy, drive and stamina, a good football brain and on the ball was nearly always effective. Roy and I were never soulmates, as most people probably know by now, but if I was putting together an XI he would be the first guy on my team sheet.

Our main rivals in 1993–94 – Blackburn, Arsenal, Newcastle – were still building their teams and we were so far ahead of the rest, in reality, that we should have won everything, domestically. We had a dip in the league when we almost let Blackburn catch up before pulling away to the title, but we squandered a potential Treble by losing in the League Cup final to Aston Villa. For that, I should take some blame. Against Charlton in the FA Cup, I had got sent off after charging out of my box to try and tackle Kim Grant and it was a stupid thing to do. There was absolutely no need to go for the ball. I had two covering defenders and there is no explanation for it.

I did try and get the ball – honestly. But with my timing wrong, I arrived foot high and arms out, clobbering Grant first with a boot, then a hand. A double red, if you like: so idiotic. Yet Fergie was furious at half-time, raging about how the ref had made a mistake, and I said in a post-match interview, 'When the referee watches it back, he'll be disappointed with his decision.' Then I got home and watched the highlights and saw this horror tackle. I felt seriously embarrassed.

I used to play in an aggressive style – unless the ball was inside the six-yard box, I was always out on my six-yard line or further when the shot came in – and one of the ideas behind that aggression was to challenge the opponent. But that day I took front-foot goalkeeping too far. It was the only sending-off in my professional career and it led to me being suspended for the League Cup final, which Villa won 3–1.

I had one other rush of blood to the head that season, leading to some behaviour that shames me to this day. Our 3–3 draw at Anfield on 4 January 1994 is held up as one of the greatest Premier League games, but as far as I am concerned it was not a great game at all. It was too one-sided for that – for the first twenty-five minutes at least.

We tore Liverpool apart. We were 3–0 up, thanks to goals from Denis, Ryan and Brucey, and it should have been 5–0 or 6–0. We should have been looking at the kind of classic score-line Bayern Munich achieved when destroying Barcelona 8–2. But we eased off and I have no idea why. It is the only time at Manchester United that we did not go for it throughout a match 100 per cent.

Anfield is the last place where you want to ease off. Once you let Liverpool back into a game there, the stadium has the ability to lift whatever team they have fielded – even if it is an ordinary one – to the next level. Nigel Clough scored twice before half-time and then eleven minutes from the end Neil Ruddock equalised with a header. They almost went on to beat us. From the position we were in earlier in the match, it was embarrassing.

For the one and only time in my eight years with United, Fergie held a lengthy dressing-room inquest. Of course, he could always go berserk at something, but the hairdryer would only come out for a minute or two before he switched back to his normal mode of being forward-looking. The post-match talk would focus on moving on. In your Pro Licence it is something they teach you: not to look backwards in a team talk but make it proactive, keep players' eyes on what is in front of them. Fergie was the master of this – but not at Anfield that day.

He was so upset about throwing it away, against *them*, that he launched into us, quickly focusing his anger on me. He attacked the quality of my goal kicks, of all things, complaining that they kept landing on the heads of Liverpool defenders. It was unfair. We ended up under so much pressure in the second half that I seemed to be taking about three goal kicks a minute and I was just trying to get the ball as far up the pitch as possible, given that we had stopped competing and they were trying to pen us in.

Of course, older and wiser, I realise he was letting off steam and I was a convenient target, but I was furious about the game too and came right back at him. There are both regrets and no regrets about what I said. What I regret is that I not only questioned him, both as a manager and a man, but I began pointing out others in the dressing room, saying they had not done their jobs. To call out team-mates, friends, in front of the group, to say to the manager that they played badly, that was not on. That is the big, big, big regret.

Not regretted is that I stood up to the manager. That was allowed. This may surprise you, but Fergie permitted that. Yet this was not the day for it, just not the time and place – and how I did it was certainly not in the right way. The disappointment is I was too naive to see all this. I should have just taken my flak from him and moved on. When I think of that day it feels almost like having a crime on my record; like something you did which you have to live with and can never defend.

It goes back to how I feel when I look at my younger self, at this intense, hectic guy who – just sometimes – should have toned it down. But hindsight is a wonderful thing. In the moment, driving home from that game, I was simply pumped with anger and adrenaline and could not see beyond the injustice I had felt when Fergie picked on me. I felt so disillusioned I even called Rune to ask him to find me a new club. The next morning, I felt calmer but still unsettled. I needed to see Fergie, but he was not at training. The day after he was, and he called me into his office. He told me he was going to have to sack me.

I apologised for my behaviour and he accepted it but stood his ground. 'It doesn't alter the fact you will have to leave,' he said. It was then that I did the only thing in the whole affair I can take a tiny bit of pride from – before we went out for training I stood up in front of everyone and said how sorry I was. Unknown to me, Fergie was listening from behind a door and he never followed through on his sacking threat.

I had some bridges to build with Eric. We were close friends, but during the dressing-room row I had said something about him which he took to heart, understandably. I tried apologising on the coach back from Anfield but he wasn't happy. It took a little time for our relationship to heal. What makes my disappointment even greater is that I told some of the story of the dressing-room row in my previous book, which meant it became public knowledge, when it was one of those things that should have stayed behind closed doors. By writing about it, I made it bigger than it needed to be. The entire thing makes me cringe: you live and learn, I guess.

The 1994–95 campaign is something else I do not enjoy revisiting. Statistically, it was probably my best season at Manchester United, but what is that worth? We ended with zero trophies – that is the only stat that counts. Between turning professional in 1987 and joining Manchester City in 2002, I won something in every campaign, except 1994–95. This might be why there are big gaps in my memory of it, and the things I do recall are negatives.

In golf, they call Saturday moving day and maybe the best way I can make sense of 1994–95 is to think of it as a moving year. Moving people in and out. Moving from one phase of our development to another. Completing one team's journey and moving to the start of a new road, one that led all the way to the Nou Camp in 1999.

We fell short in the title race for several reasons. Roy missed its closing stages because of a damaged ankle and without his drive and energy we flagged. We never had a settled replacement for Paul at right back and with Andrei losing form and focus and beginning to talk in the media about moving on, our whole right side was weakened. And, of course, there was Eric and there was Selhurst Park. I'll get to that.

Me? I am told I went twenty-six hours without conceding at Old Trafford. From January, I let in four goals at home and two of those were against Wrexham in the FA Cup, while the other was in the last game of the season, a dead rubber against Southampton. But what I remember was Stan Collymore beating me at my near post – okay, with a fantastic finish – in a draw with Nottingham Forest, and a mistake against Blackburn when I rushed out, punched the ball and it dropped to Paul Warhurst, who scored from 35 yards.

That led to another example of why I could be difficult to be around. As soon as I punched the ball, I knew I had not caught it well and was determined to get back in the goal. I was push-ing people away to get there and was convinced I'd still save the shot, but there was Brucey in my way – he was racing back to try and stop the shot too. I screamed at him. Brucey said, 'Pete, what the hell? You've just made a terrible punch.' But for me the punch was gone, I was in the next phase.

Looking back, I can see how annoying for other people they were: those hot-headed moments that led me into conflicts with them. It is kind of funny, but when I look at my old clips and see a save, I find I can't put myself back in that moment, the memory is gone, but show me a bad goal I conceded and every-thing is vivid again: the build-up, the moment, the feelings. For example, there is a soft one I let in against Colin Hendry early in 1994–95, a header. We won the game 4–2, but that goal still creeps into my mind to irk me from time to time.

The season also brought my longest spell out with injury during my Manchester United career. I was always having little problems with my back and Gary Pallister was the same – we were both tall guys who were needed for every game, playing on pitches much less forgiving than the perfect surfaces you see in the Premier League nowadays. There was more contact in the game then and even though, early in my career, Jørgen Henriksen taught me techniques to protect myself in collisions with big strikers, I still had to take plenty of hits.

I was a big guy too. I weighed 102 kilos when I signed for Manchester United and every time I dived or was bumped to the deck, my frame had to absorb all that weight on impact. In November we played Crystal Palace at home and going into the match I felt fit, without any issues. I did my warm-up and followed my established routine, sets of a few different exercises and then some practice in the goal, on reaction saves. Out of nowhere someone knifed me in the back – or that is how it felt. A stab of blinding pain. I said to Kiddo, 'Something's up,' and ran in to see Dave Fevre, the physio. He stretched me, massaged me. I felt fine again, so I decided to play.

Five minutes into the match I had a situation where I had to back-pedal a bit and catch the ball. I felt nothing. Great. Whatever it was pre-match was surely just one of those twinges in your body that mean nothing and cannot be explained. A minute later I had a similar situation. Back-pedal. Catch. The knife again. This time the pain was unbearable. At first, I couldn't move. When I made it to the dressing room I lay on a bed for the rest of the game, the back stiffening up and stiffening up, the pain worse and worse. The next day I was supposed to come in for treatment, but it took all I had just to climb out of bed and when I tried to stand, it was so excruciating I had to lie back down on the floor. I called Dave and he said to rest. Lie on my stomach if I had to, give it a couple of days.

Those were two days of torture. The pain did not subside one bit, so Dave organised a scan and I was driven there in agony. I cannot remember how I even got in the car. The scan showed I had a split disc, that the pressure on my back had made the fluid inside the disc explode through the band around the disc – imagine the filling in a roll of sushi bursting right through the seaweed on the outside. The damage was serious, as was another issue the scan identified. In my spine, two of the intervertebral discs – L4 and L5 – were misaligned. They had probably been like that from birth. It meant that part of my back was going to be prone to further damage and deterioration. Dave, the club doctor, and the specialists at the spinal clinic were very worried: they wondered if the disc would ever be strong enough again for me to play. Or would it keep bursting or popping out after impacts?

The only remedy was time and rest. I had to wait and hope that it healed and then hope the healing was sufficient. This led to weeks of lying on my stomach at home, moving as little as possible. I passed the rest of November in that state, and then most of December. By Christmas, I was able to move well enough to make it to the Cliff again and began a routine of lying on the treatment bed with my head raised while I was massaged over and over. By the second week of January, I felt well enough to rejoin the group for training.

My first day back was 8 January. I hadn't touched a ball since Crystal Palace, more than seven weeks previously, but I had done my rehab and some running. I was just happy to be back with the squad for a bit of light ball work, to do the boxes, maybe a little training game. Certainly no diving. Dave and the medics were still not clear which way this was going to go. I arrived for training and Kiddo said straight away, 'Gaffer wants you.' That was another thing – I hadn't really spoken to Fergie since my injury. When you were injured, he would say hello but leave you to it, and I understand his logic. He let the medical people do their jobs and focused his energies on the players who were fit. It was part of his mentality of continually looking forward and at what he could actually affect.

Anyway, I knocked on his door expecting 'Good to see you, you've worked hard, we're happy to have you back,' and sure enough he welcomed me in and said all that. Then after a pause he spoke again. 'How are you feeling, Peter?' Yeah, good. We talked a bit more and he asked again, 'How do you feel?' Good, gaffer, yeah. I started to twig there was something on his mind, but he wouldn't get to the point. Eventually he circled round to it. 'You're feeling okay, then? Good. Walshy [my back-up was Gary Walsh] is ill. Can you play tomorrow?'

What?

'Gaffer,' I said, 'I've been away nearly eight weeks and I haven't so much as caught a ball. If you want me to play, of course I'll play, but you have to take that into consideration.'

'No,' he said. 'If you can play, you can play. You're back.'

This was a Sunday. Our game was away to Sheffield United the following evening and immediately I started thinking about Bramall Lane. At the time it was being rebuilt and had only one big stand. Sheffield, at the best of times, is windy and this was January – there could be sleet or snow. The Bramall Lane pitch, it turned out, was frozen. These were not great conditions for a big goalie with a dodgy spine and no practice, attempting a comeback from a worrying injury.

And it did blow a gale; it bucketed down. The cold was blistering. But I was just happy; happy that, after the doubts, I had made it back onto a football pitch. In the first minute, the wind caught one of their shots and I had to scramble back and claw it out. I felt okay. Later, I made a good save, getting down to my right and tipping a crisp shot away. That was my first heavy landing – right on my hip – and I felt . . . okay. I remember standing up and checking my side, like somebody who has been in a duel looking for bullet holes. I wiggled my toes. I moved my hips. *O-kay*. And though the issue would come back in the future, I was okay for the rest of the campaign.

So, that was my 1994–95. A couple of mistakes. One career-threatening injury. Zero trophies. Twenty-six hours without conceding is an irrelevant number set beside all that.

Blackburn deserved their title. Kenny Dalglish had put his team together well. It was balanced, had energy in midfield, good defenders, a good keeper, decent wingers and Alan Shearer and Chris Sutton up front. Fair dos. We did manage to take the race to the last game, and we could have been champions if we had beaten West Ham. However, in a game we really should have won, we missed countless chances to draw 1–1. We just didn't take our opportunity. It might be the only occasion, in my career at Old Trafford, when we didn't take an opportunity.

And the FA Cup final? Where we were defeated by Everton after missing more chances and being frustrated by Neville Southall, who gave an incredible performance?

Let's not even go there.

7

ERIC AND SELHURST, ME
AND IAN WRIGHT

We need to talk about Eric. So, let me take you to Selhurst Park, Crystal Palace versus Manchester United, 25 January 1995.

To a squally Wednesday evening in south-east London and a game we needed to win – with Blackburn two points ahead of us, with a game in hand, at the top of the Premier League. Palace were a physical team who often gave us an awkward match and Selhurst Park was a difficult venue. The score was 0–0, though we were the better team, when I punted the ball up the field in the forty-eighth minute.

The kick was destined for Eric and as he reached the ball he was being manhandled by his marker, Richard Shaw. Something snapped and Eric lashed out. It was one of those moments when you looked at Eric and thought *Hmm*, because there was no need for his burst of temper, and it wasn't as if there had been any warning that he was on the edge, either in the match itself or in the build-up. Eric just had that in him, that little flame of anger that could flare suddenly and torch his good work. It was the only challenge he had in football, controlling that small part inside which made him lash out. Everything else on the pitch, he had the ability for.

The referee, Alan Wilkie, showed the inevitable red card and Eric walked off the pitch, booed all the way. Norman Davies, our kit man, was sent by Fergie to shepherd Eric to the dressing room and they were making their way round the perimeter and towards my goal when they passed Matthew Simmons.

I was maybe 30 yards away and I didn't hear anything in terms of what Simmons shouted. I just saw this fan – Simmons – running down to the front of the stand and Eric rip loose of Norman, leap over the advertising board and kick him, then punch him. I raced over to help defuse the situation and Norman and I wrestled Eric away and led him in the direction of the dressing room. As we made our way, I felt a sudden stinging – hot tea, thrown over me by someone in the crowd. I reacted as well. Eventually the game restarted and David May scored for us, but Gareth Southgate equalised for them and as we played out the rest of a 1–1 draw, the significance of what had happened did not dawn on us at all. It just seemed another Eric moment, really. We had seen those in the previous season when he was red-carded in consecutive games.

We did not resent him for the unstable side of his character. Think about our attitude to risk. Our whole culture as a playing group involved putting the positive first and recognising that this meant things would go wrong sometimes. We loved Eric because of what he could do, and if he had flaws – so be it. Ninety-nine per cent of the guy was sheer brilliance. You simply had to accept the one per cent that could blow up in your face.

It was only when we were back in the dressing room that I really thought about the incident with Simmons and said, 'Eric, what the **** happened?' The gaffer said, 'Pete, just shut up.' Everyone fell silent. I promise you, I have never been in such a quiet group of players in my life. Lee Sharpe tells another story about the incident, but it is the party version and very far from my recollections.

Martin Edwards arrived, with Maurice Watkins, the club's solicitor, and his fellow director Michael Edelson. This was unprecedented: you had the whole board in this small dressing room and Maurice understood immediately how serious things were, that Eric could face a criminal case. The atmosphere was very gloomy and stayed like that the whole way home.

The club took some sting out of the inevitable witch hunt by suspending Eric. But that was only a football punishment. In March, he was sentenced to fourteen days' imprisonment and that shocked him. Eric did not expect to be hit so hard. On appeal, the punishment was reduced to two hundred hours of community service.

Two hundred hours . . . that's a lot of picking up litter and painting walls. Eric said to me, 'I should have taken the two weeks of prison.'

I asked him many times what Simmons shouted at him and he always replied that it was something really nasty about his mother, but he never wanted to repeat it. The common story was Simmons said, 'You French bastard,' but it wasn't that. Eric would not have been so riled. Back then, that was everyday stuff.

Abuse was so common. I reckon a few players around the country might have secretly admired Eric for answering back. As a keeper, I spent a lot of time standing very close to the crowd and the stuff that used to come at you from fans in that era was not at all nice. Today, while it still exists, as a society and as a game we have some kind of grip on racial abuse, which was not the case then. Stewarding has become a lot more professional. The transition from standing to seating has made crowds calmer. With CCTV in stadiums and everyone filming each other on camera phones, people know they cannot get away with things in grounds. The idiots are still out there but have moved on to social media.

I used to hear all sorts in stadiums. I have to be honest: there was plenty of stuff to abuse me with. My nose was red. I was a big Scandinavian. So, I got all that. I was always puzzled when people said Liverpool was not a rich city – because every time I was at Anfield, they threw so many coins at me.

And food. And lighters. My goalmouth was always strewn. But I didn't mind, because if they wanted to spend all that energy on abusing me, it meant they at least were wary of my ability. My very last away game was at Anfield, in fact, and I finished my career with a lot of mutual respect between me and Liverpool's knowledgeable crowd.

I could not say the same about the audience at Elland Road. You always felt the hatred at that stadium was a little out of control. Often, it crossed the line and my worst experience with a fan came there. In 1997 Leeds beat us 1–0, with David Wetherall scoring, and the gloating from their fans was horrendous but, okay, you accepted that. However, walking to the bus in my club suit, fresh from the shower, this guy in a Leeds shirt pushed to the front of some other fans, cleared his throat and spat – all over my face. In that split second I wanted to do exactly what Eric had done at Selhurst. The police were there and the guy was in handcuffs almost immediately, but it was humiliating.

There were a few places in Europe where it felt dangerous because you never knew what was coming down from the stands. Denmark had a World Cup qualifier in Athens that was stopped because they were shooting fireworks onto the pitch. That was scary, but you had to get on with it. We escaped with the best 0–0 draw of my life. Then there was Galatasaray v Manchester United in 1993, the craziest experience. It was the second leg of a Champions League tie. During the first leg at Old Trafford, which had ended 3–3, some guy ran on holding a red flag that had been set alight and I caught him, picked him up and threw him off the pitch. What I didn't know was he was making a political demonstration, and over the next couple of weeks I received all sorts of threats. Stuff like 'Just wait 'til you get to Turkey.'

I wasn't afraid, but then we landed in Istanbul. Thousands of Galatasaray supporters were there to greet us. They had made banners. 'WELCOME TO HELL'. 'RIP MANCHESTER'. 'SCHMEICHEL YOU'RE DEAD'. Angry locals tailed our bus all the way into the city, but still I was laughing it all off. I was stupidly naive, just didn't feel endangered. Second thoughts began to creep in when we got to the stadium for the game the next day.

We set off for the Ali Sami Yen two hours early to beat the traffic and yet half a mile away from the ground you heard the singing. The place was already packed and sounded pretty lively. Okay, maybe this was going be tricky.

We stayed in the dressing room for a while and then an hour before the game I went out to the pitch to warm up – by myself, ahead of the team. I was hit by a wall of noise and a sea of faces twisted in their pure hatred for me. So, I applauded all four stands.

My idea – as always, in terms of the opposition – was to show no fear. But, my God, the atmosphere was vicious throughout the game and although none of us were intimidated, the referee was. He gave us no protection as the Turkish players got stuck right into us and ruined any chance of football being played with all sorts of gamesmanship and time-wasting ploys. It finished 0–0 and Eric was red-carded after the final whistle for letting the referee know just how *merde* his performance had been.

To reach the dressing rooms, you descended a set of steps in a tunnel by the dugouts and on our way down the stairs, Turkish police started to hit us and kick us, laying into us with truncheons. Eric got struck. Paul Parker was shoved. I tried to hold one policeman at bay while Robbo fought with another and we scrambled back to the dressing room in utter shock. *Now* we were scared. Fans you could deal with, but police? Were they going to come through the door and batter us again? Arrest us? Were we all going to get to Manchester? We stayed there for two hours, until the mayhem outside had died down and it was safe to leave. A terrifying experience.

When Eric gave his famous press conference about sardines and trawlers, I watched live on TV. I loved it. In the press, at that time, there were a couple of proper leeches – really nasty journalists, out to sensationalise and feed off the words of players – but Eric gave them nothing, no explosive quotes to make more stories from. He just threw them his sardines, then stood up and left. It was so very funny.

I like Eric a lot. We remain very good friends. We roomed together on away trips, which was great fun. He never gave interviews and did not say much around the group, and even in the dressing room some had the impression he did not speak much English. But Eric spoke fluent English, I can tell you. One-on-one he was a different guy. We had long, open conversations about everything and anything.

Philosopher? No, I don't think so. Eric has a public persona that is mysterious and artistic and, yes, those elements are in his character. He is a very good actor, I love his stuff on Instagram. But Eric is also just a basic guy. We had parallel and similar lives: we were the foreign lads of that dressing room, bringing wives from our own countries and children of similar age to settle in England. We had the same issues and talked about everyday stuff. He was brilliant company.

As for the pitch, I am proud to have shared it with him. He changed my fortunes, I guess, because he changed Manchester United's. I had first come across him at Euro 92, when Denmark met France in Malmö. Jean-Pierre Papin was their star, but in his pre-match interview he said, 'Of course it's important I do my job, but if I don't score, Eric Cantona will score.' That was when I became aware of how highly Eric was rated by those who played with him.

Talent? He is one of the best footballers ever to play in England and it was a combination of his personality and the times we lived in that stopped him becoming an absolute superstar, celebrated like a Messi or Ronaldo. The red cards and rebellious moments were used against him. In that era, people didn't like their stars controversial. I think today, in the social media age, Eric would have been an utter megastar, a Zlatan plus. The world is ready for non-conformists and individuals now.

A story that sums up Eric in many ways: I am friends with Bjarne Riis, the Danish cyclist who shot from nowhere to the very top of cycling. In 1995 he was set to be on the podium in the Tour de France for the first time and Bjarne and I shared an agent in Denmark, Ole Frederiksen. Ole said if he's on the podium, we have to go to Paris for the final race stage.

Manchester United were in pre-season training and we had Sunday off, so timing wasn't an issue. Nor was accreditation, because I had a good relationship with the Danish network broadcasting the race. We got to Friday and Bjarne was third coming out of the mountain stages, so it was clear a podium place was his. We had to go. But when Ole and I tried booking a trip, it was impossible. Every hotel in Paris was full.

On Saturday morning, at training, I told Eric, 'Can you believe it? My mate is third in the Tour de France and I have flights and accreditation but for love nor money can't get anywhere to stay.'

'Uh,' he says. 'Just leave it with me. Take the flights. Trust me. In fact, I'll come with you.'

So, on Saturday afternoon Eric and I are on a plane to Charles de Gaulle. We land. There is a chauffeur to pick us up. There are rooms in the Intercontinental. The. Inter. Conti. Nental. And the room is, like, ninety quid or some ridiculous price.

I get to the room. It's a suite, it's unbelievable. But immediately the telephone goes and it's Eric.

'Just drop your bags, grab a shower and I'll see you downstairs,' he says. 'I'm taking you for dinner.'

There are four of us plus Eric – me, Ole, Søren Lerby and Bjarne Riis's wife – and we've all got rooms. Eric takes us out and we join his friends in a discreet basement restaurant somewhere and the food is exquisite; the best meal I've ever had. Then Eric says, 'Okay, I'm going to a birthday party now, I hope you'll join me,' and he takes us to Pigalle, to this incredible bar, where we have the main table and the partying is crazy. Everyone is coming over: 'Hey Eric . . .'

Finally, he takes us to a nightclub, where we stroll to the front of this long, deep queue and the bouncer, of course, is 'Ah Eric . . .' The main table again. Eric's friends and brother are there and this is another extraordinary place.

It was five or six in the morning when I got back to my hotel room. I woke up around eleven, opened my curtains – and right there underneath my window was the race marker saying 1 km to go. Nobody in the world could have got a hotel room in Paris, and Eric got five of them – on the finishing straight.

Eric didn't bother coming to watch the cycling, by the way, he had people to see.

Eric returned from his eight-month ban in October, with the 1995–96 season well underway, and needed time to recover his sharpness. He came back into a very different Manchester United team. Paul Ince, Mark Hughes and Andrei were all gone

– offloaded by Fergie in the summer – and instead the side was full of kids: David Beckham, the Nevilles, Nicky Butt, Paul Scholes. Boys of nineteen, twenty, twenty-one.

None had even had pegs in the first-team dressing room at the Cliff in 1994–95. It was too small so, although they had become part of the first-team squad, they still used the reserve dressing room next door. For some time, we had known this 'Class of '92' was a special group of talents, though. Since many of our Premier League games were on Sundays, we were often training at the Cliff on Saturday mornings and would linger to watch the youth-team matches they played.

If you asked which United youngsters I thought would become stars, I would of course start with Giggsy. He was incredible right from the beginning. You knew Nicky Butt would make it and Gary would be a decent player, simply because of his character. Phil had more talent and you expected plenty from him. The odd ones were Scholes and Beckham.

Scholesy was a little striker in the Class of '92's youth team. It was obvious he could really play, but you wondered about his size. Nobody, not even Fergie, I think, saw he was just waiting to be converted into a midfielder – and would become one of England's best ever there. Beckham had this majestic right foot and could cross like you had never seen, but he wasn't someone who would beat a man easily and he was a pretty boy. Did we need pretty boys? A loan to Preston was the making of him. Separated from his friends and thrown into the challenges of the Third Division, he stood up to the test, did his hard yards and came back ready.

Becks had a very clever football brain and his deliveries gave us a different dimension. Scholes in midfield was an accident – his early appearances were as Eric's strike partner – but a gift. He could play the little one-twos in tight spaces that we had only played around the opposition box before, in deeper areas. That allowed us to thread possession right down the middle of the pitch. Roy very quickly caught on to his game, as did Andy Cole, who had arrived in January of 1995. And Eric was tailor-made for playing with Paul. All of a sudden, the whole centre of our team linked in a different way. At Old Trafford, we conceded just nine goals all season and did not lose a single match in the league.

Away form came more slowly. And Newcastle started the season like a train. They were 12 points clear with fifteen games to go. When trying to close such a gap there are so many elements you face, most of them psychological. Normally we won things through our risk-taking, but that season came down to the quality and relentlessness of our defending, which is why it is one of my proudest seasons. We ground Newcastle down with twelve clean sheets in those last sixteen matches, with Eric popping up to score important goals.

We won the title by four points and, of course, Fergie won the mind games with Kevin Keegan. When I worked under Keegan later, at Manchester City, I learned how emotional he was. A key moment in 1995–96 came when Liverpool beat Newcastle 4–3 and Keegan reacted with such naked devastation to Stan Collymore's winning goal that, watching at home on TV, as he slumped in the dugout, I felt like I had just won something.

Then, after a match against Leeds, he went off on his infam-ous 'I will love it' rant. What managers need to remember when they give post-match interviews is that the most important group of people they are speaking to is their players. They need to deliver pre-planned messages that set the tone in the dressing room – where everyone will be watching on a TV or on their phones. Fergie was a master: he never spoke to the cameras until he had spoken to us and he would rehearse the stuff he was about to tell the media by saying it to us first.

So when Keegan jabbed his finger at the camera lens and tearfully said he would love it, love it, if Newcastle could beat us to the title, his own players would have lost a little belief, while we, watching in our houses, came away with the sense that our manager was beating their manager, that he was stronger than the other guy and we were stronger than them.

Psychology also played a part in us beating Liverpool in the 1996 FA Cup final, to win the Double. There was Eric's wonderful goal, but my biggest memory of Wembley that day was the moment we saw Liverpool's cream suits. We were gobsmacked. *Wow. Look at that lot. We cannot lose to those suits.*

In the build-up, Brucey was called into the manager's office and came out ten minutes later, saying, 'Eric, Peter, Roy, Pally – gaffer wants us in there, now.' Once we were assembled Fergie told us he had a special tactical plan for the game. He was going to play Phil Neville as a man-marker for Steve McManaman. In some ways, this was no surprise because Fergie was terrified of McManaman. McManaman was the only opposing player he *ever* paid attention to in the Premier League. I mean, he would mention Alan Shearer and other major opposing players in team talks, but never with any fear. However, McManaman always had him in a sweat. And, to be fair, Steve was a fantastic footballer. Fergie's thinking was always that if you took McManaman out of the game, you took Liverpool out.

The trouble was that, in our experience, when we tried changing our tactics in domestic matches it just didn't work. So, after Fergie revealed his 'Operation Stop McManaman' scheme there was a silence, and then I said, 'Gaffer, this is a bad idea.' But Fergie stuck to his guns.

'No, this is what we're doing,' he affirmed.

Then Eric spoke. And Eric *never* spoke. He said, 'Gaffer . . . bad idea.'

Fergie said, 'Aye . . . okay, we're not doing it. Lads, off you go.'

What an incredible person Steve Bruce is. He was so team-orientated that he did not reveal to any of us that in his one-to-one chat with Fergie before we were all called in, the gaffer had told him he wouldn't be playing at Wembley – that he wasn't even going to be on the bench. Brucey had just returned from injury, but he was our captain and the cup final was to have been his last game before leaving the club. And he was not even on the bench . . .

I know the gaffer always regretted it, but that is precisely who Alex Ferguson is: with him there was never any sentimentality. His decisions were always objective, and it was always about the next win and the next trophy.

Another league title arrived in 1996–97, but it is a season I look back on with mixed feelings. We lost our biggest games – 1–0 to Borussia Dortmund in both legs of a Champions League semi-final – and there was that weird patch at the end of October and start of November when we were beaten 5–0 by Newcastle, 6–3 by Southampton, 1–0 at home by Fenerbahçe and 2–1 at home by Chelsea. The Southampton defeat was our second in consecutive visits to the Dell, the first coming in April 1996, a 3–1 reverse remembered because of the infamous grey kit we wore.

On that day, the sun was bright and because the Dell was a small stadium, with no big stands casting shadows, you got the full glare of the sun on the pitch. In the match we genuinely could not see each other. When David was on the right wing and I looked to find him, he just blended into the background. Fergie went berserk at half-time, but not at us, at poor Albert Morgan, the kit man. As if Albert had been the one who had come up with the design of the shirts! Eventually Fergie yelled, 'Get them changed,' and we went out for the second half in the extra strip – blue and white – that Albert had brought along. After trailing 3–0 at the break, the second forty-five minutes were at least a bit better.

The most uncomfortable part of the 1996–97 season was what happened involving me and Ian Wright. I need to give you a bit of background here. Ian was a great striker, but he had never scored against me. There was a special feeling of 'me against him' when our teams played, a one-v-one rivalry that was only a factor with a very select group of strikers I faced: Wrighty, Robbie Fowler and Filippo Inzaghi. Between me and Inzaghi it was probably honours even across our encounters, while Robbie – I hate to admit – had the upper hand on me. But I had the upper hand on Ian. He made no secret of his desire to get goals against me and I made some incredible saves against him in our games.

I had fun on the pitch with that, knowing the more I kept him out, and the more I made my shows of 'arrogance' against him, the more he would get wound up. I have to stress, though, that on my part the rivalry was always purely professional. Wrighty has admitted hating me in those days (though only for the ninety minutes on the pitch) but I am being honest when I say that, personally, I had nothing against him. In fact, I admired him. I thought he was a real player. And John Jensen, who is one of my best friends, always told me Ian was a really good guy.

On 16 November 1996, Manchester United beat Arsenal 1–0 at Old Trafford. There was a situation where I dived at Ian's feet and he followed through, planting his studs in my hand. He was booked and I stood there, chuntering, still annoyed about the challenge. That evening, after seeing it on *Match of the Day*, a viewer in Croydon believed they could lip-read me saying something racial and reported it to the police. The first I knew about it was when I had a call from an officer a week afterwards. He outlined the complaint and said they had to carry out an investigation.

I was sure I had done nothing wrong and spoke to Maurice Watkins, United's lawyer. The club was very supportive and Maurice told me not to fret. A fortnight later – for some reason, I remember being in a music store in Warrington when the call came – the police officer rang again to say the investigation had come up with nothing and I wouldn't be charged.

I thought that was that, but on 19 February we went to Highbury and early in the game, Ian chased a through ball and I came out of my box to try and clear. We both went into the tackle fully committed and ended up in a collision that sent us both spinning off to the side. The ball stayed put and Ian recovered his footing to get to it first. He was laughing. He was finally about to score against me and roll this ball into an empty net. Except the ball was punctured. It had burst with the force of the tackle.

That frustrated him and so did missing two further good chances. Then came another tackle. I reached the ball first, kicking it away, and Ian jumped over it, sinking his studs down hard into my legs. It was seriously sore. In fact, it might have been a career-ender for me had it not been for the fact I liked to wear special shinpads that went higher up the leg than normal ones. Those pads are in the Old Trafford museum, and visible on one pad are a set of stud marks that go right to its top. Where the marks stop, that's where Ian's studs went into my knee. I still have the scar.

In today's game, Ian would have been sent off and faced a lengthy ban. Then? He was not even booked for the challenge, and I believe if the referee had handled the incident properly, the whole regrettable saga of what came next could have been avoided. Instead, Ian played on and had two more opportunities, one a header into the ground that bounced up and I tipped over the bar. I laughed at him. He shouted, 'How's your ******* leg?'

The game finished and I did something completely out of order. I consider myself innocent, except for this: hearing the whistle, I charged after Ian and said to him, 'Don't you ******* do that again.' I wish I had not. Anger got the better of me.

Ian ran away, all the way to the tunnel. Now, the Highbury tunnel was narrow and there was always a policeman stationed at the top. Ian reached this policeman, stopped, stood beside him and then as I entered the tunnel shouted, 'And don't you ever call me a black ******* again!' Everyone in and around the tunnel, including the journalists whose desks were nearby, would hear Ian's words – as well he knew. It meant the whole controversy re-erupted, dominating the next day's headlines. There was talk of me being investigated again.

The truth? I did not say what I was accused of at Old Trafford. The lip-reader claimed I mouthed 'black *******' at Ian. Those are utterly detestable words and I would be very disappointed in anyone who said them. I am not a racist. I abhor racism. Racism was never part of my environment as a child or my later life. When I came to England, I was so impressed by how multi-cultural the country was and, coming from Denmark where there were problems with attitudes towards equality and immigration, I saw a society where it didn't really matter who you are and I was proud of being part of it.

In the aftermath of Highbury, the Football Association talked about punishing me and the police were under pressure to reopen the case. After talking to Maurice Watkins and the manager, we put out a statement. I was adamant I had done nothing wrong and I did not want to be connected with racism at all. That was why I rejected a request from the Football Association that Ian and I should pose for a picture, shaking hands. I did not believe the FA seriously or sincerely wanted to deal with racism and it felt like their proposal was just a publicity stunt – and taking part would imply I was accepting guilt.

The efforts of the Professional Footballers' Association were even more pathetic. Their chief executive, Gordon Taylor, stepped forward to show what a world-class opportunist he is. I needed support and I'm sure Ian did too, but instead Taylor suggested the pair of us should meet up and stage a show of reconciliation in front of assembled journalists. I said I wanted Ian to apologise for what he had accused me of, but Taylor replied we both had to take responsibility. I said, 'What for? If I do that, I'm a racist – and I am not a racist.' A few weeks later, at Mark Hughes's testimonial dinner in Manchester, I met Taylor coming out of the toilet and pinned him against the wall. I told him straight, 'You're the worst kind I've ever seen.'

For a number of years, Ian and I had nothing to do with each other. But I knew that what happened at Highbury was a regret to him. Johnny Jensen relayed to me that Ian was sorry and wanted to apologise but, while I was still playing, I was quite hard about it all. My line was 'I don't want Ian Wright's apology unless Ian Wright does it publicly,' and it is a regret. I should have been more open and met up with him in private – and just talked.

But you get older, you grow up, you mellow. I think that happened to both of us and in 2002 we found ourselves part of the BBC punditry team for the World Cup. Knowing our history, Niall Sloane, the BBC's then head of football, had gone out of his way to separate us in broadcasts so we were never even in the same building at the same time.

Our studio was in London, where we would analyse the games that were being broadcast from South Korea and Japan. I was in a hotel near Television Centre, sitting at the bar having a cup of tea, when Ian walked through the lobby and towards the lifts. I ran after him, grabbed his shoulders and turned him round and said with a big smile, 'Don't you ever ******* kick me again.'

That was the ice-breaker. Wrighty said, 'Pete, Pete, Pete, I'm so sorry. I never meant to do that, it was just the moment.' I said, 'Hey, it's cool, don't worry about it,' and in the same instant we said, 'We should do a show together.' I went back to the bar and called Niall, but he said, 'Yes, yes, you both want to do a show . . .' Ian had already called him.

We did the show and really enjoyed being on with each other. Most of the 2002 World Cup games were at breakfast time in the UK and nearly every day Ian, Alan Hansen, Gary Lineker and I would go off after we had broadcast and play golf together. Wrighty and I became good friends and have stayed that way. In fact, I would go as far as to say I love the guy. How can you not love someone who can spray the ball everywhere in a round of golf yet still be in contention coming off the 17th – then phone his golf pro, from the buggy, for tips on his final drive?

I want to put this to bed. I hate racists. I hate what black footballers have had to go through. I hate how they were abused back in my day. I'm glad football – while it still has many problems – is a better place now. As for Ian, even at the peak of our battles, I felt no animosity towards him. I thought he was a superb player and one of our toughest opponents, hard-edged but full of passion.

I always saw in him someone with feelings similar to me regarding the game. To him, football, his club and competing to win seemed to mean everything and I was the same. In his interviews as a player, he spoke from the heart, which I both loved and envied, and he took that approach into broadcasting.

He is one of my very favourite pundits because he is so passionate, to the point and honest. Not many people get away with being truly honest and 100 per cent themselves on television – but he does.

So, if what happened nearly a quarter of a century ago was a source of pain, if you say the name Ian Wright to me now my first thought is *I am so glad he is my friend*. And my second is *My God, I would love to have played with him*.

8

THE LONG, MISTAKEN LEAVING OF MANCHESTER UNITED

Manchester United was everything I ever wanted – but I did think about leaving a couple of times.

It was nothing to do with money or ego, and I knew there was no better or bigger football club than the one I was already playing for. But I did have an obsession, one that grew during my seasons at Old Trafford and became my reference point for measuring our success.

Europe.

I burned to win the Champions League and complete our journey as a team. Yet by the summer of 1996, I found myself with three Premier League and two FA Cup winner's medals in my pocket, but a European resumé with Manchester United that was just a document of disasters. It included exits in knockout ties to Torpedo Moscow, Galatasaray, Atlético Madrid and Rotor Volgograd, and our only attempt at a Champions League group phase resulted in failure to qualify from a section topped by IFK Gothenburg. I had done better with Brøndby.

My mentality was that you should always be pushing towards the next level. For me, that meant Manchester United had to move on from dominating England to winning on the continent. Otherwise, what were we doing? Stagnating? I was fed up with being shown up in those European forays, fed up with our naivety, and I knew Fergie was dissatisfied too. His team-building was increasingly with the Champions League in mind. However, I was reaching my mid-thirties now and I could not wait for ever for him to get the formula right.

I took a call one day from Rune. 'Fancy Barça?' he said. Barcelona needed a new keeper and were looking at me. They signed Vitor Baía instead but their interest got me thinking and by the end of the 1996–97 season I was feeling unsettled again: all because of Europe. United's Champions League campaign had begun well. We felt we had cracked it. We escaped an awkward group, hammered Porto in the quarter-finals and faced Borussia Dortmund in the semis. I thought it was our year. But we let Dortmund do a job on us and exited to Ottmar Hitzfeld's canny side without scoring, home or away. The disappointment hit me hard. In November I would turn thirty-four and when I pondered what I still wanted to do in my career I kept coming back to one thing: winning the Champions League. I wanted it so badly that when I try to recall the seasons leading up to 1998–99, I find myself struggling with details of our Premier League campaigns – but I can remember every single thing about our failures in Europe. Europe was my priority.

This was why, as the season was coming to an end, I asked my agent to let me know of any interesting options – I was certainly willing to consider them. Unbeknownst to me, he told Fergie about my feelings and one day Fergie called and said, 'Come to my house.' When I got there, he came out with it straight away.

'You can't leave now.'

'What do you mean?'

'You can't leave,' he said. 'I've spoken to your agent and you want to leave. You can't.'

We talked about Europe and he said he knew how to make us better there, that he was working on ways to evolve the team. Increasingly, his signings had been with the Champions League in mind – Jordi Cruyff, Karel Poborský – and he had his eye on a few more. Then, just after the season finished, Eric announced he was quitting – retiring from football at just thirty – and while Fergie made the right noises, he did not put up any great fight.

There had been a pattern to our European exits and the semi-final with Dortmund in April 1997 had laid it bare. I missed the first leg in the Westfalenstadion after my back seized during the warm-up and I watched from the bench as we did not even come close to scoring. It had been similar in those exits against Volgograd, Torpedo, Atlético and Galatasaray: we had been goalless and carried little threat in the away legs. Fergie needed to make the team more incisive in such games. Tactically, we had never quite been good enough in Europe and Eric's departure meant there would have to be a change of approach.

I was going to miss Eric. As his friend, though, I knew that leaving football was probably something he needed to do. His appetite for the game had slowly evaporated and in Eric's mind, I don't think he was ever a footballer anyway. The way he saw it, football was just a station on the way to becoming what he truly wanted to be: a figure in the arts. I remember him taking up the trumpet and the first thing he tried to learn was 'My Funny

Valentine' because that was Chet Baker's song, and Chet Baker, that's how he saw himself – on the cooler side of things.

Goals were not our only problem in Europe. The old UEFA 'three foreigners' rule was always a headache for the manager. There was only one time, in all our years together, when I would say he lost the plot in terms of decision-making – and it came at the Nou Camp in November 1994. There was no indication of the brainstorm that was coming when I saw him at breakfast in our hotel in Barcelona on match day. He was full of the usual chat – 'It's a big game, blah blah' – and gave no indication of what he was considering: dropping me.

I was rooming with Eric, as usual, and when I returned to the room after breakfast Eric wasn't there, in fact he hadn't been there all night. That was not a problem, because he was suspended and had friends in Barcelona. He was no doubt with them. But I didn't know his whereabouts. There was a knock on the door: the manager. He asked, 'Is Eric here?' and I said no, not giving anything away about Eric's absence since the previous evening. 'Okay,' said Fergie, 'well, tell him I've got the tickets he wanted,' and he went away. It was strange. Fergie almost never went to players' rooms. The only other time he contacted me in my room was in Southampton, when he phoned to say my room-mate wouldn't be coming, having had to leave camp for personal reasons.

In Barcelona the weather was nice and we were staying at a marina, so I decided to take a walk. On my way out of the hotel I bumped into Fergie. Quite casually, he dropped the bomb.

'Oh, Peter, by the way – you're not playing tonight.'

The night before, when talking about plans for the game, I had been in the team – something had caused a sudden rethink.

At Tivoli Gardens, in bow tie – and nappy.

With my mother and my sisters, Margrethe and Kathrine, before my first day at school.

Me by the Little Mermaid in Copenhagen, 1968.

Aged 12 or 13, rocking that mid-1970s hair.

Tolek Schmeichel, at the back, in one of his bands – Dad was an incredible musician.

Hanging with my mother, Cecilie and Kasper. I love this photo.

Bowling at Old Trafford: it's not cricket but my very first appearance at the Theatre of Dreams, in August 1991.

My neighbour Steve Bruce after scoring against Sheffield Wednesday in 1993, the late winner that sparked the concept of Fergie Time.

We've just beaten Forest at Wembley to win the League Cup in 1992, my first medal with United.

Eric Cantona's influence on the boss's baby-faced brood – here (left to right) Beckham, Solskjær, Giggs and Butt – was immense.

Sent off in a 1994 FA Cup tie against Charlton – yet I still ended up with my first winner's medal in the competition.

And another one: we returned to Wembley for the 1996 final against Liverpool, won by a brilliant goal from a certain Frenchman.

Above: To say Ian Wright and I had a combustible relationship at the height of United's rivalry with Arsenal would be an understatement.

Right: A once-unthinkable picture: Wrighty and I are now friends, TV colleagues and occasional golf partners.

January 1999: Dwight Yorke's last-gasp winner at Charlton proved a momentous step in our Treble pursuit.

Barcelona: Mario Basler scores early for Bayern Munich in the Champions League final in May 1999, a lead they hold for 85 minutes.

Mehmet Scholl thinks he's put Bayern 2–0 up and turns to celebrate, but his chip hits the post and rebounds to me.

It's now or never, so I charge upfield for a corner in stoppage time, and the pressure leads to Teddy Sheringham's equaliser.

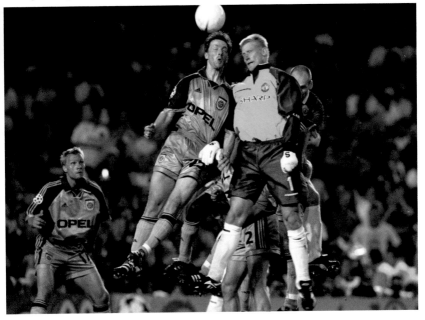

Above: The Trebble is ours! Ole turns Teddy's header into the roof of the Munich net to complete the most incredible comeback.

Left: Rapture, and perhaps relief and disbelief, is written on our faces as the gaffer and I raise the European Cup to our fans. Has there ever been another manager like Sir Alex Ferguson?

'We need our foreign players outfield,' he said. 'We're going to try and win the game.'

What?

'Okay, gaffer, but that is a really, really stupid decision,' I said, trying to stay composed. 'I'm very disappointed.'

'Okay,' he replied, 'but I don't make the rules and this is my decision.'

I was fuming. *Fuming.* Let me remind you of that Barcelona side. Romário. Hristo Stoichkov. Gheorghe Hagi. Ronald Koeman. Pep Guardiola. José Mari Bakero. Guillermo Amor. Manager: Johan Cruyff. Why would you go away from home against them and not defend, not try and be as secure as possible? Why would you go to the Nou Camp and go all-out to win the game?

Well-placed in the group, with games against Gothenburg and Galatasaray to come, a point would have been great and that is where Fergie, I believe, got himself in a tangle. He was impatient for Europe to see how good he was, to make a statement on the big stage. Taking chances was a very important element in his management and not one I would ever have changed. But there is a time and place to roll the dice. The Nou Camp, versus Romário, Stoichkov and Cruyff, is not it.

Barcelona destroyed us. They were Cruyff's so-called 'Dream Team' and one of Manchester United's worst European nightmares unfolded, a 4–0 drubbing. Subsequently, Fergie has claimed it all went wrong because Paul Ince did not do his job defensively. I think he is being kind to himself. The foreign player he chose instead of me was an attacker, Andrei Kanchelskis, and his words before the game were 'I want to win.' He wanted to surprise Barcelona in their own stadium, which was ridiculous.

There was nothing wrong with Fergie's judgement, however, when he went into the transfer market to replace Eric. He bought Teddy Sheringham, a wonderful – and I think still underrated – player. This meant we entered the 1997–98 season with strong striking options: Teddy, Andy Cole – back to fitness after two leg fractures – and Ole, who had been a revelation in his debut season in 1996–97.

The campaign proved a frustrating one, though. It featured a fair bit of bad luck. For instance, a weird injury kept me out during the festive period. I went back to Denmark for a Christmas lunch and, having had a few drinks at it, went out the next morning to cleanse my system with a run. I was jogging in a park when I knocked against one of those signs that tells you to keep your dog on a leash. There was a rusty nail sticking out of it and I gashed my hand. Paranoia kicked in. If I went to A&E it might become a story in the Danish press, so I decided to call Per Bjerregaard. Remember that as well as being Brøndby's chairman he was a trained doctor? 'Come over,' said Per, and he cleaned the gash up and put stitches in the wound.

On 21 December I played against Newcastle, with the stitches in. Afterwards the hand just ballooned. I ended up in a private hospital in Manchester with my hand bandaged and suspended in the air for three days to let the fluid drain. Lying there, I listened on the radio as we were beaten 3–2 by Coventry on 28 December. I was on pills, antibiotics, all sorts.

Injuries ruined our season. In the Premier League, we were overtaken by Arsenal, who found incredible form in the run-in and beat us in a decisive game at Old Trafford, for which we were missing so many players. The final nail in our coffin was a 1–1 draw at home to Newcastle after which Fergie exploded in fury – at Ole, of all people.

I was injured and watching from near the dugout when Rob Lee went through on goal in the last minute of the game. Ole sprinted after him, caught up and took him down on the edge of the box. Uriah Rennie showed him the inevitable straight red and he trotted off – after a pat on the head from Becks – to a standing ovation.

I never saw Fergie so angry. He detested cynical play. As soon as we got to the dressing room he screamed at Ole, absolutely bawled him out. 'That is NOT who we are. We're Manchester United. We don't do that!' he yelled, and even in the middle of this hairdryer hurricane I think all of us – Ole included – respected his values.

The most painful part of the season was not surrendering the title, though. It was blowing it in the Champions League yet again. In the group stage we played so well, finishing ahead of Juventus, with Teddy giving us the same ability to thread passes through the middle that Eric had done, but bringing more out of Coley, who scored freely.

Then we met Monaco in the quarter-final. They had some great young players, including David Trezeguet and Thierry Henry, but we should have had too much for them. Instead, they shut us out in the away leg and in the return game at Old Trafford – which I missed through injury – they scored early through Trezeguet. Pressure told on us. Ole equalised in the second half, but we toiled and went out on away goals after the game finished 1–1.

The season petered out in a very deflating way. Out to Monaco? It felt that in Europe there had been no progress at all. Sitting at home in Denmark, reflecting on things before joining the national team for the 1998 World Cup, I was really low. Those thoughts about leaving surfaced again.

I was not the only one. There was a feeling among a few of the United players that our team was coming to the end of a cycle, and in the back of our minds the World Cup was an opportunity to show any interested clubs what we could do. Personally, I looked at my age and felt I had a limited number of years before retiring. I did not want to finish playing without winning everything I could.

Europe. Winning a European medal at club level – it came back to that. It was my first World Cup and I wanted Denmark to do well and for me to show the world I was still at the top of my game. And if, off the back of that, there was a big club out there who liked what they saw and were interested in recruiting me . . . well, put it this way, it would have been an interesting conversation.

This is not a book of regrets, but of course I do have some. Who doesn't? One involves how I let fatigue, pressure and negative thoughts build up during 1998. It led to the biggest mistake of my career. United's European issues were only one part – the smaller part – of why I began feeling I needed out of Old Trafford. The bigger part is that I simply felt pushed to my limit.

In the seven years between joining Manchester United and the end of the 1998 World Cup, I had played 342 club games and 64 internationals, been to three tournaments and had only two proper summer breaks. I had not had a real rest since summer 1995 – in 1997, though there was no tournament, I had an operation on my knee and spent much of the 'holiday' recuperating and rehabbing.

Playing in the Premier League, in those days, meant slogging through the winters on heavy pitches, being battered in big collisions. I had a chronic back issue, aching joints and had been in more planes, airports, coaches and hotel rooms than I cared to remember. It was becoming a blur, a grind. My kids were school age now and deserved more of my time, and their mother felt she had never properly settled in England. I was out of bandwidth. Physically and mentally, I was tired.

The World Cup turned out to be one of the times of my life. The Danish team had an idyllic base in the south of France and a relaxed, avuncular manager in Bo Johansson. We played well on the pitch and enjoyed the golf course at our fantastic hotel. Our families were around, the sun shone. It was a taste of the good life. The idea of a different way of living was still in my mind, and it was hard to shake out of it when the time came to go back to the pressure and graft of United.

When you met up with the national team, you would have casual conversations with other players over dinner and hear about the attractions that certain leagues in Europe offered: the different conditions, lifestyles, weather, winter breaks. Little things like those, when you added them all up, might mean an extra year on your playing career and, putting everything together, the notion of trying something new grew in attraction. When Denmark lost in the quarter-finals to Brazil on 3 July it was my fifty-fourth match in eleven months, and when you exit a tournament you always face that call to your club manager: 'Okay, we're out. When do you want me back?'

Fergie's reply was: 'Pete, our two most important games of the season are early on, the first one and the fourth.' He gave me ten days off.

I don't blame him for that. He had no option. The games he was talking about were the two legs of our Champions League qualifying tie versus ŁKS Łódź, and of course it was essential he should take no chances with his team selection and get through those. But it meant I faced going almost straight from the World Cup into pre-season. Just ten days of holiday, having not had a proper vacation in three years? I knew the 'break' would not be enough. Still, I tried making the best of it. The day I arrived back in Copenhagen with the Danish squad I went to our house there, collected the family, repacked and flew back to the south of France the following day for a bit of time at the beach.

There, I attempted to wind down, but the World Cup was still on every TV screen in every bar and restaurant and there was no getting away from football. At the end of every season, a player needs a period when they rest the body to heal all the little nicks and niggles and allow the mind to settle and process all the necessary questions: *How did we perform? What was my contribution? Am I still good enough?* The process requires time and, after just ten days, I did not even get halfway to where I needed to be in terms of recovery, either physically or mentally.

On 14 July I was driving to the Cliff again, thinking about what lay ahead. I knew I was about to embark on another intense campaign and it would be ten months before I got the extended break I needed. I thought of my Denmark team-mates who played in Italy and Spain and how they were starting their seasons later *and* would have winter breaks. For a few days of pre-season I turned it all over in my mind, then came to a decision: one more season. I'd do one more season of this.

I called Martin Edwards. I had two years left on my contract, but could I make this the last? I explained to Martin my reasons. He needed to think about things. On the way to training the next day he rang. 'Okay,' he said, 'you came to us on almost a free transfer, you've been absolutely brilliant for us, so we're going to let you go on a free next summer. But one condition – you don't sign for another English club.'

At the Cliff I went to speak to the manager and the conversation was a little tense, because I'd gone to Martin and not him and he did not like that. Although he claimed, years later, 'I could see in Peter's eyes how he was feeling, blah blah blah,' actually it was a very short and businesslike meeting where we went into no great depth. He just said, 'Okay, I accept it. You'll go at the end of the season. But make sure it's a good one, eh?'

And that was that.

I have to say, the process I followed in taking a step as enormous as leaving Manchester United really was not right. I did not speak to my family, I did not speak to friends, I did not speak to my agent. I didn't speak to anyone, in fact. I just made up my mind and acted. Bang. Done.

So, yes, this one is a regret, perhaps the only big one of my career. On reflection, maybe the manager was right, perhaps I should have gone to him first; spoken about my feelings and the fatigue and the pressures that were sapping me. I should have talked to other players, spoken to my loved ones more – basically just involved more people, taken a range of advice. One of the problems was that I did not know exactly what I wanted, not really. I just wanted a change. To push that red button and stop the treadmill.

In the modern game there is a different culture. Players are encouraged to talk, to be open about their thoughts and feelings. From youth level up, teams have psychologists. Open communication – between managers and players, between players and players – is worked upon. Every top footballer is surrounded by a team of people, but my era was different. You didn't talk. You cracked on. The stuff inside was your business to handle.

Another difference is that today's players have also grown up in a system where rotation is normal, where even the biggest stars are not guaranteed to play every game, but in my day the mentality of a top player was 'I play every game.' At United, that is certainly how eight or nine of the first team saw it – me included. I had worked so hard to get those United and Denmark shirts – why would I give someone else the chance to wear them? But of course, in hindsight, such thinking was wrong. There should have been less fear about asking for a rest.

The bottom line is I should have been tougher on myself. I wish I had asked myself harder questions, but I had a lot of pride. We often talk about pride as a positive tool in football: pride in performance, pride in being on top, pride in never being beaten. But can it also be a negative? What I felt was that if I started to talk about my vulnerabilities with other people, I would show them weakness – and I didn't want to show weakness. Not to anybody. Not ever.

I wanted to be this strong guy, this big, broad-shouldered goalie who never broke down, who was always in your face, who had no chinks in the armour. That was the younger Peter. I was full of a sense of self that I had started to develop from the early days at Brøndby. We were Denmark's first professionals, we were pioneering, every day we were blazing a trail. So we had to be more than the rest. We had to be strong.

And it also went back to childhood. Being an alpha: that came naturally to me. I grew up in a house where being the best was important. It was important to my father. I grew up feeling I had to be extraordinary and that having the weaknesses which ordinary people had was not for me.

But there is a reason I keep talking in terms of no regrets. 'Regret' is a word I dislike. To me, regret is complaining, regret is blaming. Those are the last things I want to do here. I take responsibility for my career – and how can you 'regret' the career I had? But you *can* be unhappy with some decisions you made and admit you made a wrong call – and here is one. I just never should have left Manchester United in 1999. It was wrong for me, wrong for the club, as simple as that. And it could have been avoided if I had sat down with people and talked.

The positive is it is one of those big wrong turnings in life that you learn from – and so it has always been important for me to make sure that Kasper thinks decisions through comprehensively, takes views from a circle of people that he can speak to openly, gets proper advice. He does all of this very well. My long leaving of Manchester United? Mistaken. But a lesson used to help him.

It stayed between me, Martin and the manager. Once we'd had our brief discussions and agreed 1998–99 would be my last season, that was that. We didn't tell the press. We didn't tell the squad. Not until November did we make the announcement that I would be leaving. Between us, there were no follow-up chats, no checking in – again, if that sounds strange, it is just how football was. Something I was always able to do was compartmentalise, to put things away in a box and take them out only when I needed to, and it is what I did in this situation.

Problem: *burnout*. Solution: *new club*. Follow up action: *none*. Current status: *in a box*.

Now get back on the pitch.

Making a decision did give me a feeling of having dealt with things. But only for a very brief period. In September I made an error away to Bayern Munich in a Champions League group match, coming out for a throw-in and gifting Bayern the chance to score. A feeling began to grow that I just wasn't myself, wasn't performing well. In darker moments I even had that nagging voice saying, *Pete, maybe you just don't have it any more.*

The media were beginning to speculate that I was coming to the end. I was about to turn thirty-five and they were asking: do

Manchester United need to start looking for a new goalkeeper? It was not as if I was throwing the ball into the net and costing us goal after goal, but there were little things in games: bad decisions, iffy moments. Inside, I felt very strange: insecure, not able to trust my instincts, hoping they wouldn't shoot.

Hoping they wouldn't shoot.

What on earth was I doing feeling that? Such doubts were completely alien to me.

In October, I missed a couple of games through injury and came back in time for a Champions League double-header against Brøndby. This meant a lot of tiresome media hullabaloo around me: requests for interviews, pieces focusing on me playing against my former club. I didn't enjoy it and I struggled into November. On the 21st we played Sheffield Wednesday at Hillsborough. It was a bright day – I remember the sun in my eyes – and a noon kick-off, which added to the disorientation I experienced on the pitch. Throughout the game I had that out-of-sync feeling of someone who has just woken up.

I felt tired and not completely 'there'. My timing seemed off. I felt physically inhibited, had put on tracksuit bottoms and deep down didn't fancy going all the way in challenges. The only thing I can compare it to is that rusty feeling you get in your first one or two games of pre-season, except without the comfort of there being a logical explanation for it. Fourteen minutes in, Niclas Alexandersson fired an easy shot, straight at me, from the edge of the box.

I dropped it into the net.

Just dropped it in.

Jesus. What was wrong with me?

Everything was weird. 'Straightforward . . . even for the goal-keeper in a pub team on a Sunday morning, but not, it seems, for Schmeichel,' said Jon Champion in the BBC's commentary. Early in the second half, I was slow off my line to make a block and Wim Jonk put Wednesday 2–1 up. Then Alexandersson almost chipped me from 35 yards, from out by the touchline. Late in the game, he rounded me easily to give Wednesday a 3–1 win. I had never felt worse on the pitch.

On the Monday I knocked on Fergie's door:

'This isn't working for me, gaffer. I have felt this coming for some time. I've made some bad decisions and not played as well as I should. You know it and so do I,' I said.

He let me continue.

'My performance on Saturday was really bad. I'm really sorry about that, but I'm so tired. Mentally tired. I haven't had a break in years.'

I always liked the way you could knock on Fergie's door. Whenever you did so, he made time for you. If he had other people in his office, he would introduce you and say to those people, 'I just need to speak to Peter here, can you go outside and give me a minute.' Another thing I liked was that with personal matters, instead of arguing he would trust you. So, when I spoke about needing a break he listened, then said, 'Let me look at the fixture list.'

He got his planner out. All our games were marked there. He ran his finger across the boxes on it and got to January. 'Okay, Pete,' he said. 'Look. You can take this week off.' It was after FA Cup third round weekend and it would mean missing a home game against West Ham. I walked out feeling suddenly better, somehow lighter and, you know what, I immediately began to play okay again. I was able to get through the next six weeks. Then on 4 January, the Sunday morning after beating Middlesbrough 3–1 in the FA Cup at Old Trafford, I flew to Barbados with the family.

It was wonderful.

I came back on 14 January, a Thursday evening. As soon as I got through the door of the Cliff the following morning, Kiddo was there, saying that the manager wanted to see me. I knocked on Fergie's door. 'How was it?' he said, smiling. 'You've been in the papers, looks like you had a great time. Can you play tomorrow?' We had Leicester away. I went home, collected my suitcase once again and soon was back on the team bus en route to the Midlands – and I felt my old self. The next day, in a 6–2 win at Filbert Street, I played okay and over the remainder of the season I got back to my best.

Nowadays, there is awareness about athlete burnout. There is more sympathy for footballers shouldering workloads. My workload in the 1990s was not too unusual, and nor was it too much. I wanted to play all those games. I was a goalkeeper, a No 1, I didn't want rotation in my position. My club dealt with me the best it could and I played for the best man-manager in the game.

The issue was simply that back then the game did not have the culture or tools to help me – or other players in my position. The regret is I didn't do more to help myself, that I didn't reach out. The one guy I spoke to when I was at my low point was Jørgen Henriksen, and he was always very good at putting extra confidence in me – but confidence wasn't the problem.

I just needed a break, a period to process and regroup. My instincts were telling me that. I should have shared them a lot earlier with Fergie. Had I done so, I might not have left Old Trafford in 1999, because when I finally did share, he showed such great understanding. Few managers would say, like he did, 'Here, take this week.' Most would say, 'If I give you time off, I'll have to give everyone time off.' But that was Fergie, willing to treat you differently when he had to. He managed every single player individually, according to their character and needs, while keeping the group absolutely united, and I've never come across anyone else with the ability to do that.

Has anyone? Have we ever come across another Alex Ferguson?

9
TREBLE

Our immortal season had the most memorable ending of all time, at the Nou Camp, and brought games of unforgettable drama at the Stadio delle Alpi, San Siro, Villa Park and, of course, Old Trafford. But who remembers Charlton away? Let me tell you about one dark, wintry afternoon at the Valley that may have held our best ninety minutes of 1998–99 – in a certain way.

There are games that characterise a football team. There are moments a campaign hinges on, even if nobody realises at the time. There are memories that stick in the brain long after seemingly bigger ones have faded and gone. Charlton away.

It was 31 January, a cold, dry and gloomy Sunday, a 4 p.m. kick-off. We had spent a total of three days at the top of the league since the season began and arrived in south-east London sitting third. Charlton at the Valley was a tough fixture. They had a cautious, disciplined team, organised by a canny manager in Alan Curbishley, and nothing was happening for us in the game. I dislocated a finger and our doctor popped it back in, then it dislocated again. I signalled to the referee, who stopped play for a second time to allow the doc to repeat the procedure, except this time strap the hand up. The Valley was an older stadium, where the crowd always felt on top of you and the goalmouths were muddy. Charlton kept slogging towards their nil-nil.

And then.

In the final minute, Gary Neville pumped a long diagonal into their box to set up a last attack. Charlton lumped clear. Gary returned the ball to Scholes, who shimmied into space and chipped to the far stick. Yorkey, with the most finely judged header, angled it home off the post. We went top and, apart from a fortnight in spring when Arsenal had played more games than us, would not relinquish that spot again. There are days when you just have to keep going, keep chasing, keep trying things, and that was one. And Scholesy, who proved our lock-opener – he was a substitute.

We kept winning games in that mode, pushing to the end and finding the answers off the bench if we needed to, all the way to Barcelona.

It is in tough, unglamorous settings like a muddy goalmouth at the Valley on a dark January afternoon that titles are won. Apart from that, I only have really clear recall of a handful of other league games from 1998–99: a 2–2 at Anfield; Ole's four goals coming off the bench in an 8–1 win against Nottingham Forest; a draw at Leeds; and the day we clinched the title, at home to Spurs. Those, plus our 3–2 defeat by Middlesbrough at Old Trafford on 19 December – our worst performance of the season and the very last game we lost.

The manager wasn't at the match. He was in Scotland for his sister-in-law's funeral and we were in a period of change on the coaching side. Brian Kidd had left to become Blackburn boss and Steve McClaren had yet to join as the new assistant manager. Jim Ryan was trying to fill in, but it's difficult to go from reserve-team coach to first-team No 2. Fergie was still furious about Kiddo, so there was a bit of an atmosphere at training, and we all missed Kiddo – he was the glue who bound things together at the Cliff, who stood up for the players to the manager, who provided training that was always inspirational. He was like his name says, a Kidd. He had a youthful enthusiasm.

Against Middlesbrough, and I don't know why – was it the manager not being there? – we played a terrible game. In the dressing room afterwards we sat embarrassed, looking at the floor. Eventually eyes began to lift and we started talking. 'How did we play so *badly*?' From there it developed into a discussion, for the first time, about what we wanted from the season, what we were trying to achieve. The consensus was we had just not been good enough: we were eighteen league games in and there had been more draws and defeats than wins. We had to improve. We said, 'Let's just agree between us not to lose another game.'

From there grew a routine of which Yorkey was a very big part. After Middlesbrough somebody quipped, to laughter, 'Thirty-one wins, and we'll have an unbelievable season!' and that started it. We would look at the number of games left, and someone – Yorkey usually – would chirp up with the comment. We beat Forest: 'Thirty wins, boys!' Then drew with Chelsea and beat Middlesbrough in the cup. 'Twenty-eight wins!' It seemed a bit of a joke initially, but it built and built and Yorkey loved the chat. After Charlton there he was, grinning.

'Hey, boys . . . twenty-four wins!'

Yorkey was pure, 24-carat dressing-room gold. He had the biggest smile you could imagine. Our spirit was fine before his arrival, but the young guys were their own gang, with their internal banter, and us older guys were another group. Yorkey's smile became the glue that bound everyone together. He had a lively social life and was never shy about telling us what he had been up to. Just a fun guy; he was always in a good mood. The dressing room became a happier place.

There had been talk about buying Ronaldo or Patrick Kluivert, someone with international status and the clout to help us win in Europe. Dwight's signing came in under the radar but was one of Fergie's very best: the connectedness he gave the dressing room led to better connection on the grass, both in training and games. Watching the team in front of me, I could see it immediately.

He was someone Andy Cole related to. Their partnership was as good as anything I've seen and just sparked; you saw it in training straight away. It was not practised but born from an intuition between the two. I called them The Twins. They had the same movements and a telepathic understanding.

I'm a really good pal of Dwight's. I always liked and respected him. Like me, he was an incomer to England. You have me, this Scandinavian who wants to do everything right, and him, this Caribbean guy whose laid-backness almost cost him at times, and in our friendship we probably bring something different to each other. I was always impressed with his ability to mix enjoying his life with high performance. I could never do that. I had to keep things straight and routine.

Jesper Blomqvist and Jaap Stam were our other signings. Jesper would play his part and Jaap proved to be what Søren Lerby and Frank Arnesen, who knew Dutch football, had told me: the real deal. You never saw a better defender in your life: big, strong, loved to tackle and block, but with the ball at his feet, he could really play. He added speed to the backline too. The only thing he didn't provide was goals. He scored one in 127 appearances for Manchester United and needed us to be 5–2 up at Leicester before he sneaked one in. We celebrated as if it was the winning goal in the Champions League final.

His great partnership was with Ronny Johnsen. Ronny was an odd one: a real worrier in the run-up to games, nervy in the dressing room, yet ice cool once he stepped on the pitch. Henning Berg was also a deceptively good player. He was not quick, not big, not intimidating – but he had character, personality, leadership and bravery. He proved important too.

Henning and Jaap were our centre backs when we faced Liverpool in the FA Cup fourth round, the week before Charlton away. It was an early kick-off; I hate early kick-offs. I had a routine for 3 p.m. kick-offs and a routine for evening games. Breakfast, a chat, a nap – I kind of liked to ease into the day. But if you're playing at midday, you're at the stadium for 10 a.m. and leaving the hotel at 9 a.m., which means no time to enjoy your food – and I'm a big guy, I always enjoy my food – and no time to centre yourself.

And, of course, three minutes into this horrible midday kick-off there was a little kid scoring. Little kids, you know how they are: always waking up before everyone else to annoy the hell out of you.

Before Jaap and Henning had got settled, Michael Owen nipped between them to score from a Vegard Heggem cross and Liverpool clung to that lead. We were on top. Roy headed against the bar and Incey – a Liverpool player now – cleared off their line. Giggsy went close, Coley went close, Roy hit the woodwork again, I made a decent stop from Patrik Berger. With two minutes left, Beckham stood up a lovely chip, Coley headed across goal and Yorkey banged it in. We pushed forward again and Ole won it in stoppage time, with one of his speciality finishes through the defender's legs. A potty Stretford End and broken Liverpool hearts. It was brilliant. Oh my God, it was brilliant.

When Yorkey equalised, you could smell the hot dogs. The hot dogs? That's a Brian Kidd thing. As soon as we won a big FA Cup tie he would sniff the air and go, 'Mff mff mfff, I can smell the hot dogs, boys.' Think of the old Wembley. In my day, when you arrived at the stadium you went past the concession stands and as you were going through the door you – literally – could smell the hot dogs.

Liverpool, followed by Charlton away – that was the week we showed what we were. Which was: relentless, positive to the last. You could challenge us with anything – the kick-off time, an early goal, ninety minutes of the toughest Premier League grind – and we would still come through. We weren't going to break the commitment we'd made on 19 December, when there were still thirty-one (in the end it was thirty-three, because of FA Cup replays) games to go.

We beat Fulham in the next round of the cup and had Chelsea in the quarter-final. Di Matteo got sent off, Scholesy got sent off. We missed chances. A nil-nil. In the replay at Stamford Bridge we had one of those strange bits of luck. A cross came in that I couldn't quite reach and Dennis Wise went to tap it in. But Tore André Flo, who had jumped with me, slid as he landed, blocking Wise's shot. We got bombarded in that game, but won 2–0 through a Yorke–Cole special and a sublime Yorkey finish.

Arsenal in the semi-final. We were neck and neck in the league and the build-up was all about our rivalry. Whoever wins the cup tie will win the league, the media said – and internally we shared that feeling. Everyone remembers the replay, but the initial game was brilliant too. Roy scored a perfectly good goal that was disallowed for the weirdest offside – Yorkey was fractionally off but nowhere near interfering in the build-up – and Nelson Vivas was sent off for elbowing Nicky Butt. Arsenal showed what a good side they were by regrouping and shutting us out, all the way through to the end of extra time. Clear in my mind is us sitting in the dressing room afterwards, agreeing it was the most interesting nil-nil we had played in our lives.

The replay was three days later, same place, Villa Park. It began with Teddy holding off close markers and setting up David for a brilliant strike, and then you couldn't take your eyes off the game. There were incidents everywhere. Seaman made an exceptional save from Ole, Dennis Bergkamp equalised via a deflection and I made a bad mistake, fumbling a shot for Nicolas Anelka to score – he was offside, thankfully.

Roy got red-carded for two bookings. Arsenal had the momentum. In stoppage time, Phil Neville tripped Ray Parlour – never our favourite player – and Bergkamp had a penalty to win it. In the moment, I did not understand that everything was on the line, there and then. I thought there were ten minutes left or something. I hadn't seen the board for stoppage time go up. I thought that, even if Bergkamp scored, we would have time to chase an equaliser.

Bergkamp was a great footballer, but in that moment I did not care who he was. With penalties, I never thought about the taker, never researched what side he liked to put it and all that. My approach was to focus not on my opponent but on me: that way, I put myself in control, not them. I would make a clear decision about which way I was going to dive and stick to it, so that it was my call, my responsibility, about me. And there was my arrogance – or rather, the conscious way I used arrogance as a tool. Don't look at the taker. Treat them like air. Act superior. Let them know: if you want to score against me, you have to be at your best.

Bergkamp put the ball to the side where I was diving, at a nice height, and I pushed it away. Players came to congratulate me, but if you look at the footage I'm screaming at them to go away. *Guys, guys, the ball is in play, get upfield.* I was surprised when the ref blew for full time straight away. And so we plunged into extra time: the FA Cup and probably the Premier League, thirty minutes, us or them.

Let me tell you about Giggsy. You can't compare anyone with Maradona, and Lionel Messi has played in an era where geniuses are protected. The pitches are lovely, opponents can hardly tackle and the game is played on the floor. Ryan played in the mud, at a time when defenders could smash you and not even get a yellow card, but his technique was amazing.

For a dribbler, Ryan was a big guy, tall and skinny and quick. He had an unusual way of moving with the ball. He looked a little bit bouncy, almost like he was not in control of it at times, and that made opponents think they had a chance of taking it off him. So, they would dive in and he'd just whip it away from them, because he always *was* in control and his balance was exceptional. He might be Manchester United's greatest player, and the only thing that stopped him being one of football's megastars was Wales not qualifying for tournaments. Had he played in one, the whole world would have woken up to how good he was.

FA Cup semi-final replays were scrapped after 1999 and I think Andy Gray said in commentary that if Ryan's winner was the last semi-final-replay goal we would ever see then so be it, because his goal will be up there with all the goals we talk about until the end of time. I had the perfect view. As soon as he collected Vieira's stray pass in our own half, I could see something was happening. It was the way he ran, the purpose in his movements, the acceleration with which he set off – with Arsenal stretched.

It was a killer sniffing blood. Ryan bobbed past the first man, Lee Dixon, then wove past the second, the covering Vieira. Then when Dixon got back, Ryan went past him again. He left Martin Keown on his backside, then veered away from Tony Adams. We played with Mitre balls in the FA Cup, which weren't great, and it was a bumpy pitch, yet Ryan just flew across the ground. Seaman was fantastic across the whole semi-final and beating him took something special. I know his process in that moment: as a keeper you come out, cover your angles and make sure you show the attacker almost nothing of the goal. There is one compromise. You bend down a little to spread your body and make yourself big and that leaves a little bit of space around your ears. It is very rare an opponent will try and beat you high because they could easily put it in Row Z; most will hit it low, and all you do is stay in your position because with one small movement you'll make the save. Seaman does all that, Seaman does everything right. But Ryan just blasts it – over his head into the top of the net. What a goal. Crazy good.

I don't think I'm revealing any secrets in confirming that Fergie did not love Arsène Wenger at that time. I think he was worried Wenger would be considered a better coach than him. Wenger was superior tactically and came from a background where football was played in a more subtle way, so when we played Arsenal Fergie had an extra intensity about him. But between the teams there was a great deal of respect. We knew how good they were, they knew how good we were, and Keane versus Vieira came later. At that time United v Arsenal never had the edge meetings with Liverpool did, but they were of the highest quality. The hype was probably right: winner was going to take all. Had we lost, I believe it would have stopped the roll we were on and then the momentum to win the league but, instead, after winning such an epic, we felt unstoppable. 'Hey, boys . . . ten more wins!'

A week later came another second game of a semi-final, against Juventus in the Champions League. Our European campaign was also becoming epic. In the group stage we scored twenty times and got through a tough section that included Barcelona and Bayern. Finally, in those European games, we had goal power and were becoming a team who took advantage of weak points of the opposition. Our quarter-final was with Inter Milan. What a team they were. Ronaldo, Iván Zamorano, Youri Djorkaeff, Javier Zanetti, Diego Simeone, Roberto Baggio, a young Andrea Pirlo . . . The way we got past them showed all the learning and experience we had acquired.

Inter played a back five. Yet, early in the first leg at Old Trafford, the intelligence of his movement won Yorkey space. I've never seen a player cross a ball like Beckham, not with the consistency of brilliance in the delivery. For me, it was a gift: I got to practise defending and coming for crosses against the best the world. Before half-time, with two near-identical crosses, one somehow delivered as he was falling over, David found Yorkey, who scored with smart headers. Then we dug in for the second half, dug deep, shut Inter out.

We were pushed to the limits of our resilience in doing so. A cross from Fabio Galante found Zamorano arriving six yards out in prime position to score. I was coming from the other side of the goal and saw everything clearly, knowing that it was the biggest chance for Inter so far. Zamorano sent a powerful diving header towards to my left. I set off flying across the length of the goal, my eyes fixed on the ball, my body spread in a star shape, reacting in time to get my left hand to the ball. Wrist strong, I clawed it away and landed, ready for any rebound.

I am often asked what my best ever save was: well, there you have it. If it was not the best – and I think it was – it was definitely the most important one. I had to make another stop when Nicola Ventola went through, but the ball ran to Francesco Colonnese, who tried to finish, only for Henning Berg to sprint back and clear off the line. Henning: the looks of an accountant but a warrior's heart.

Two-nil would set you up for a comfortable second leg against most teams, but Inter were too good to relax against and there is never comfort at the San Siro. It was seriously hostile. Everything was thrown at me, lighters, water bottles, food, coins. Eighty thousand Italians bayed for our flesh and there were a few nasty players in their side. Colonnese put in one challenge that in today's game would be worth anything between five and eight red cards but just got a booking. Simeone tried to provoke Beckham. Again. Benoît Cauet and Zé Elias were nasty.

Inter started with Ronaldo, but he clearly wasn't fit and lasted only an hour. His replacement, Ventola, scored immediately and we had to hold out for thirty minutes, with Inter just needing a goal to get to extra time. They were diving to try and win penalties, but the French referee, Gilles Veissière, was strong. Henning was heroic again and Fergie showed he was beginning to crack Europe tactically, playing Ronny Johnsen in midfield and letting Ronny run himself out before sending on Scholesy, who equalised, after David's cross and Coley's set-up. 1–1 it finished.

We graduated as a European side that night and I would say it was the best game we played all season. I don't mean in terms of beautiful football but mature, hardened, professionalism. In both legs, we kept the pace at Premier League level but combined it with the defensive organisation needed in Europe. At the San Siro, Inter's tactic was to maintain a high tempo. They had six balls at the ready and every time the ball went out, a ballboy threw a replacement on. That played into our hands. We loved the game being fast. You could feel them tiring with twenty minutes to go.

Juventus were a more measured side. Carlo Ancelotti was their coach, Zidane their star and Inzaghi their absolute pain in the neck. As Fergie observed, that guy was born offside. He scored many annoying goals against me, scruffy, poacher efforts that were the worst to accept. Juve also had Edgar Davids, Antonio Conte, Didier Deschamps, Gianluca Pessotto, Angelo Di Livio, Nicola Amoruso, Paolo Montero – for sheer quality, the best starting XI in Europe. Conte scored twenty-five minutes into the first leg at Old Trafford, when they surprised us by not being measured at all for a few minutes but coming at us hard from kick-off. We recovered and started plugging away. We had chances: Roy had a shot deflected just wide, Teddy scored but was just offside, Scholesy missed two opportunities and Ryan had a strong penalty appeal turned down.

In the end, our sheer relentlessness told. We kept pushing; they kept falling further back, inviting us to pile ever more pressure on. In stoppage time, with the ball in their box again, Juve cracked, their left back, Mirković, messing up a clearance. David lobbed the ball back in and two tired Juve headers couldn't get it away. Ryan arrived to slam high into the net. 1–1. Our lifeline.

What sticks in my mind even more than the game is what happened in the stadium after Conte scored. I never experienced a better atmosphere at Old Trafford. People talk about fans as 'the twelfth man', but when you are an athlete who works to the limit on every part of your game, it is hard to admit the crowd makes you better, because what does that make you?

Does it make you someone who doesn't actually give their best unless you get help?

What I think happens is you don't so much play better as play braver. We were willing to take little risks, spurred on by an incredible wall of noise. We had just been to the San Siro and I had never heard anything louder than the sound when Inter scored, but our fans took things beyond that level as they roared us on to chase Juventus down. The eruption of noise, when Ryan's goal went in, I'll remember for the rest of my life. For me, in terms of atmosphere, that game is the benchmark for big European nights at Old Trafford. On paper, 1–1 was a first-leg result that favoured them, but our feeling, coming off the pitch, was 'We'll do this.'

The Juventus home leg was the second in a sequence of fourteen games we would play in fifty-three days, finishing at the Nou Camp. And every one of those matches was all-or-nothing. It was like playing a cup final every 3.8 days over a period of seven weeks. When you have momentum, you feel like a snowball thundering down a hill, and we hit that mental sweet spot. For me, things had felt quite different since my holiday and I was loving rolling from challenge to challenge. Managers then did not rotate the way modern ones do, but Fergie had a genius for resting one or two players every game, and thereby keeping everyone fresh, happy and motivated at the same time. This ability was crucial in that period, as was his knack for keeping our minds clear of everything except the next game. On the training ground Steve McClaren, with his fresh and imaginative approach, was showing his worth too.

The Stadio delle Alpi, where we would play the second leg, is not the San Siro. It is out of Turin and the pitch is too far from the stands, so it wasn't a pressure cooker and, having played group-stage matches there in 1996 and 1997, it held no fear for the team. But it did inspire foreboding in me, personally.

I had a thought coming into the game that I hated myself for. I had once filmed a commercial for Sugar Puffs at Juventus's stadium, in which the premise was I was playing in goal, got injured coming for the ball and the Honey Monster came on to replace me. He performed a Higuita 'scorpion' save while I was shown sitting on the touchline, my leg in a plaster cast. I never liked the idea of pretending I was injured; I didn't want to give myself the kiss of death. As soon as we were drawn against Juventus, though, this little voice spoke in my mind: *Stadio delle Alpi, eh? Going to break your leg, are you, Pete?*

We started well, very well, in fact. And went 2–0 down. Bloody Inzaghi. His first goal followed the only mistake we made in the whole game, when we were disorganised as they took a short corner. I still think about the cross: could I have got to it? I'd been drawn to my near post and the ball came in at pace. Inzaghi scored at the back stick. Then there was a nothing situation. Inzaghi hit a shot that was going straight into my gloves, but Jaap put a boot out, the ball skimmed off the under-side of his studs, bounced into the ground and the spin took it over me and in. Two behind, ten minutes gone.

Honestly? I was annoyed but not too worried. My thinking was simply that if we could score, we'd be right back in the tie, because we were creating chances, we were opening up an Italian team at home, a brilliant Italian team at that. When Roy got booked it changed the game. He would be suspended for the final if we went through, so now he went at Juventus with an energy and ferocity they could not answer. He headed home to make it 2–1 and I just knew – we weren't going to concede another and they had used all their luck. Our best was better than their best. We'd crack them again.

The Yorke–Cole partnership was all about little one-twos, and if Yorkey was the better header of a ball, Coley was incredible in tight spaces. There was another lovely dynamic: such was their friendship, they didn't care which one scored. They just loved playing for each other and it was Coley who crossed for Yorkey to head in for 2–2 before half-time, and Yorkey who went through to set up Coley for 3–2 before the end.

Because of the high profile of those three wins – Inter, Arsenal, Juve – they might seem to be the best performances of the season. But I can't get away from Charlton. You think about it: we won the Premier League by a single point from Arsenal. We don't score that last-minute goal at the Valley and we don't win the title. There is no Treble. Charlton 0 Manchester United 1 (Yorke 89) – it was not a high-profile victory, but it absolutely summed us up.

Eight more wins . . .! After Juventus, we drew three of our next five Premier League matches, but the manager judged it perfectly. We won just enough points to stay ahead of Arsenal and he tweaked the line-up, resting legs, with the climax of the season in mind. On 16 May, a bright Sunday afternoon, we arrived at Old Trafford with three fixtures left. Tottenham in the league, Newcastle in the FA Cup final, Bayern in the big one, in Barcelona. Win those three and we . . .

The trick was not to think ahead but to focus on each job individually. To be certain of winning the title, we had to take three points from Spurs, and when Les Ferdinand lifted a brilliant finish over me to put them 1–0 ahead after twenty-four minutes, I felt the same calm confidence that we would be okay as I had when we went 2–0 down in the Stadio delle Alpi. I was certain that, with plenty of time in the game, we'd be okay – and Beckham scored beautifully to level just before half-time.

Two minutes into the second half, from what Gary Neville claims was a pass but I suspect might have been a clearance, Coley lobbed Ian Walker: a sublime finish, fit to win the championship. Credit to the manager. He always recognised the importance of celebrating achievements. Even when you're going for a Treble, winning the league is very special and after an improvised get-together that evening we were given Monday off to go out in Manchester and celebrate properly. Albeit under strict instructions: behave yourselves. We had a big week ahead, which included a media day to preview both the Champions League finals and the FA Cup final at Wembley.

Roy did not appear to have got the memo when he turned up at the pub where we gathered in Deansgate, the last to arrive and very drunk. As soon as he stepped through the door, Gary Neville said to me, 'Oh God, look at the eyes, this is trouble.' In the next pub, Roy got into an altercation with a bloke and two girls. It was a stitch-up by a tabloid newspaper, with photographers waiting outside. We phoned Ned Kelly, our chief of security, who arrived quickly and calmed everything down. I went straight home. There was no point in staying out.

The next time we were in was the press day. I'd never seen so much media at the Cliff and they weren't there to talk cup finals. The manager got us in the dressing room and was absolutely furious with us. With us! First for letting something happen, second for calling Ned instead of him. That was not a great day. The media event was a disaster. Here we were on the brink of history and all they wanted to speak about was Roy. We said nothing.

Typically, having had his say, the manager moved on, as did we – to the FA Cup final. It was my ninth trip to Wembley in seven years and we had sort of built up a routine. We would arrive two days before the final and stay in the Oakley Court hotel on the bank of the Thames in Windsor, a nice place. The manager always put on entertainment, a way of emphasising we were in a final and had achieved something special. This time, we went clay-pigeon shooting. A guy came and set it up for us on the river.

Our families would be in town in a different hotel and I loved the morning of the game – you wake up and put the BBC on and the pictures are live from the hotel. You open the curtains and the outside-broadcast truck is parked in the grounds. You breakfast, go for a little walk by the river, have the team talk, a pre-match meal, a bath or shower. Then you get dressed up in your new cup-final suit and get on the bus: you have a police escort and TV helicopter following you. You arrive, go past the concession stands and there it wafts, the smell of hot dogs. And it is such a strong smell – not a great one, actually – but part of the whole special experience.

Yet Teddy was not in any 'isn't-this-special' mood that day. Disappointment oozed out of him. On that bus journey from Windsor to Wembley – and it is quite a long one – he was seriously unhappy. He sat, stone-faced, almost as if he had separated himself from the club at that point. The reason was the manager had named him as a substitute and was playing Ole and Coley. Knowing that the partnership against Bayern would be Cole and Yorke, and having been subbed at half-time against Spurs, Teddy felt the FA Cup final should be his opportunity.

Roy, though, was injured six minutes in and for some reason, instead of putting another midfielder on, Fergie summoned Teddy. Teddy told me later that he could not believe it: 'Roy is coming off and he is looking at *me*?' He said he got stripped and onto the field as quickly as possible, before the manager changed his mind.

Teddy scored within a few minutes and, truthfully, the game was easy. There is no way of being kind to Newcastle and saying otherwise. I am still a bit mystified why they were not more motivated and competitive. They had good players, but it was as if they were not there. Teddy set Scholesy up for 2–0 and we strolled the rest. I remember very little detail of the game – a shot from distance by Andy Griffin that I saved, another fairly harmless effort by Didi Hamann – nothing else really. We went up to get the trophy and straight away the T-shirts were out: '2 DOWN, 1 TO GO'. Mentally, the preparation for Bayern Munich began the moment we collected our medals.

The Treble came down to substitutions. Coley for Teddy against Spurs: Coley scores. Teddy for Roy at Wembley: Teddy scores and assists. Then, of course, Teddy and Ole at the Nou Camp. And substitutions are about your squad. Ours had evolved over my seven years since arriving from Brøndby and when I think of how good Ole and Teddy were, it makes me think how strong the squad was for those two not to be first-choice players.

Teddy was elegant, both as a footballer and a person. For a long time, I thought he was arrogant, but then I realised he was just shy and that his remoteness was a shield. He is one of the most intelligent players I played with; the way he saw football was very un-English. He was an amalgam of Mark Hughes and Eric.

Then you had Ole. When you're struggling, not taking your chances, look up and see Ole getting stripped to come on and you think, *Yeah, I like this*. He is the best finisher I ever saw. He drove me mad in training. It was his cleverness in knowing precisely where to be and precisely when to strike the ball – which is why he popped so many finishes home through defenders' legs. From the bench, he analysed the game so well that he knew exactly how to exploit the opposition's tiredness. If he needed to go on and be a target player, he'd do that. A link man, a poacher – he'd perform those roles too. He would be whatever the situation demanded.

That it came down to substitutes was fitting, because the Treble was a triumph of the collective, of trying everything until something worked, of keeping going, of the manager's brilliant gambling in games, of that risk-taking mode we could click into, especially with fresh forwards on and opposing defenders on the back foot. Another thing about

Fergie: to keep players of Ole and Teddy's quality happy while not starting them was man-management genius – the sort I benefited from when I destressed on a Barbadian beach.

Wembley was my last game for Manchester United in England. The Nou Camp would be my last game for Manchester United full stop, and with Roy out, I was going to be captain. After beating Newcastle, we went to the Metropole hotel on the Edgware Road for a big party, a club event, before we left for Catalonia the following day.

Our families were at the hotel, so too all the ordinary club staff who had come to mean so much to me since my arrival in 1991, but I am not big on goodbyes. I was presented with a trophy with an inscription thanking me for my 'legendary achievements at Manchester United', or something like that. I was brought up on stage and handed a microphone, and it nags me to this day that I didn't make a proper speech. I just said, 'I really appreciate this, but I'm not quite gone yet. I do have one game to go and I'll speak to you after that.'

I imagined there would be another club event after the Champions League final, but instead there were informal, more spontaneous celebrations. If I am being honest, I was a little irritated at being summoned to the stage in the Metropole, because it felt like something sentimental, almost a distraction. It felt like the end.

It was not the end. It was far from the end. To all the people I neglected to thank properly for my time at Manchester United that evening, I apologise. But the Nou Camp was to come. We were boarding Concorde the next day. And as soon as the final whistle blew at Wembley, I was absolutely in Champions League final mode.

10
THE WILD BOY

I was quite an unruly boy; born on the wild side, you might say. I was never a fighter, never a vandal or thief. I did not break laws. I was just wild. By the age of fourteen, I had been to a few schools.

I needed outlets for my energy and ways to express the independent spirit that adults sometimes found difficult to control. If another kid could do some physical feat that I had never attempted before, I made sure I could do it too, only better. I threw myself into any challenge.

In Høje-Gladsaxe, where I spent most of my childhood, behind our block of flats were some small man-made hills. In winter, they were brilliant for daredevil sledging, full of holes and craters that the snow would cover. At other times of year the challenge was to climb one of the mounds, take a run-up on the flat ground at the top and launch yourself off the edge to see how far you could jump. You did not know what you were landing in and cuts, scrapes and bruises were inevitable. Of course, the lunatic who could always jump the furthest was me.

There was a little playground for my block and the block next to it, which parents from the apartments had helped build using telegraph poles. It had swings, climbing castles and monkey bars, and I could do all sorts of crazy stunts. I would sprint and jump onto something or leap off from any height, no matter the risk. Deep inside, I know being that boy led to what I became, because the control I had over my body and my physicality, the balance and assertive bravery I possessed as a goalkeeper, it all came from there. But I was hard to handle and my mother might have welcomed me being a little less boisterous and reckless. Parents' evening was not her favourite date in the diary.

That started from when I was six. I never went to kindergarten, so my first taste of anything like organised learning and play was pre-school. Halfway through the first grade the teachers called my mother in and asked if she could enrol me somewhere else. I was too restless, too untamed, too cheeky. My mum found a nice way to tell them to go **** themselves.

She did move me, by the way. But that was because she thought the teachers were no good.

If I am like my father in looks, in character I am most like her. Think about the girl who ignored the rules and just hopped aboard that boat to Poland; who boldly strode up to a stranger to score a theatre ticket. The independent spirit, the willingness to follow instincts wherever they might lead: that is her, and that is me. She is the kind of lady who would say, 'I need a break', jump on her bike and not stop cycling until she felt like stopping. Once she kept going all the way – 120 kilometres – across the breadth of Zealand. She is tough and headstrong, but considerate and a brilliant mother. She tells me that as a child she was on the wild side too.

At the State University Hospital she was not just any nurse; she was a nurse in a children's cancer unit, in charge of four wards, and the work could be harrowing. The staff needed to be not just caring but brave. She looked after terminally ill kids and coped with their loss, and two of the children she watched pass away were from families in our social circle. Big heart, tough core: that's Mum.

The self-reliance that was another quality which helped in my career was forged early in childhood. Our family were outliers, and not just because we were one of the very few in the estate to be mixed in nationality and culture. My parents' working patterns made home life unconventional. My mum's shifts were in the evenings, seven days on and seven days off. My dad's gigs were in the evenings and at night. From a very young age, us kids were left in the flat to look after ourselves, with a neighbour looking in to check all was okay.

I would have been four years old, five at most, when this routine began. My older sister was six or seven, my middle sister two or three. Mum left for her shift at four o'clock and Dad fed us before leaving for Tivoli at six. We were then alone. We would play for a couple of hours, then take ourselves to bed. In our block were neighbours with children of similar age and the spirit was that everyone looked out for each other. It was a safe place. These were the early to mid 1970s, the hippy era, when living in bigger groups was a social aspiration – and if the manner in which we were left to fend for ourselves seems wrong by modern standards, it was in keeping with the ideas of the time.

My very early years had been in Buddinge, a suburb in northwest Copenhagen. We moved to Høje-Gladsaxe when I was seven. Høje-Gladsaxe is all concrete, glass and landscaped greenery and was one of the largest housing projects in Denmark. It was regarded as an attractive place to live in the late 1960s and a little more expensive than other estates. It comprised five wide tower blocks of fifteen floors, two eight-storey buildings and ten three-storey buildings. We lived in one of those small three-floor blocks and these sat behind the high rises, with green space, including football pitches, in between.

I crossed the pitches to get to school. Then the development grew, the planners built another school and my whole class relocated there. I was restless in class but happy in general, comfortable among kids I had grown up with. When we moved again, this time to new-build housing in Smørumnedre, another 20 kilometres out of town, it set me back. My parents had a dream of living in a house and my sisters and I liked the idea of having our very own garden, so our move was a dream for everyone . . . that didn't work out for anyone. None of us settled. My parents were caught up in the financials – the value of our house decreased and their mortgage interest was something incredible, like 19 per cent. They were trapped and we were stuck.

It was a disaster, schools-wise. We were part of a large influx of families to the area and there was a new school, far bigger than my old place in Høje-Gladsaxe. So many kids. There were twenty-eight in my class and eight classes in my year, and we were children arriving from all parts of Copenhagen, all fight-ing for position in the pecking order. I learned nothing. There was so much noise, so much fighting and disruption, and the teachers gave up on many of the kids – while the kids' mentality was sod the teachers, sod homework, sod rules. I fell in with that and was virtually kicked out after an argument with a reli-gious studies tutor. I made no real friends and played up to my personality, trying to be one of the loud ones, one of the dominating guys. That was my seventh and eighth grade: a waste.

Conventional school was just not for me: sitting still, learning things slowly and repetitively. I prefer to go by instinct, and after the school in Smørumnedre I was at a crossroads. My older sister, Kathrine, got involved. She had heard about a school run by the state which headhunted outstanding teachers and tasked them with developing new materials to roll out across the Danish curriculum. It was called Statens Paedagogiske Forsogscenter (SPF), which translates as the National Innovative Centre for Education, and it was in Islev, west of Copenhagen city centre, about 15 kilometres away. My mother was keen; the drawback was I would have to redo eighth grade there, but we had some long heart-to-hearts, I applied and I got in.

This was 1978. I was fourteen and a half. Every summer my mum took my sisters and me on holiday to Thisted, to stay for two weeks with her parents and for one week with her aunt. It was a long drive to the north of Denmark and we borrowed the old van my father used to ferry his instruments and equipment to gigs. There was always competition to sit at the front beside Mum. In the back, there were no windows or seats, just mattresses we slung down to perch on for the whole long journey.

Ten days before our annual trip I woke with a terrible pain that spread from my hip to my thigh and down the right side of my leg. It was so powerful. My mother gave me some tablets and it briefly disappeared, but then it returned with full force. The pain would come in waves, sometimes with a few hours between them, sometimes just an hour, sometimes only twenty minutes. The waves were relentless. I had never experienced such agony before, nor have I experienced it since.

Mum took me to A&E, where I had blood tests and X-rays, but the doctors found nothing. I was back at A&E the day before our holiday, the pain absolutely excruciating – but still the medics could not pinpoint anything wrong. They said it was okay for me to travel, but the five-hour drive to Thisted was unbearable. I lay on a mattress, the soreness intensifying. I felt no better once we got there and spent days lying on a sofa, barely able to move. When I needed to get up and go to the toilet I had to use my aunt's old walking stick.

Three times, my mother called doctors out to see me. On each occasion they recommended I should go to hospital, but I refused: there was no way I wanted to be stuck there. Then on the last day of the holiday something crazy happened: all my discomfort just disappeared. I was outside my aunt's house, playing a ball game we called 'kerby' with the other kids. I was so elated. I don't think I had been so happy in my life to that point.

Back in Copenhagen, we kept an appointment for me to be checked out at hospital that had been made before our trip. The pain had not come back – weirdly, it never did – but this seemed the sensible thing to do. We were there for six hours. They took blood tests which had to be examined in the lab and looked at by specialists. Finally a doctor delivered the bad news. I had an extremely serious infection somewhere. My levels of a certain indicator were a crazy number like 120 or 130, whereas in a healthy body they would be between two and eight.

I was placed in a hospital bed and ordered to lie there, as still as possible, in case moving helped the infection spread. In the meantime they would try and determine exactly where the infection was. I was kept like that for two and a half weeks, while staff tried different investigations and antibiotics without success. I was more miserable than I had ever been in my life to that point.

For my mother it was hell. Years of nursing children with cancer had given her some frightening ideas about what my problem might be. Finally, the doctors decided on an operation. They bored right through the bone into the centre of my hip and took a sample – which told them that the source of the infection was right there. Antibiotics were prescribed, but they had to be given by injecting me, three times a day, with an enormous needle. The pain when the needle plunged into my muscle was beyond description.

During the op, they had also inserted a drain to collect and pump away the pus, but the procedure was not done properly. The drain was misaligned, meaning the poison stayed there, bubbling up over its sides. One day a doctor came in and was furious with his colleagues' handiwork; he took out a pair of scissors and cut my skin open and all the pus came gushing out.

Two weeks later, I was allowed home on crutches. I was forbidden to put any weight on my leg for fear the hip bone might crumble and collapse because of the hole from the operation. But there had been eight weeks of this nightmare; I'd had enough. I was nearly fifteen; I was supposed to be a big, strong football player. I could walk normally – nobody needs to know I have crutches, I thought. The day after getting home, I decided to go to the youth club and hobbled on my sticks all the way there, a distance of one kilometre. I hung out with my pals and milked the attention, before hobbling back. The next morning, I woke, completely drained, with red spots all over me and a fever of 40 degrees. A combination of no exercise in almost two months and the pills I was on had knocked me over.

I was taken straight back to hospital and they wanted to keep me in again, but I couldn't face that. What saved me was my mum being a nurse. She promised to look after me using her professional skills and the doctors said okay. They also changed my meds: it turned out I had an intolerance to the first ones. It took me six more months – through to February – to be completely better, and I wasn't able to play football the entire time. When I think back now, I guess it was as close as I came to an injury or physical problem robbing me of my career: until it healed fully, the fragile hip could have gone.

Not that I saw the big picture back then. I just hated my crutches. And I would have to start my new school late and, for the first few weeks, hobble in like some weedy guy on them.

My new school was incredible. The lessons were different. It wasn't quite, 'Hey, let's sit outside among the flowers all day,' but the educational methods were experimental. The teaching was fresh, the classes were small and the teachers cared about the pupils. My tutor, Ib O. Petersen, was also the headmaster and he taught general education – about how society works. He understood me straight away. He saw this boy who, yes, had an untamed nature but who also showed promise in many things, like maths, music, drama. What this boy was not good at was listening. So he got through to me. At football, I was starring for my Gladsaxe-Hero boys' team, and the Danish newspaper *Politiken* had a comprehensive Monday sports section which printed every result from the Copenhagen area, right the way down to the smallest kids' games. Every Monday morning, Mr Petersen would wait for me at the school gates, say good morning and make some comment about our result. It forged a connection. For a kid of my type, he had found the ideal bit of psychology to deploy. I felt responsible to him. I felt, *I'm not going to let this guy down.*

I began to love school. Every Wednesday you pursued an optional subject. I was in a small group who loved music and theatre. Wednesday mornings, we practised music and Wednesday afternoons we did drama, and in the evenings the school opened to the general public for various night classes and we persuaded it to keep the theatre open so we could effectively spend the entire day – from 9 a.m. to 10 p.m. – creating or rehearsing shows. My role was usually that of music director, and in one of our productions I used a melody my father had composed. When we performed the play for our parents, he was so very proud.

Early in my time at SPF, we had an exchange programme with a school in Milton Keynes called Stantonbury Campus. I loved Milton Keynes. It was not too different from the planned, concrete villages I had lived in and, most important, it was in England. It's weird, but from an early age I always felt a connection to Britain. Denmark imported a lot of BBC and ITV shows and they were my favourite television: *Fawlty Towers, Monty Python, Not the Nine O'Clock News*, Benny Hill, Tommy Cooper, the David Attenborough nature documentaries.

I stayed with this brilliant family in Milton Keynes. It pains me that I cannot remember their names, because I have thought about them a million times. I think the boy might have been called Mike. He was cool. One of my first conversations, around their dinner table, was about football. Who do you support? *Manchester United*. It became a theme; to them it was fascinating that this kid from Denmark had such an obsession with all things Old Trafford. I loved rock and pop – Supertramp, Dire Straits, Toto, Led Zeppelin, ABBA – and one day all the kids on exchange were scheduled to go to London, with the highlight being a trip to HMV on Oxford Street. It was all we had talked about for months and I had been as excited as anyone about visiting the store, but my biggest obsession was getting my hands on a Manchester United jersey. My host family, bless them, drove me to a sports shop in Northampton so I could buy my shirt.

They were lovely folk. They took me to a pub and to visit the castle in Nottingham, where I went to a market for the first time. I bought a trick deck of cards, a Manchester United scarf and a mirror with the Manchester United crest on, which went up over my bed at home. The idea that England was where I wanted to be just got multiplied after that exchange.

Football was my anchor. It gave a shape and focus to my pre-adult years that school only belatedly did. On the pitches of Høje-Gladsaxe there was a sports club of the same name and a number of my classmates began playing for its boys' football team, with their parents getting involved in the organisation. I went to a training session and the coach, a guy called Sven-Erik, watched me for a couple of minutes and said, 'Try going in goal.' It was immediately clear that I was a natural. We played in full-sized goals, but I was tall, agile and brave as hell. There were no linesmen, so you just shouted, 'Offside!' and I proved a natural at winning those decisions too. I didn't have a clue about the rule – but I did have a very loud voice.

My first proper match was in a tournament on a pitch in front of my apartment, on 7 August 1972. I know the date because my mum was getting ready to go to hospital for the birth of my youngest sister, Hanne, who arrived the next day. Mum packed her overnight bag while looking out of our window, watching me play. At the end of the tournament, a few of the parents began telling me how talented I was. Some even said, 'You'll play for Denmark one day.' Before long, giving me a lift home in his car after a school game, a teacher told me the same thing and I was quite prepared to believe all the compliments.

The example my dad set was that you should strive to be the best and expect it of yourself. He felt he was the best pianist around: while he never made that claim explicitly, it was implied when he talked about all his competitors. The way he saw it, they were rubbish compared to him. So, I grew up in an environment where to be the best was important and it became a driver in my football career.

Another was a feeling of being accountable to those who told me I would go far. Because of their faith, I should therefore look after my talent and make the most of it, I believed: otherwise, I would be letting people down. That sense of obligation followed me every day for the rest of my career, as did the sense that I was special. As a kid I felt the other boys would never score: *Come on, shoot – I'll save it.* And I felt that every day until I finished playing.

I threw myself into becoming a footballer. Høje-Gladsaxe were a new club, starting in the bottom division, and the level was too easy. In our first season we won every game, scoring 267 goals, thrashing opponents 35–0 while I stood against a post watching the fun. How many did we concede that season? Seven. Disappointing, hey? In one game, the opposition coach just walked off rather than stay to the end of the hammering. 'Sorry, boys, I'm going home for dinner,' he said. Another time, one of the opposition was playing in wellies.

A bigger club played on the other side of the tower blocks. They were called Hero and after two and a half years with Høje-Gladsaxe, where we never lost a game, Hero invited me and my best pal, Peter – Peter K. Nielsen – to join them. People from our area remember Peter for two things. One, he was the only black kid where we lived, and two, he was both a football and handball player of jaw-dropping talent. He idolised Pelé and he was my first real friend and my best friend. I often slept at his place. He lived with adoptive parents in a nice house with a garden on the edge of the estate, and we shared a lot of our youth together.

Peter's story is both sad and beautiful. National team footballers of my generation ask after Peter. He was a left-footed midfield player and his talent was widely renowned, but he went off the rails after his adoptive parents divorced and he moved with his dad to one of the tower blocks, then somewhere else, from where it became complicated for him to get to training. He dropped out of football but stuck with handball and was beginning to break into the best team in Denmark when he started getting involved in serious trouble. Soft drugs, car theft, petty crime. He spent time in prison, he met a girl called Ae. They had a daughter, Tatiana. One New Year's Eve, Ae fell backwards, hit her head on a kerb and died, leaving Peter to look after this tiny girl. He made a decision: to put Tatiana's life before his own – and the pair of them made it. It was never easy for them. Peter had to take menial jobs, educate himself and stay out of trouble – but he now works as a security consultant, while Tatiana grew up to be a wonderful young woman.

I played handball too and, in winter, indoor football. I loved that game. In Denmark, it is popular. You play four v four, shooting into a handball goal, but can only defend with two players and the goalkeeper. One of your players must stay in the opposition half. It means that you always defend a man down and the keeper must organise the players in front of him tactically and look to throw quickly to the man upfield to counterattack.

This helped develop my style in the outdoor game. Handball shaped it as well. In handball, nobody except the keeper can step inside a semicircle in front of the goal, but outfielders are allowed to be in the air inside that zone as long as they release the ball before they land. So, you defend that goalmouth using your presence. If an attacker jumps into the zone, they might be three metres in the air and with just a slight turn of their wrist can throw the ball either way, at speeds up to 100 mph. The keeper has very little control. The only thing you can really do is try and trick the attacker into putting the ball where you want it to go, and you learn to do that by making your own movements first, to trigger their throw. It is all about being proactive and you save with any part of the body that you can. There are also rules to stop time-wasting, so when you are in possession it is about mounting fast attacks and you rehearse running certain patterns for when you break. The keeper is a real playmaker.

We practised so that as soon as the opposition took a shot, my wingers would start running and I would catch and immediately throw the ball to one of them. So many of our goals were scored on the counter, and the guys on the handball team were basically the same as the guys on the football team. That handball style of play naturally filtered into our footballing game. I played both indoor football and handball almost up until I turned pro with Brøndby.

Hero had an excellent team. As well as Peter and me, there was Lars Schöne, whose son Lasse would play for Genoa and with Kasper for the Danish national team. Lars was a big talent too and the first of us to graduate to the Danish top flight. I have mentioned the national cup semi-final we played against KB and their star player, Michael Laudrup. Torben Piechnik was also in their side. In the game, we were winning 2–0 when our player who had been man-marking Michael got injured. After he went off, Michael scored twice to force a replay, which KB won.

Following a merger, Hero became Gladsaxe-Hero. The club belonged to the Zealand football association and we won its youth championship, the YKS League, my first significant honour – I was sixteen. The club's senior side were in the Danish third division and were relegated to the Danish National League with five games to go in the 1980 season. Its new coach, Svend Aage Hansen, decided on a clear-out and to promote seven players from our youth side – but not me, at least not for the first match. This was despite telling me I had a big future. Although he promoted me for the game after that, for years the humiliation gnawed at me, until I finally asked, 'Why on earth did you not pick me that first game?' He explained the opposition were the side who had run away with the title and he hadn't wanted to expose me to a potential hammering on my debut. When I did make it, I got Man of the Match, so perhaps he knew a thing or two. He became my father-in-law: Bente, my first wife, was his daughter.

Svend Aage managed us for two seasons. A team-mate was Christian Andersen, a classy defender who had played in Belgium and was now thirty-six and winding down his playing career while taking over his father's business. He was a great influence and with him playing in front of me, I could learn from someone who really knew the game. My best performance for Gladsaxe-Hero was a relegation-decider on a miserable day and I was flying left, right and centre, saving everything. We won 2–1 and when I meet with Christian now, he still says, 'Bloody hell, what about that game?' Our winner came when I saved a penalty, gathered the ball and threw it up the left wing to the eventual scorer – who was a mate from my handball team. An absolute handball goal.

I played two full seasons in the first team. Svend Aage had contacts at Hvidovre, a club with a record for developing young talent, and spoke to Jørgen Henriksen, their goalkeeping coach.

He started scouting me. Jørgen had played in Holland with his best friend, John Steen Olsen, and when they returned to Denmark both opened shops on the same street in Copenhagen, next-door-but-one to each other. Jørgen's was a fashion boutique, while John Steen's was a sports shop. They were quite a duo. After watching me for a while, Jørgen invited me to meet him at John Steen's shop and I sat in the back room waiting for him. I looked at a massive photo on the wall and it was of John Steen scoring an overhead kick – against Jørgen.

John Steen became Ajax's Scandinavian scout, discovering, among others, Zlatan Ibrahimović. Jørgen, I guess, can say he found me. When he arrived at the back of the shop, he said he liked what he had seen of me and I had to sign for Hvidovre. He fixed up a meeting with their board, who had a contract ready for me, and that was that: I became a Danish top-flight player. Jørgen would be my goalkeeping mentor for the rest of my career, and by a lovely coincidence he lives 400 yards away from me now. When Denmark play at home, the national team are based in our vicinity and he, John Steen and I meet up to go and watch training.

I had a connection with Jørgen immediately. He believed in me from day one and coached me in precisely the way that fitted my personality: he was original, unconventional and positive in his thinking. I went straight into Hvidovre's first team and in my debut was full of confidence, making my saves, coming for crosses with total self-belief. The headlines were along the lines of 'WHO IS THIS GUY?'

My second game wasn't so good. It was a four o'clock kick-off against Aarhus and the sun shone straight down the field into my eyes, so I wore a cap. Aarhus played a ball over the top and as I ran out to meet it, the wind whipped the cap off my head. I reached for it instinctively. That split second was enough to make me mistime everything. The ball went past me, past the leg I flicked out in one last desperate attempt to knock it away, and this little shit of a striker ran round me and just rolled it into our goal. Seriously embarrassing. The next set of headlines was 'WHO THE **** IS THIS GUY?' That little shit of a striker is one of my best friends today: Tommy Christensen, who played for Leicester and Portsmouth and ended up as my team-mate at Brøndby.

After that mishap I calmed down and played better and better. I became a star of the team. However, at the end of our second season we were relegated. We were all part-timers and my job in the real world, at that point, involved selling adverts for a local newspaper. One of my customers owned a small supermarket. He called and asked me to come and meet him, and when I arrived, another guy was there – a member of the Brøndby board. This guy said, 'We want you, can we do something?'

The trouble was that just one week previously, I had signed a piece of paper promising I would stay with Hvidovre. I could have forced the issue and ignored it, because in my actual contract there was a clause saying I could leave if we were ever relegated. Brøndby was the biggest opportunity going – Denmark's only fully professional team and runners-up in the league that year. I went to see John Steen Olsen, who was

Hvidovre's chairman then. I said to him that this was a big, big opportunity and I really wanted to take it. He said he would not stop me but that he was very disappointed: I had put a promise in writing and Hvidovre needed me in order to try and get immediate repromotion. I thought about things and turned Brøndby down. I had to keep my word. I would like to think I am a person who always does.

Maybe it was another of the several decisions I have taken in my life that were a little unusual, but the independent spirit has served me well. I think back to how I was at fifteen, when I started with Gladsaxe-Hero and was in my first year at the National Innovative Centre for Education. To get there for lessons, I had to be on a bus at 6.56 a.m. in order to catch a train, ride three stops and jump on another bus. An hour's journey. It was an hour's journey back. And Gladsaxe-Hero was an hour in another direction.

I trained three nights a week and every time faced a choice – do I go home after school to eat or go straight to training? There was a cafeteria at the club, but my parents did not have enough to give me money for snacks, and if I was really hungry the only way of eating was to go back home. There would barely be time to run through the door, stuff something in my face and head straight back out again. I had to work things out in advance, each morning asking myself, 'Am I coming home today or going straight from school to training?' and if the latter, then take my kit.

All the decisions and planning at that young age – the routine continued until I left school at seventeen – fostered further independence and are a reason, maybe, that I am comfortable when I have to think on my feet in the face of adversity. I was always having to scheme and think. The buses home from Gladsaxe ran every half an hour and if I missed one, it would be another half an hour before I finally got home to eat and sleep. I became a living encyclopaedia of travel timetables. I knew the departure times for trains and buses from Ballerup, Gladsaxe, Jyllingevej and Islev. I could work out alternative journeys on the spot if I missed a connection and I got to know bus drivers by name. There was one connection where, if I could persuade the driver to speed up for the final section, I could jump off at the stop and sprint to another one to get my next bus, saving me half an hour. Every second time I was successful; on the other occasions I had to walk fifteen minutes to another stop.

I was cared for by my family but left to work things out for myself. By my mid-teens I was living a completely independent life from my parents and sisters: making my own decisions, on football-training days leaving the house before seven in the morning and returning at eleven at night, at weekends very often sleeping at friends' places. Again, this might seem jarring by modern standards, but that is how life was for a lot of young people of my generation – no mobile phones, certainly no helicopter parenting, a lot of independence and taking of responsibility. Those last traits are powerful resources in a professional football career and one of the challenges in the game today is developing them in young players who have grown up in a different society.

I was glad I kept my word to Hvidovre. We won promotion straight away and I was Player of the Year. I can't help feeling I missed the 1986 World Cup because of my decision – I was on the national team's radar by then but was not going to get called up playing in the Danish second division. I left Hvidovre on good terms, though, and that is important to me. In March 1986, as my final campaign there was starting, I signed a pre-contract to join Brøndby for the following season and, on 5 November 1986, Kasper was born.

On the same day, Brøndby knocked out Dynamo Berlin to reach the last eight of the European Cup: now I knew my first game for them would be a quarter-final, in the greatest of club competitions, in March.

On 1 January 1987, I joined Brøndby formally: a dad, and professional footballer at last, at twenty-three.

11
BRØNDBY

When I did my famous Reebok advert, posing as a Danish pig farmer, some members of the public got confused. They thought that as well as being a footballer, I actually did farm pigs. I wish I had kept the letters. I got one from a real farmer saying he had seen me on TV and was so happy to note how well I was treating my animals, that they looked in great condition, congratulations. Wonderful!

But I did do a number of 'proper' jobs after leaving school. My mother wanted me to keep studying but I was never going to do that, and my first paid work was in a fabric factory, working on a jigger machine – with all kinds of nasty chemicals and no protection. The hours were 7 a.m. to 3 p.m. one week and 3 p.m. to 11 p.m. the next. I lasted four months before leaving to be a dish-washer in Nimb, the restaurant where my father played piano in Tivoli Gardens. After that, I worked at a supermarket, collecting bottles for recycling, and my aim was to start with the store in that lowly role and work my way into an apprenticeship. It was exceptionally boring, though, and I left to become a cleaner at an old people's home. I quite enjoyed that, staying for nine months. I started at 7 a.m. and finished at noon every day and I hardly cleaned anything. I spent most of my time talking to the residents.

Next came a stint as a shopkeeper, with the World Wildlife Fund, at their store in central Copenhagen. They needed someone to package up the stuff customers bought by mail order – stickers, teddy bears, pandas, all kinds of junk – and the woman who ran the shop decided to leave, so the WWF entrusted it to me. That was stimulating. I had to find new lines to sell and arrange my store in the most appealing way. It was like running a little business. I stayed for eighteen months, spanning my last season with Gladsaxe-Hero and my first with Hvidovre.

The problem with that job was getting to training on time. I had to shut up shop and race from downtown Copenhagen to Hvidovre in the south-east of the city and it was a struggle. I asked my father-in-law for help. I said I would do any job, I didn't care what, as long as the hours fitted with my football. Svend Aage had a carpet-fitting business and gave me an apprenticeship. It was the toughest work I have done in my life. I could be on my knees gluing and stapling for six hours, then play in the Danish first division in the evening.

We had two big clients, one the HQ of Denmark's military, the other a remand prison in Copenhagen. I spent four months working in the jail and hated every second. It was a truly horrible place. There was a stench of old food and bad hygiene – I always said it was the smell of despair. It made me sick to my stomach.

We were there to lay new linoleum on the stairs between floors. I was vulnerable because I was issued with keys to the doors leading in and out of the building and my tools included knives, hammers, nails, tacks: all the goodies a desperate prisoner might want. I felt threatened every time I was in there.

They were locked in cells for most of the time, but there was always a traffic of prisoners coming and going. They had one hour of exercise per day, when we had to clear the area, accounting for every last tack and blade. The Blekinge Street Gang, a group of communist activists who robbed banks and post offices and sent the money to the Popular Front for the Liberation of Palestine, were at the height of their notoriety in Denmark and a famous member, Carsten Nielsen, who had been blinded in a car accident while acting as a getaway driver, was in the prison. That was sobering: seeing a criminal you had read about in the papers, a few yards away.

Both physically and psychologically I found that job tough. On days Hvidovre were not playing, my shifts could last ten hours, and when I was playing, though I would knock off early, I would get home from my game full of adrenaline and hardly sleep. Then get up first thing in the morning to lay flooring again.

The only career I had ever really fancied, footballer apart, was in graphic design. My mum's father and stepmother were incredible amateur artists and bought me books on how to draw and paint. Art was not offered as a subject in my schools until SPF, where I chose music and theatre instead, but it always fascinated me. It is a hobby of Laura's and mine to go and see art. We love galleries. At seventeen, I applied for several graphic-design courses, even trying a college in a town a long journey from home, but found them oversubscribed and I didn't get in.

I explored a little of my artistic side in my final job before becoming a fully professional player. The carpet-fitting became just too hard, so I went to Hvidovre's chairman at the time, John

Steen Olsen's predecessor, Niels Erik Madsen, who owned the local newspaper, and asked if he had anything going. He did, but the role was not well paid. No problem, I told him. I just wanted out of the prisons and off my knees. The newspaper sold advertising. There were two main salespeople and a junior – me – who looked after the smaller clients. To gain new customers, you went round local shops trying to sell them ads. If someone bought one, you would sketch it out yourself before handing it to the graphics team to put together professionally. I loved that.

Then there was national service. I was at Gladsaxe-Hero when I was called up and our chairman negotiated for me to avoid going into civil defence – an eight-month posting – and join a scheme that involved one block of four weeks' service and another of two weeks' work, fulfilled at a future date. Local Civil Defence, it was called. By the time of my start date, I had just joined Hvidovre; it was February and we were due in Portugal for a pre-season camp. I went to the top officer, knocked on his door and explained I needed a week off to go to the camp. Fortunately he was a football fan and knew who I was. We brokered a deal where I could come back and complete that week's service over two weekends down the line.

They made me a fireman. My job was to operate the pump. Pumps are pretty simple. They suck or blow and that's just about it. One day we emptied a flooded farmer's field, which involved me turning up in the morning, hitting the 'suck' switch and sitting there all day. There was a bit of training – how to clean up and stabilise buildings struck by bombs, how to firefight in those circumstances. I found that interesting. Then we received orders for where to report if Denmark ever went to war, and that was the end of it.

Those jobs developed my work ethic. They taught me about early starts and late nights and the real graft people do in the real world. They gave me perspective on exactly how good a life being a footballer is, and I was able to use that on those days in a career when you just do not fancy training or you are struggling for motivation. Most Scandinavian players of my generation and before it were similar, which was perhaps why the region produced so many footballers with strong mentalities, whereas now Scandinavia is just like anywhere else. Boys with football talent go straight from school into the full-time professional game and immediately become kings of their own small kingdom, wealthy before their time and adoptive of a certain lifestyle. Not all of them handle that well. But our generation learned about life. We grew a broader perspective. I would not have changed it.

That said, arriving at Brøndby in early 1987, a pro at last, was some feeling. My wages were around 20,000 kroner (£2,400) per month. My combined pay at the newspaper and Hvidovre had been more, but this was a big step towards the dream. My debut was quite a proposition. Brøndby were in the European Cup quarter-finals, drawn against Porto, with the first leg away from home in the Estádio das Antas. A 40,000 crowd. I had never played in front of more than 6,000 before. I had never played in Europe either and Porto had some fabulous players: Paulo Futre, Walter Casagrande, João Pinto, Fernando Gomes, Rabah Madjer.

For me, the test was more than just the step up in quality. It was wrestling with something that had plagued me since starting in senior football five years earlier – nerves. This may surprise people, given the persona I would later adopt on the field, but as a younger footballer I was wracked, and very nearly wrecked, by doubt. Most of Hvidovre's games kicked off at 7 p.m. on Sunday and for me that meant, from leaving work on Friday afternoon, an entire weekend of worry about the match. The fears seemed to go away after kick-off, but the build-up to games was almost unbearable sometimes.

The first leg in Porto was on 4 March, Brøndby's first game after the winter break, and the hype around it in Denmark was huge. The club chartered a flight, with a big gang of journalists on board with the team, and it was suddenly redirected to Lisbon. Knowing what I know now about how Portuguese football works, I wonder if this was a coincidence. Anyway, we had to scramble to get up to Porto by bus, a three-hour drive, reaching our hotel late. Not ideal preparation. The journey to the stadium on the day of the game was also chaotic. The roads were crazy, we had a police escort and our coach thundered down the middle of the highway, between lanes of traffic, with the police forcing cars out of the way.

I had never seen anything like it, never had a police escort, never played a big game abroad before. I had an aisle seat with a clear view through the front windscreen. As we hurtled down the middle of the road I was terrified of an accident, and yet a weird inner voice was saying, *Crash, crash, go on . . . crash*, because it occurred to me that if we did, I wouldn't have to play this game and I could relax. But we did not crash and by the time I was changed, gloved up and ready to warm up, I was sweating. There was a tunnel from the dressing room to the pitch and I took a few steps into it before having to stop and suck in deep breaths. As I was doing this, I suddenly had that odd feeling of being able to look at yourself, for a moment, from the outside – and what I saw was this big, supposedly dominant goalkeeper, shaking like a frightened child.

I grabbed hold of myself and gave myself a talking to: *Pete. This is what you've always wanted. Big game, people in the seats, people watching on TV, all the papers talking about the game – and you on the pitch. So what are you nervous of? You should be enjoying this.*

Something clicked. I continued through the tunnel, up the steps and onto the pitch. I looked at the crowd. I thought, *Yeah.*

I played well. We lost 1–0 to a second-half goal by Madjer and ran Porto close in the second leg, a 1–1 draw in Copenhagen. Per Steffensen put us 1–0 up and Juary, their Brazilian striker, did not equalise until sixteen minutes from the end. Porto went on to win the competition and the tie demonstrated Brøndby's growing potential. We were a team of upcoming players: me, Lars Olsen, John Jensen, Kim Vilfort, Kent Nielsen, Brian Laudrup – all future Euro 92 winners. The club had been fully professional for only a year when I arrived and it shared a gym with the Danish Institute of Sport. We worked out beside wrestlers and badminton players. Our training runs were in a forest, which you reached through a tunnel under a motorway, so there was still much growing to do – but what we did have was Per Bjerregaard.

He was an incredible communicator and manipulator. He could persuade us to believe anything, convincing us that Brøndby was definitely on the right path whenever there was a bump on the road. Because he was club doctor as well as chairman, he even sat on the bench. We needed him. Breaking new ground is seldom done by committee. Leaders force you ahead. Nowadays, I have two ways of thinking about Bjerregaard. I think about the guy who screwed me on a couple of occasions. But I also think of him as one of the most important people in the history of Danish football. A visionary and sometimes a bastard. A love–hate figure.

We talk to this day and when we meet, there is no animosity on my part. All gone. This guy is incredible. He had terminal leukaemia and survived. Who does that?

The uniqueness of his character was evident the moment I signed. I found a mistake in my contract. 'Oh, let me redo it,' Bjerregaard said, and, by hand, he wrote out three contracts from start to finish: one for me, one for the club, one to be lodged with the Danish Federation. All in the neatest and most beautiful handwriting. So, he was in ultimate charge and Ebbe Skovdahl was the coach – and the late Ebbe was a lovely man, mild of nature but with a strong personality underneath. He was ahead of his time, playing an intense pressing game with specific triggers to lure the opposition into traps. Everyone is impressed with Pep Guardiola's 'six seconds' rule – where his players have to regain possession in that time or drop back – but we were doing that in 1987. We won the championship with five games to spare that year with a starting line-up so strong that Brian Laudrup, who was only eighteen, spent most of the campaign coming off the bench.

There was Claus Nielsen, an incredible striker who was never quite the same after moving abroad, and Bjarne Jensen, whose drive made up for what he lacked in finesse. Henrik Jensen was a very good forward, who I'd already played with at Hvidovre, and Steffensen had personality – he became an agent and was always going to go into that kind of work. John Jensen was the Dwight Yorke of the operation, the effervescent character who made the dressing room tick. He was born-and-bred Brøndby. His mum, dad and sister were in the training complex every day – the whole family were in with the bricks of the club. Then there was Lars Olsen, my room-mate and our leader; the heart of our defence.

For me, the difference was playing for a team that was winning. That changes you as a goalkeeper. You have to find ways to improve your concentration, so that you are always engaged with the game, even when play is at the other end. With us pushing forward a lot, I also learned how to come out of my box and develop sweeper-keeper skills. In a dominant team, I was able to come for most crosses, improving those techniques too. Our desire to attack required me to distribute quickly and positively – allowing me to dust off those old handball moves.

Ebbe left for Benfica before we secured the title and Birger Peitersen guided us home, but Ebbe returned for the 1988 campaign, when we won the league easily again. But 1989 was not so good; we were second to Odense and it was totally ridiculous to concede the championship to them. We also went out of the European Cup to Club Brugge in the first round. At New Year 1990, a new manager arrived, Morten Olsen. He was as intense as Ebbe was laid-back.

On Morten's first day we were told to report to the clubhouse at the training ground. The media was there, as was a big tray of champagne glasses. *What?* I knew Morten. I had spent three years playing with him for the national team and knew what kind of character he was: serious, *very serious*. To get a laugh out of him you had to tell the world's funniest joke. Yet now the most serious guy I had met in my life was serving champagne to the media: what was going on?

Bjerregaard introduced him and Morten took over. He said he was proud to be Brøndby manager and was looking forward to the challenge. The aim, he said, was to drink more champagne. 'Because,' he said, 'when you win trophies, you drink champagne . . .' Then he put a glass to his lips. 'Mmm, this tastes so nice.' He handed the glasses round. 'Let's drink,' he said. 'Because this is the last time we'll be having champagne until we win something.'

At the end of this pantomime, he sent us into the forest for a run. This was midwinter. On our normal route, there was a point where we turned right, went over a little hill and through the tunnel back to the clubhouse. 'No,' barked Morten when we got there. 'Today we go left.' We went left, all the way down to the beach and back again, which was crazy, crazy long. Some players had never run so far in their lives and came back with injuries.

It was an accurate taste of what Morten was going to be like. He had a knee injury and, having played in Germany, wanted to prevent us sustaining knee injuries by using German techniques. Every day after training we sat up against a wall, our posture 90 degrees, and raised our legs, holding the pose – for five sets, first of twenty seconds each and building up to one minute. Training started with a yoga exercise that we repeated ten times. In pre-season, one group ran in the woods for thirty minutes while another did circuits, then swapped, then swapped again. That was our morning session: ninety minutes of gym, ninety minutes of running. The afternoons involved more running and finally some ball work.

The weak players fell apart, but the strong ones became among the fittest footballers in Europe and we destroyed domestic opposition, winning the 1990 title and then again in 1991. Positionally, Morten did something interesting. He created pairs on the pitch. Carsten Jensen and Erik Rasmussen, two new midfielders, became a pair: the idea was each pair would move as a unit, with tactical responsibilities they shared. He played Kim Vilfort deeper, with great success, and strengthened the defence with Uche Okechukwu, an incredible player, the future captain of Nigeria.

Uche arrived at the club in an unusual way. With Brian Laudrup having left for Germany, Brøndby were looking for an attacker and through an agent heard of a Nigerian winger, Friday Elahor. But Friday refused to come on trial unless he could bring his friend. They arrived and in the trial Friday was okay but nothing special. The club sent him back. It was only a few days later that something popped into the coaching staff's heads: 'Forget Friday . . . what about his mate? How good was *he*!' They called the mate – and he wouldn't sign unless Friday signed too.

That was Uche. He was miles, miles ahead of everyone else at centre half in Denmark. He was a bit like Jaap Stam and good enough – easily – to have played for Manchester United. The opposition bounced off him and he brought another level to our team. Laughs too: we northern people are so stiff, whereas Africans can be so wonderfully easy-going. It came to club vehicles. 'Do you have a licence?' 'Oh yeah,' said Uche and Friday. 'Good, you can have a car.' Turned out they had never driven one. Sometimes, they cooked directly on the stove, not bothering with pots and pans. I have images of winter training and Uche and Friday just lying in the heaps of snow by the side of the pitch, laughing.

In the first round of the 1990–91 UEFA Cup, we thrashed Eintracht Frankfurt 5–0 in Copenhagen. Uche scored and it was funny watching him swat big, fit German players aside as he bullied his way through to put us ahead. The second leg was different. Eintracht had underestimated us in Copenhagen but were ready now and they went 3–0 up after half an hour, but we scored and after that were okay.

We were too good for Ferencváros in the next round and in the last eight travelled to Bayer Leverkusen, 3–0 up from the first leg. The team talk was a Morten special. Our pay was modest and our bonus scheme was not great either, and Morten started off with a few remarks about standards and playing for each other before suddenly changing gear and bringing up the subject of cash.

'We play for pride . . . but also our livelihood,' he said.

'IT IS ALSO ABOUT MAKING MONEY!'

His voice was booming now, and when he flipped over his flip chart there were twenty 1000 kroner bills pinned to it, arranged in two fans.

'THAT!' yelled Morten. 'THAT IS WHAT YOU WILL MAKE IF YOU GET THROUGH TONIGHT.'

A 20,000 kroner bonus? Nice: 20,000 kroner was our monthly wage.

Bjerregaard was there, watching, the colour draining from his face. He pulled Morten aside, asking why he had not cleared these huge, unscheduled bonuses with the board. Morten said he didn't give two flying pfennigs about that. 'If the club won't pay it, I'll pay it from my own pocket,' he said. We thought, *Yeah*.

Super-motivated, we went out and secured a 0–0 draw. I had a great game, coming for crosses, dominating my box. I was playing with more and more maturity and as I mentioned earlier – I was Player of the Year in Denmark that season.

After the break between domestic seasons we had quite a schedule. The Danish top flight was being revamped as the Superliga and its entire programme would be played in a short-ened period, to sync up with the international calendar. Meanwhile our first game was a UEFA Cup quarter-final first leg at home to Torpedo Moscow. Morten went into overdrive, working us super-hard in a crazy pre-season in which we trav-elled around Europe to find grass facilities to train on. Our stadium had no undersoil heating and the groundsman impro-vised a way to defrost the pitch, but it worked only to a certain point. The club put up temporary stands and 16,600 came to see us play Torpedo – we scraped a 1–0 win through a Jens Madsen goal. Then we went to Moscow. My God. It was minus five million degrees. They scored with four minutes left, to take the tie to extra time, which ended with us in a penalty shoot-out. In its last two kicks I saved from Gennadi Grishin and then Kim Christofte converted: we were through, the first Danes to reach a European semi-final.

After our long flight home to Copenhagen, Kim and I went out. We were heroes. We stayed up drinking all night and went for breakfast. Across from the café, there was a newsagent which had morning papers. Kim was on the front of one tabloid and I was on the front of the other. We went in and bought every copy we could. Oh, and two beers. We stood in the street, clinking bottles, giggling and looking at ourselves in the newspapers. This was 9 a.m. People hung out of office windows clapping us.

This was the point when the profile of footballers was really beginning to change. In Denmark, Brøndby were becoming bigger and bigger. Soon I would be in England, where the fame level for players was different again, but we were still a generation who were not, primarily, in the game for stardom or money. We were there to win. And now we were in the last four in Europe, drawn against Roma, a great team featuring Rudi Völler, Aldair, Thomas Berthold and Giuseppe Giannini.

We drew the first leg 0–0 in Copenhagen and in Rome went behind but equalised – an own goal – after an hour. With three minutes remaining, we were going through, when there was a scramble in our box. A shot flew up off the feet of one of our players, who was trying to block, and struck my chest. It dropped to Völler, who beat me – only just.

In fairness, Roma were the better team, but we had come so close to the final. So much was down to how Morten had driven us. We were tactically improved and his ways left us super-fit. I put on eight kilos of body mass in eighteen months, all of it muscle, thanks to the gym work.

Having been focused on Europe, we turned our attention back to the league to close out another title, my fourth in five seasons, clinching it in our final game against Lyngby, our main rivals. It was a memorable match. Lyngby, like us, did not have four proper stands and their stadium was packed, thanks to temporary seating. Early in the game, their Nigerian midfielder, Emeka Ezeugo, jumped with me for a ball and planted his right knee in my hip. I couldn't move properly after that. Bent Christensen put us ahead, but with seven minutes left, Per Pedersen scored for them – with a long-range shot which I was too injured to get across to. I played out the final minutes a bag of nerves. This was my last match for Brøndby and a Lyngby win would have given them the title. I didn't want my final act for the club to be one that cost us a championship.

That grounding with Brøndby set me up for everything which came after. It made me a player who was fitter, more professional and in the habit of winning. Brøndby also helped forge my idea of what a football club should be, for it was a family place, where wives and kids were as bonded with each other as the players; a place of camaraderie, common purpose and soul. Bjerregaard was the father of it all.

But some parents find it hard to let their offspring grow up and prosper without them, and my second power struggle with Bjerregaard was a result of his compulsion to control. Towards the end of my time at Sporting Lisbon, in 2001, I thought I had found what my next career move would be. I was invited to return to Brøndby as player-manager. The proposition really excited me.

Not long after my departure from the club in 1991, Bjerregaard had made a disastrous decision. He correctly understood that football was changing and, to be a leading club, you needed to generate income outside of the game. His solution was to buy the Danish bank Interbank, which would have been far from a bad idea had he enough funds to complete the deal. Money for the purchase was supposed to come from qualifying for the European Cup group stage but Brøndby went out in the final qualifying round to Dynamo Kyiv.

Before the second leg, Per had come into the dressing room and told the players, 'This is the most important game you'll ever play,' only adding to the pressure. Brøndby faced bankruptcy and when another insurance company stepped in as saviour it was on condition that Bjerregaard stepped down as chairman.

In 1997, Ole Borch took over the role and it was Ole who called me in 2001. He was in Lisbon and asked if I fancied meeting up for a chat. Ole had a bold idea. 'Pete, I want you back at the club; you can be player-manager,' he said. I spoke to my adviser, Ole Frederiksen, and we agreed this was a great opportunity – exactly what I wanted as a challenge and perfect in terms of personal meaning: Brøndby are the only club who share space in my heart with Manchester United. We started negotiations and I came up with a very specific plan for how I wanted Brøndby to develop on the football side of things. Borch believed in me and would protect me.

I travelled to Denmark, in secret. We had a contract agreed and I was to meet Ole to sign the paperwork and finalise details. We assembled at Frederiksen's offices, in a back street of Copenhagen. The meeting had to take place outside normal business hours so that nobody would spot us and make a connection.

In the room were me, Ole Frederiksen, Ole Borch – and Bjerregaard. The way Brøndby was structured, its stock was divided into 'A' and 'B' shares. The 'A' shares were controlled by a mother company, of which Bjerregaard was chairman, so he still pulled Brøndby's strings from afar. One of the details in my plan was that Bjerregaard should step down as club doctor and no longer be involved in matches from the bench. This was a new, more professionalised, era in the game and it was time to move on from all of that.

This stipulation was written down in the contract I had thrashed out with Ole Borch and initially the meeting with him and Bjerregaard seemed to go well. Everything appeared to be agreed. By now it was evening. I was about to sign. Then Bjerregaard said to Borch, 'I need to speak to you.' Borch suggested they step outside, but Bjerregaard said he would prefer to go to Borch's offices, which were a ten-minute walk away. They left. Ole Frederiksen and I twiddled our thumbs. Finally, Borch called.

'We can't do this,' he said.

'Why?'

'Per won't support it.'

'What? We had everything agreed.'

'He thinks you're too inexperienced.'

'You're kidding me. We've been through all that.'

'Sorry,' Borch insisted. 'He just won't do it.'

What had changed? Power. I think Bjerregaard suddenly saw the control he had exerted over Brøndby slipping away, potentially. So, the same guy who in 1991 cheated me out of what would have been another year at Manchester United blocked the best offer I have ever received to go into management. And we would cross yet again, in the years to come. I have no hard feelings towards Per Bjerregaard – but enough water has flowed under our bridge to fill the North Sea.

12
EURO 92

I t all began at Brøndby. At the start of summer, in 1992, Denmark
had a friendly booked against CIS for 3 June. The players who
were not involved in the Superliga – which was still ongoing –
were training on Brøndby's pitches with Richard Moller Nielsen,
Denmark's manager. The vibe was: let's get this game out of the
way and go on our holidays.

We were having lunch in the Brøndby cafeteria when Richard
took a phone call. He came off it and just said, 'We're playing,' in
his matter-of-fact way. I can't paint you a picture with any more
drama than that. There was no big announcement, no celebrations and no great sense of shock – even if we were a bit surprised.
For weeks, there had been rumours that the international
community might exclude Yugoslavia from sporting competitions and, if so, we would be given their spot at the European
Championships.

We weren't going on holiday after all. Denmark were going
to Euro 92. If, in the end, it was not unexpected, I don't think
any of us truly believed it would happen until it did. Except
Richard, perhaps. Richard was never a man to leave himself
unprepared. In our training at Brøndby he had had us doing
double sessions and, though he had not mentioned the Euros,
I think he had them in mind. He wanted to be ready, just in
case.

None of us were jumping up and down when he said, 'We're playing,' because from a sporting point of view, it did not sit right with us that we were taking Yugoslavia's place. The Yugoslav team had beaten us fair and square in our qualification group and the war in the Balkans – the reason they were being sent home from Sweden before the tournament – had nothing to do with them. We felt sorry, maybe even guilty, towards their players.

I was also still deflated from how Manchester United's 1991–92 season had ended. All I wanted to do was get away from football and get some new energy into my system. My immediate reaction to Richard's words was: *I can't find the enthusiasm for this.* I was really low. I didn't have a holiday booked, but we had just spent our first year away from Denmark as a family and were looking forward to a relaxed summer in Copenhagen, enjoying home. The idea that our squad 'came off the beach' in '92 is a myth because nobody was away at the point our participation at the Euros was announced – but certain players did ask Richard not to pick them because they had vacations booked. It is well known that Bjørn Kristensen was one and he never started for the national team again. But Bjørn should not be remembered negatively for his decision. His wife was about to give birth and the call he made simply reflected where a lot of us were – mentally – at the time.

We went into camp the next day, moving into the Hotel Marina in Vedbæk. Before then we had been staying in our homes. Even after camp began, there was a haphazard nature to things – for example, our domestic-based players did not join up until after the last round of the Superliga was played on 8

June. And so, just three days before our opening Euro 92 match versus England in Malmö, I sat with others from the squad in the stands at the Gentofte stadium watching Lyngby beat B1903 to become champions.

The CIS friendly, a 1–1 draw, was a non-event. Our Euro 92 opener against England was a poor game too. They were terrible. Having gone in thinking a draw would be a good result, we came off the pitch disappointed not to have won. We were much more ready to play at tournament level than we had imagined, and the feeling was we had missed a big opportunity. In the dressing room afterwards, there was a change in the group that was brilliant to experience. Everyone sat talking things over, agreeing we should have taken two points and had nothing to fear. It was an awakening – us waking up to the idea that we could actually do something at the finals.

We played the game in the Under-21 team's kit – that is how last-minute things were. Our tournament strips were not ready and I had to wear a jersey that was a little too small and shorts with padding. I hated that. Padding on your elbows and shorts? Can you imagine playing in English conditions wearing that? You would dive once in a pool of water and the pads would be heavy with moisture for the rest of the game. Padding? Your diving technique should be good enough not to need such protection.

After the England match, our ambitions multiplied. Eleven of our twenty-man squad had played for Brøndby at some point and the Brøndby culture was one of pushing beyond your limits. We also had players from Bayern Munich, Borussia Dortmund, Monaco, Cologne, Schalke and Manchester United – players who in their club lives competed for trophies, expected success. So, we were far from a happy bunch of tourists leaping out of our deckchairs. And if we were disappointed after England then, oh my God, we were furious after Sweden.

We lost 1–0 to our arch-rivals in Stockholm, despite playing them off the pitch. We created so many chances. They had good players like Roland Nilsson, Jonas Thern, Tomas Brolin, Martin Dahlin – but we were better. We just could not find that edge in front of goal. On Danish TV, the commentator, Jørn Mader, uttered a line that became infamous: 'And that is the end of the adventure, Denmark are out of the Euros!' The dressing-room mood was very dark. A number of us asked the stewards to lead us to a back exit so we could leave the Råsunda stadium and go straight to the hotel, without speaking to the media.

But when the emotion faded we looked at things calmly. Were we in the tournament or out? In. Our point against England meant we would progress if we beat France in our final game. They were the Euro 92 favourites, with incredible talent like Jean-Pierre Papin, Manuel Amoros, Laurent Blanc, Didier Deschamps – and Eric – but we were getting better with every game. That we were having goalscoring issues was normal, when we thought about it, because when you are undercooked, those final few inches of sharpness that you need for finishing will always be among the last elements you find. Between Sweden and meeting the French in Malmö, Richard had us doing a lot of finishing practice.

Training was very happy. We had taken over Yugoslavia's hotel bookings for the tournament and our base was a spa in Ystad. It was right on the sea, built round a courtyard with a swimming pool, a nice place but not a fancy one. The rooms were basic and I shared with Lars Olsen, the two of us in a small room with single beds that were too cramped for a proper night's sleep. The hotel remained open to the public and we mingled with holidaymakers, eating from the hotel buffet in the same dining room as everyone else. The modern philosophy is always to shut players away, but football carried a different meaning then. Fellow guests left us alone; there was nobody bothering you for an autograph as you went up for eggs at the breakfast buffet. No mobile phones, no selfies in those days: that makes a massive difference.

You could have dumped us in a two-star motel and we would have found ways to enjoy ourselves. We were a squad that liked being together. Many of us had come up at the same time, through the Under-21s and Olympic side, for which Richard was coach. International get-togethers were something you looked forward to, and I noticed, in the Manchester United dressing room, that made me a rarity. There was not a lot of looking forward to international weeks among my fellow United players.

The focal point in any camp is the treatment room. Players gravitate there. All our entertainment, the TV, videos, books and games, were integrated with the treatment area and if you wanted company, that was where you could always find it. The place was buzzing in Ystad.

Richard did not want us cooped up, going mad. He took us to play mini-golf and, on one occasion, to McDonald's. Every day, on our way to training, we drove past the restaurant and each time we passed it – for a laugh – all the players shouted, 'Let's.

Go. To. McDonald's!' One day, Richard told the driver to take the turn-off – he had secretly organised for us to go in for burgers and fries. McDonald's may not be the top recommendation of sports nutritionists, but a little treat like that does wonders for your mental state and makes you love your coach.

Copenhagen is just over the water from Malmö and an hour from Ystad. We knew the vibe back home was special too. It was a summer of incredible weather and for once little Denmark was the centre of international attention. As well as our Cinderella story at the Euros, the Queen and Prince were celebrating their twenty-fifth anniversary and there was a referendum, in which Danes voted against accepting the Maastricht treaty and closer ties with Europe. When we won Euro 92 this led to one of the quips of all time from our foreign minister, Uffe Ellemann-Jensen, who observed, 'If you cannot join them, beat them.'

Apparently, against England, I made a fine save from Tony Daley – but I have no memory of it. I tell you what I do remember from that game: John 'Faxe' Jensen. He had four shots. Two went to Copenhagen, another ended up in Stockholm and another hit the post. Afterwards, we had a lot of fun with him. 'Bloody hell, the chances we made . . . and they all fell to JJ! He'll never score. His shooting, hahaha.' But John has such a great, positive character, he is someone who will always keep trying. He just laughed along. I love him. In Denmark's dressing room he was one of two great rays of sunshine. And sources of mischief. The other was Flemming Povlsen, and that pair were always on the lookout for something that would put a smile on people's faces. They were a dangerous double act.

A prime target for Faxe and Flemming's teasing was our team doctor, Mogens Kreutzfeldt. One day at training Flemming pretended to tackle Faxe hard. Faxe rolled around, screaming. He had hidden a sachet of tomato ketchup in his sock and as Mogens raced onto the pitch, Faxe squirted the ketchup on his head. Poor Mogens saw all this red stuff dripping and Faxe almost in tears with the pain. 'Oh my God. BLOOOD,' Mogens was saying. 'Call an ambulance!' Only when he got his fingers in there did he realise it wasn't blood at all and we all burst into hysterics.

The France decider would be my fiftieth game for Denmark and further motivation came when we detected a whiff of arrogance about our opponents in the run-up to the game. As we were lining up to go on the pitch, one of their players – a teammate of his at Monaco – said to John Sivebæk, 'Hey, go easy on us, we have to play Holland next.'

'These *******,' said Johnny, 'they think they've already won,' and it pumped us up. Richard had made little adjustments to our line-up which helped the fluency of our attacks. We scored early through Henrik Larsen, and Henrik Andersen was exceptional, keeping Eric Cantona quiet and linking with Larsen when we went forward. Denmark had always struggled with finding good left-footed players and our left side always felt weaker than our right, but Larsen and Andersen, two underrated footballers, were tremendous that summer. France found us hard to break down and hard to stop when we countered.

They were rated the best side in the world, but it was not a game where I had to be anything special. Without ever bombarding my goal, they eventually equalised through Jean-Pierre

Papin. What a player he was. Then the pressure came, but Richard put on Lars Elstrup, a wild card in many senses. We broke at speed, Flemming Povlsen got the ball out wide and played an inch-perfect cross to Lars, who was making the inch-perfect run. Arriving at exactly the right moment in front of goal, Lars slotted home, to send us to the semis. It was the only thing he did in the tournament, but how important it was.

Lars was an incredible finisher, with a remarkable nose for where to be to take chances. I'm not going to go into his issues as a human being, only to say that you never quite knew psychologically where he was, which made him very difficult for a coach to use from the start, but he was a great X-factor to introduce at the right moment. Richard deserved immense credit for that substitution. To those who suggest Denmark were 'lucky' in '92, I say watch the France game. You play the pre-tournament favourites, with great players, managed by a legend in Michel Platini, in a winner-takes-all scenario and you match them man-for-man before taking the spoils thanks to a great goal and a brilliant tweak from our coach.

Winning felt like confirmation of the growing sense within us: that we might have stumbled accidentally into these finals, but we certainly were not out of place there. We were a good side and now we were in the last four. After frustration in our first two games there was this sudden feeling of release – we left Malmö stadium as if on wings.

From the moment Elstrup opened his body to side-foot past Bruno Martini, the memories hardly seem real. Everything that happened in Gothenburg, where we were based for the last two games, feels like something from a movie. Our hotel was beautiful, perched on a marina with a restaurant by the water's edge. We had individual rooms looking out on the bay, and the treatment room was one of the nicest I've seen, an ample space with a big screen on which Eurosport played coverage of the tournament on a loop. You gazed out at the marina, watching people go by in the hot sunshine, knowing you were doing your country proud, and felt life could barely get any better.

Holland were ... decent, you might say. Just Marco van Basten, Ruud Gullit, Frank Rijkaard, Ronald Koeman, Dennis Bergkamp, Frank de Boer and a few others to worry about. Reigning champions too. But we had Brian Laudrup, who after five minutes got to the Dutch byeline and crossed for Henrik Larsen to head in. Bergkamp equalised from a shot which I only saw late, but then from a header by Brian, Koeman cleared straight to Larsen, who converted again. Henrik was amazing that summer.

The Dutch had too much talent and experience for us to contain them, like we had France. They put us under the cosh. With twenty minutes left, Van Basten challenged Henrik Andersen and they clashed, knee against knee. Henrik screamed, the sound was terrible, ringing out over the pitch. Andersen's kneecap had split in two – a freakish, horrific injury to the guy who had been our best player in the finals to that point.

You don't just shrug it off when something terrible like that happens to one of your team-mates. The injury knocked our focus and we were on the back foot when, with four minutes left, a corner kick took a couple of ricochets in my box and Rijkaard equalised. He slotted his shot underneath me as I leant back, putting the ball in the only place where he could score.

The mentality of extra time is strange. You want to finish the job because you don't want the lottery of penalties, and yet that lottery does promise you a chance, so you kind of hold back. It is football played in psychological no man's land. I had a save from Brian Roy, but there was little real action in those added thirty minutes and the moment the final whistle blew, I made my picks: (1) left, (2) left, (3) right, (4) left, (5) left.

That was which way I would be diving for their penalties.

With shoot-outs, I always decided it like that.

Think about a shoot-out from the goalkeeper's point of view. You don't put the ball on the spot. You don't pick the angle of the run-up. You don't choose which foot to kick with. You don't decide the timing. You don't control how hard the ball will be struck, at what height, with what kind of shot or to where in the goal the ball will be directed.

You are literally out of control, and control is the one thing you always want to have. It may work for other keepers, but for me research on the opposition takers is pointless. If a coach ran up to me with a little list – 'This is where so-and-so puts it 57 per cent of the time', 'Such-and-such has missed 24 per cent of his last year's penalties' – I'd want to kill them on the spot. The taker can change their mind. With all that info, you still have no control – only muddled thinking now.

So what *can* you control? Only one thing: which way you dive. This is why, in advance, I always made my selections and made them randomly. Left, left, right, left, left. See? Now I know something the opposition does not. Now I have a tiny feeling of the upper hand again. Fretting over a taker and their history would also go against a golden rule I had: *It is about me, not the opposition.*

With my method, I just need to sync up with the taker once. Go the right way just once. I backed myself, if I did so, to make the save. And, more often than not, you just need one save in a shoot-out to help your team go through. Holland scored their first penalty but when Van Basten walked up for their second I wasn't thinking, *Oh, it's one of the world's greatest players.* To me it was just a guy wearing orange and I was diving left.

I went left, he went left too. It was a good penalty, but I was across so quickly that I pushed it out. When you save one in a shoot-out, it's play-acting time. Time to strut, to project to everyone that you're unbeatable, that you're Super Goalie. So you stand tall and look arrogantly at the crowd. *Yeah, this is what I expected* is your vibe. Holland's keeper, Hans van Breukelen, clearly had the opposite approach to mine. His method seemed to be all about the opposition. He spent most of his time trying to intimidate our guys and, honestly, I would have been disappointed not to save three of our efforts. But he only got a hand to them. Spending less energy on mind games and more on saving might just have helped him.

But our guys did their jobs: Larsen, Povlsen, Elstrup, Vilfort – all scored. Elstrup was our best penalty-taker, and I know people would have been nervous about Povlsen, because he had not scored in the tournament, but if you know Flemming you know he is mentally strong. Unbreakable. Vilfort? Nobody could ever doubt how great Kim's fortitude is.

Kim Christofte was on our last kick. For me, it is one of the moments of the tournament: he spots the ball and then he points to it. The ref comes over, Van Breukelen comes over and Kim says, 'Oh, oh dear – the ball is not in the right place.' The absolute nerve. He knows if he scores, we're in the final, and he milks the moment like nothing else. Then he takes three steps, saunters up, waits for Van Breukelen's movement and casually rolls the ball down the other side. Before twirling on the spot doing a comical jig.

The whole thing was to psych out Van Breukelen. Having watched all his crap, Kim thought, *I'll turn it back on him*. A normal person would have walked up and tried to get the job done, but Kim is not a normal person. He is always a bit different from everyone else, but different in a good way. He was elegant and had a sort of arrogance in his play. 'You might be Germany, but I am Kim Christofte.' He was ahead of his time: a ball-playing, technically excellent centre half who calmly thought his way through matches. He would have been perfect in the modern game. That penalty: three decades later, I am still shaking my head at how cool it was.

Back at the hotel, on the screen in our treatment room, the Holland game was played over and over again. We would gather round to watch and every time you could see more and more detail and appreciate just how well we played. But we had a problem and it was to do with the treatment room's main purpose – injuries were now a massive concern. Henrik Andersen was clearly out – he would not play again for months – and Kent Nielsen had been ruled out of the Holland semi by a muscle problem. His tournament was supposed to be over.

Then there was Sivebæk. Against the Dutch, he had pulled his hamstring, an injury that normally takes between six and eight weeks to recover from. And there was Lars Olsen, who in a collision with Van Basten and me had taken a knee to his hip. It hurt his nerve and after dinner that evening in the hotel restaurant, Lars found he could not stand when he tried getting up from the table. He said that my knee had caused the damage. I told him it was Van Basten's – but no one was having that. So I had to carry him up to his room.

Now, Lars is a six-foot centre back and I had to put him on my back and haul him up fifty stairs: my punishment, everyone said. Of course, the next day when they replayed the game in the treatment room, everyone could see the knee which hurt him *had* been Van Basten's all along.

I say 'the next day', but that is not entirely truthful. Because in fact it was 6 a.m. when we finished downstairs and I carried Lars up. And, actually, we didn't go straight to bed after dinner but went to the bar. Then got on the piano. Richard Møller Nielsen had a reputation for being strait-laced, but he really loosened up that summer and allowed us the reward of a few beers after our Dutch exploits. It was midsummer and the hotel was full of Swedes in party mood and we sat at the piano, singing away to everyone. Me, Lars Olsen, Kim Christofte and a few others. At 6 a.m., Richard came down and said mildly, 'Okay, boys, we're training at ten – maybe you should get some sleep.' I grabbed a couple of hours, but I know Christofte did not. He kept going – then rolled straight to training.

It was another moment, like dining on Big Macs, when we bucked sports science, but also another moment when Richard understood that sometimes the psychological outweighs the physical. He could have gone hard on us, but what would have been the point? We were five or six guys having a few beers. Okay, and a sing-song too. But with all the adrenaline still flowing from the penalty shoot-out we may not have slept anyway, had we turned in at midnight, and the coach knew that once we had released a little pressure, we would train hard again, we would be ready.

Brøndby was a family. A family of families. All the wives, girlfriends and children of players were part of the clan. Line was the first kid, Kasper was the second. I joined the club when he was a baby and there was only one child around at that point, a year older than my son. That was Line, Kim Vilfort's daughter.

Being the first one, the first to arrive, the first to walk, the first to talk, she delighted us. Everyone took to her. She was a good girl, a funny girl. After every home game, there would be a huge meal, players and their partners around the table, the kids running around, and something magical to come out of that period is that those kids – our kids – are still in contact with each other. They are in their twenties and thirties now and meet up, have WhatsApp groups. And Line is with us all still.

By Euro 92, she was very ill. She was in hospital receiving treatment for leukaemia – in fact, she was on my mother's ward. When you are in your twenties you don't have much grasp of mortality. At eighteen, I lost a friend in a traffic accident – Carsten Sunstrom, an incredible sportsman and the captain of Gladsaxe-Hero. But that was different. Kim was a close friend, one of our Brøndby gang, but we couldn't begin to relate to what he was going through. Somehow in the tournament he was finding the strength to perform brilliantly and after the semi-final he flew back to Copenhagen to see Line and Minna, his wife. We didn't know if he would come back. He spoke to us about Line sometimes and we tried to support him, but I think what enabled him to keep going, keep playing, was the togetherness and strength he and Minna had as a couple.

Minna and Line encouraged him to return to Gothenburg for the final, and from somewhere he found the ability to separate his football from what was happening in his life. Line did not pull through. She left this world a few weeks after the final. I don't know how, but Kim and Minna found the strength to carry on with life and move forward through it while always continuing to honour her memory. I have an admiration for them that I cannot express.

On the morning of the final, Sivebæk, Nielsen and Olsen had some news for Richard. They were fit – or so they said. Olsen, you could get your head round. A tough player can shake off a dead leg. But the other two being able to play? The chances were so remote that I think it was out of respect more than anything that Richard said, 'Okay, go and have fitness tests.'

Sivebæk and Nielsen . . . passed. Don't ask me how.

Our physios were fantastic guys: Kim Christiansen and Alan Poulsen. Laura goes to one of them for treatment even now. I am sure those guys had something to do with the miracle of Sivebæk and Nielsen's returns, but 95 per cent of it was down to adrenaline, mind over matter. I have no rational explanation for how they played otherwise. It is something I have been thinking about for ever – did they tell white lies to Richard and the medics to get themselves on the pitch and, if so, was that wrong? My conclusion is I would much rather have two players so driven to play that they would do anything to get on the field than two guys who accept sitting in the stands.

Did they take a gamble with the biggest game of our lives? Who cares: if so, it was a gamble that paid off.

Attention on us had been building throughout the tournament. When we played our first game, against England, people were nice. Oh good, Denmark are here. But the better we played and the further we got, the more support came our way. In Gothenburg, there was red and white everywhere. Danish fans had not been allocated tickets because Denmark were not supposed to be at the party, so I still don't understand how all those supporters of ours got there. They dominated the Ullevi stadium when we played Holland, and once Sweden went out every Swede became Danish too. And, of course, when our opponents in the final were Germany, then all of Europe became Danish as well.

The pre-final press conference is the biggest I have ever been involved in. Everybody, in their life, fantasises about going out and grabbing something that wasn't really theirs to grab – and that is what little Denmark were doing. We represented something to the rest of the world, and it felt like the rest of the world was with us. I didn't feel pressured. My only worries regarding the match itself were about Lars, Kent and John and their fitness. Their involvement was so touch-and-go that on match day minus one, when Richard went through set pieces as he always did, we practised without those three in our defensive line-up.

On that day our kit man, Simon Rasmussen, sprang a surprise. He called me into his room and said, 'Look, I've got you a new shirt, it's up to you if you want to wear ... this.' I always had my own ideas of what a goalkeeper's strip should look like. Against Sweden I had been given a conventional green one to wear, which I did not like at all. I played other Denmark games in blue. I had training shorts (which were bigger) made up into match shorts and that kit made me look huge, strong, athletic – every message that you want to send. White socks: I always wore white socks because white socks make you look quick. And, because I used my feet and legs a lot to save, the colour – white against a green pitch – would stand out, be emblazoned on strikers' minds.

We called the jersey that Simon handed me the harlequin shirt. It was dotted with fluorescent colours, like a Tour de France cyclist gone psychedelic. I loved it the moment I saw it and said, 'Oh, *yes* – please make sure you get permission for me to wear it.' It was certainly not everybody's cup of tea but, for me, it was the best shirt I ever had.

Germany were the world champions. Denmark had never won anything. But Richard was his usual, low-key, unflustered self. The day was incredibly hot. Again, the Ullevi was red and white. Sivebæk, playing after four days of rehabbing an injury that takes two months to heal, somehow lasted sixty-seven minutes. Kent? There was a situation where the ball was chipped over me and Kent got back and, at full stretch, knocked it away at the far post. I watched, thinking, *How did you even do that?* With his injury, it was impossible.

And the miracles did not stop there. After eighteen minutes, Flemming teed up a shot for John Jensen. And this is why John Jensen is one of the most important players ever to play for Denmark. He was a clever footballer, who stayed within his limits and had a golden character, a mindset that told him not to be embarrassed by all the shots he had been spraying during the tournament, but to carry on. His was not blind confidence: anyone who played and trained with Faxe over a long period realised that he could catch those shots right sometimes – and when he did, they were unstoppable.

He caught this one right.

It flew in.

And John . . . this is why I love the guy. Find the footage and check out his celebration. He is not 'Bloody hell, I've hit the target!' No. He is running off, twirling his finger, with a grin that says to the world, 'Told you so.'

When you take an early lead you always face a dilemma. Do you sit back, or keep playing? We kept playing, kept trying to get the ball forward and ask the Germans questions, but they came at us. My God. The bombardment began. We were scrambling and they had chances. At half-time we spoke about being ready for more pressure, but I will never know what happened to them next. It was really weird. In the second half the big German push just did not materialise. I made a few saves. The best was when, just after John scored, Jürgen Klinsmann cut in and shot for the far corner. I got down and with a fingertip touched it past my post. It was a difficult save, physically – you are moving to your left and have to get down to your right – and an important one psychologically. Had Germany equalised at that point, we may not have held out. Momentum would have been with them.

I felt invincible on the day. Like I always did as a kid. Like the opposition would never score. Mind you, I felt that in most games . . . until proven wrong. The press always focus on saves but, in that game, just as important was my command of the box. I was coming for everything, closing angles, clearing players out of the area. Given our injury issues in defence, it was necessary that I took control in there.

I remember another save, again from Klinsmann, from a second-half header. I tell you what I liked about it: his reaction. His face says, 'Oh, this isn't our day.' Being Germany, they were used to wearing the opposition down. That was the moment they played for: an equaliser to break the little guys' hearts, from which they would go on to snatch a winner.

Claus Christiansen replaced Sivebæk. He had not played too much international football, and yet he was the guy who won the header which set up Kim Vilfort for his immortal moment. Not long before, Kim had gone one v one with Bodo Illgner but scuffed his shot wide, and it was like being punched in the gut – we thought we were about to win the game, only for that chance to go begging. But now Kim took the ball, turned his markers and, from the edge of the box, hit a shot that looked so impure, as if it was bobbling away harmlessly, that Illgner was taken by surprise. When Kim struck it, he didn't look back. He knew his angle was perfect and the connection was good enough. The ball bobbled beyond Illgner and went in off the post: 2–0, twelve minutes to go. They were done. We were . . . what . . . *European champions??*

The final moments were incredible. The atmosphere around the stadium was something else. The referee screwed us a little by not giving us our moment to milk the full-time whistle. He finished the game abruptly, picking up the ball and jogging off. The feeling was unreal. I went to Illgner and swapped shirts, which meant I was walking round the pitch in a T-shirt and that annoys me, still. What was I doing? I should have been in my fantastic new jersey – and I gave it away. Another reason I get embarrassed when I look at the footage is that, at the presentation, I was so eager to touch the trophy, I was pushing people out of the way.

In the dressing room Henrik, Prince of Denmark, and his sons, Crown Prince Frederik and Prince Joachim, arrived to congratulate us. We had cigarettes and beer with them. The last thing I saw before being hauled off for the press conference was Kim Christofte, wearing just his underpants, striding over to the royalty: 'Hey, Henrik, what about that, wanna beer?' All protocol out of the window.

The following year, I did an autograph-signing tour of Denmark and was in Aarhus, which is where the royals have a summer residence. They play tennis with my adviser Ole Frederiksen's friend, Knud Rodin, and we were invited to challenge them in a game. I was recovering from a cartilage operation, so had to decline, but they asked us over for a glass of wine and we arrived while they were still on court. I have to say, it was not the best tennis you will ever see. When the princes finished, we chatted for an hour – it was nice – Ole and I arranged to meet Knud Rodin for dinner later.

When we sat down for that, Rodin looked at me and said, 'Do you know something, I've been playing tennis with the prince for twenty years and it is only this year that he said to me, "Herr Rodin, I think we know each other well enough now that you can call me *du*."' Danish has two forms of the second person pronoun 'you'. There is *du*, which is informal, and *De*, which is very formal and rarely used these days. 'So, after twenty years, I can finally call the prince *du* and there you are, having just being introduced to him, using *du* for an entire hour – and he never corrected you. I have known him for thirty years and this is the first time he did not tell someone to please speak to him formally.'

What could I say? I can only suggest that when you've had beer and cigarettes with someone, sitting next to Christofte in his Y-fronts, then the usual barriers get broken down a little.

Ah, Kim Christofte. We called him the Media Shy. It was because he never wanted to speak to the press. After the final we partied all night in our hotel and after almost no sleep had to be on a bus from our hotel to the airport. We waited for him, but Christofte wasn't there. No one knew what had happened to him. With hundreds of thousands of people waiting in Copenhagen for our victory parade, in the end the coach driver said we had to go or we would miss our flight. Christofte would have to make his own way home. We got to the airport and were taken straight to the tarmac and our plane. As we were boarding, in the distance, a bus started coming towards us. There was only one guy on it. Out stepped Kim.

He was carrying a massive, human-sized teddy bear. On his head was a straw hat. Under one arm was the match ball from the final. There was a camera round his neck. Oh, and he wore sunglasses and a casual smile. He looked like someone trying to attract the maximum attention – the Media Shy. Of course, the whole costume had stayed with him since the trophy presentation. And it was somehow cool. That was Kim.

13

DENMARK

You never want to be on an aeroplane that makes an aborted landing. Except when you are Denmark and you have just conquered Europe and the football world cannot believe it and Copenhagen is going mad. When our flight from Gothenburg came in to Kastrup airport, the wheels of our plane barely touched the tarmac before the pilot took off again. He wanted to circle above Copenhagen so we could see the spectacle from the air: the streets were jammed with crowds and had been redecorated in red and white. We could not quite take it in. Since early morning, people had been packing the route for an open-top bus parade that would take us from Kastrup to Copenhagen Town Hall. There were thousands waiting at the airport itself, where all its red fire engines were parked in a guard of honour.

The parade went on and on. After the final there had been an informal dinner for the squad, staff, DBU (Danish FA) people and families, which had turned into one long partying session. On the open-top bus we carried on in that vein, singing, drinking and smoking cigarettes. We leaned over the sides to steal the hats off policemen. But after a while it stopped being so enjoyable: it was 30 degrees, we were tired and everyone was desperate for the loo. At the Town Hall we piled onto a small balcony and dangled the trophy above the crowd. I shudder at that now. The trophy had a marble base, connected with a screw which had got bent in the celebrations – it could easily have come loose, fallen off and killed someone. And the balcony had a sign that I only noticed once twenty-five big football players were already crammed aboard. It read, 'MAXIMUM EIGHT PEOPLE.'

We wore the worst green DBU-issue shirts you have ever seen and, in the heat, soaked them with sweat. In the photos, we don't look so attractive. Christofte continued clowning with his sunglasses, hat and camera. The speeches from the mayor and dignitaries seemed to last hours, and by the end of it all we were very drained and very bored and escaped back to our bus via a back exit. Everyone met up later that evening in a restaurant called Copenhagen Corner, which had a little basement dining room tucked away from the eyes of the public where, without anybody knowing, we rounded off our adventure with a chilled-out dinner. Just us.

'Ninety-two bonds all of us together, to this day. The official and unofficial meals, the get-togethers, events and receptions – they carry on. Personally, once a year is quite enough for reunions. Nostalgia does little for me. I mean this without arrogance, so forgive me if it sounds that way, but winning the European Championship was fantastic, unbelievable – but it is not the only thing I did in my life. I have always felt that if I stop to enjoy something I did before too much, I might stagnate and not make the next moments count too. I am in no way prepared to be an old man. So, every time the invitation to another '92 bash comes in, I always think twice, though I generally go.

For years we had a group which went by the acronym, 'EMMA'. We, the players of '92, would meet up in summer, usually at a coastal place in Denmark's Summerlands – where Danes traditionally take summer vacations – and play a match against a local team. There would be a massive party in the evening, with top Danish bands playing. Then it got to the point where it was difficult for us to play, so the meet-ups became smaller, but in 2017 there was a twenty-fifth-anniversary celebration which started with breakfast at Copenhagen Town Hall and walking back out onto that balcony. A crowd was waiting in the square to see us again, a pleasant surprise. We drove to Ystad for a party at our old hotel. It was nice.

Richard Møller Nielsen passed away in 2014 and only after his death did he get included in the Danish Football Hall of Fame. Can you believe that? The DBU did it hastily and out of shame. I was invited to make the speech marking his induction and chose my words carefully. I could have been stronger in my language, but I made clear my disappointment that he had not been honoured while he was alive. The audience contained all the FA nonentities who disliked him and were responsible for him being overlooked. My old boss and friend might have enjoyed the squirming in seats.

The treatment of Denmark's most successful ever coach is a national embarrassment. In 1992, Richard was European Coach of the Year and World Soccer Magazine Manager of the Year – but not Danish Coach of the Year. Incredible. It typified the country's lack of appreciation for the man behind its greatest achievement in sport. Yes, Richard had his ways. He was not cuddly or clubbable, nor did he charm the TV cameras. He was different, but sometimes difference is the precise ingredient you need to achieve something special – and he did.

Denmark can be a superficial place. Danes have a knack for celebrating people who are irrelevant, who have contributed nothing real to society, while failing to recognise those of true value. It is one element about my country that I do not like. We should honour our real heroes and not be jealous of them. Richard Møller Nielsen, make no mistake, is a real hero.

Richard's detractors seek to isolate winning the Euros from the rest of his career, but he began building for that success in 1984, when as Under-21 coach he brought together the spine of our team, continuing its development via the Olympic side. Sepp Piontek, who was in charge of the 'Danish Dynamite' side that played so entertainingly at the 1986 World Cup, was revered and included in the Football Hall of Fame long before Richard, but he was essentially a big, loud, old-school manager. 'Fight! We will win!' He happened to be gifted with a generation of incredible talent, like Michael Laudrup and Preben Elkjær, but he did not nurture talent and I have never made a secret of my feeling that he should have taken me to Mexico in 1986, to help bring me on.

It was Richard who, as Sepp's assistant, was interested in development. In '86, I was twenty-two, playing well for Hvidovre, a target for Brøndby and had served my Under-21 apprenticeship. Richard wanted me to be at the World Cup. In the months leading up to picking the squad he took to driving from his home on the island of Funen to Copenhagen to train me three times a week. We met at Hvidovre stadium at precisely 11 a.m. and every time, Richard was positive and smiling. This was twelve years before the Storebælt Bridge linking Funen with Zealand was built, meaning Richard had a three-hour journey, involving a ferry crossing, each way. The exercises we did, if I am completely honest, were boring. Catching, diving, simple functions: four drills done in repetitions of eight. Every rep had to be completed flawlessly, and that is how Richard was: everything had to be done in the correct way or it was a waste of time. When Piontek did not select me for the '86 squad, Richard was more disappointed than me, taking it as a personal defeat. We used the setback as motivation to work even harder and for me to get better.

Richard continued putting me through those drills after becoming manager of the senior national side and, dry as the exercises were, they gave me so much confidence in catching the football and diving in the best way, elements that became strengths of my game. Yet there was more to Richard than his serious and professional side. He, above all else, was a lovely person. When he let his guard down he was very funny. His party piece was to take the microphone on the team bus and sing us songs, and these were old Danish comedy numbers: smutty and full of double entendres. A favourite involved the story of a young virgin with three beefeater hats displayed in her entrance hall. He gave us that one on the way back to our hotel in Gothenburg after winning the '92 final. We sat with cold beers, as drunk on our success as from the alcohol, happy to have such a coach: an unusual man who looked after us, inspired us, and now and then entertained us with his kinky little rhymes.

Back in the autumn of 1986, following the World Cup, Piontek had approached me at a training camp for the Olympic team and said, 'I've been thinking about picking you.' By that point I was pretty annoyed about not having been in his squad before. In my mind, I was the best goalkeeper in Denmark, and I was even more disillusioned when he added, 'I want to see how you do in these next matches.' What kind of motivation was that? He spun things out before finally giving me a senior debut against Hungary one month before Euro 88. I played okay. I went to the championships as No 2 goalkeeper but returned from them the No 1, after Sepp promoted me following a 3–2 defeat in Denmark's opener against Spain.

Overall, I appreciate what he did in improving the national team's mentality and raising Danish football's profile. Without '86, Brøndby would never have gone full-time, so I was a direct beneficiary. But his lack of interest in development led to Denmark's decline at the end of the 1980s and he was not always in my corner. In 1989, to mark its centenary, the DBU arranged a tournament with Brazil, Sweden and England which clashed with a Brøndby tour of South Korea. Some players were allowed to go with Brøndby, but I was one of those who had to go to the tournament. But Sepp told us, 'I've got to be fair, I'll play you in one game each, then we'll see.' I thought, 'What?' I was the No 1 and wanted to play every match of a competition involving big opponents like that. He picked me against England, but I was on the bench for the Sweden game and was not involved against Brazil. Brazil! Every player wants to face them. And Sweden is our derby. The experience hurt.

After we messed up the qualifying campaign for the 1990 World Cup, Sepp departed and Richard was the obvious and logical replacement. But the DBU wanted to be clever. It botched an attempt to appoint Bayer Uerdingen's Horst Wohlers and wooed several other foreign coaches. The chairman, Hans Bjerg-Pedersen, said, 'My grandmother could have achieved the same results as Richard Møller.' This undermined Richard with the press and public before the DBU ended up going back to him.

I am not going to say that everything about Richard was brilliant. His team talks could be long and drawn out, a lot of repetition, a lot of boring stuff, but that was him, the attention to detail. As Brøndby players you compared him with Morten Olsen, who was dynamic in the dressing room and could surprise you – with those fans of money, for instance. Morten would never sit down for a team talk, whereas Richard would start seated and slowly get to his feet as the lecture neared its end. He was not a man for risk mode, not a coach who would say, 'Let's attack.' The forwards found his cautious ways hard, and when Michael Laudrup was among seven players who quit the squad after defeat at home to Yugoslavia in our third qualifier for Euro 92, I had sympathy. His decision was wrong, but I could see his viewpoint: you play for Barcelona one week and the next you play for Denmark, where all the pressure is on your shoulders, you are always the scapegoat for the media, and yet you are not playing in a system that allows you to be the best version of yourself.

It said a lot about Michael that he was able to swallow his pride, repair relations with Richard and come back to be our captain at Euro 96 and the 1998 World Cup. And it said a lot about Richard that in 1991 he could bounce back from being undermined by the FA, starting badly and losing seven star players, to win our last five qualifiers and finish second to Yugoslavia in our qualifying group. And then, of course, there was his brilliant management at the Euros themselves.

At our '92 reunions, we players have often spoken about our disappointment that Richard was not acknowledged properly in his lifetime and I think that lack of appreciation did hurt Richard personally. He was a very proud man, who would never show feelings like those, but at his funeral there was a surprise. The priest revealed Richard went to church four times a week, and they had deep conversations, not necessarily about religion but about life. I am sure these formed part of Richard's way of dealing with the footballing rejection he suffered.

Failing to reach the 1994 World Cup took some of the gloss off '92. We were the first reigning European champions not to qualify for a World Cup. It allowed people to claim we had got lucky. Denmark's biggest challenge as a national team has always been scoring goals and in the qualifiers we just did not take our chances, drawing 0–0 in Latvia, Lithuania and at home to Ireland. We conceded just twice in the whole campaign, and missing out is still something that hurts, really hurts, because you only get so many chances in your career to play at a World Cup and we were good enough – with Michael's magic added to the '92 team – to have really done something at what was an open tournament in the USA.

The manner in which we ultimately missed out was terrible. Our last qualifier was on 17 November 1993, in Seville. A draw would have taken us to the World Cup. After eleven minutes Spain had Andoni Zubizarreta sent off and we just had to hold off ten men, but in the second half, at a corner, José Mari Bakero obstructed me and Fernando Hierro scored. An obvious foul.

Not only did the Greek referee decline to give it, he booked me for protesting. Years later, Bakero admitted, 'Of course I blocked Schmeichel,' and it was no consolation when he did. The day after the game was my thirtieth birthday and was the most miserable birthday of my life. We stayed in Seville's Expo, which was a ghost town, and the despair as we sat in our deserted hotel trying to come to terms with the defeat was unbelievable. It was one of the lowest points in my life, let alone my career. I did not watch one second of the 1994 World Cup. I had zero interest.

I did experience one day of joy with Denmark in 1993. I got to play a competitive match against Diego Maradona. He was my greatest hero, in terms of outfield players. The first foreign football to be screened properly in Denmark was Italian, when in the late 1980s TV2 began showing Serie A matches on Sundays. Maradona was at his peak with Napoli and, in those days, in Italy you almost had to kill someone on the pitch to get a yellow card. Every game, the opposition seemed to try. Maradona was kicked, hit, grabbed, barged and provoked, and yet there he was, on screen every Sunday, jumping, dancing, rising above it every time. It was poetry, ballet.

In 1987, Brøndby were hired to play in Saudi Arabia against Al-Ahli, for whom Maradona was given $1m to be a guest player. The whole thing was a birthday present for one of the Saudi princes from his father. At a dinner we were given medals and Maradona was presented with this great gold, jewel-encrusted sword. Before kick-off, he shook hands with every player in our line-up, before the prince and his father came along. The dad had spent so much on the extravaganza that he felt he could ask Maradona anything. He said, 'Do some tricks,' and Maradona began. 'More,' the father said. Maradona did more. This went on, five minutes, ten minutes, fifteen minutes, Maradona still juggling the ball, but the thing was, he was not embarrassed or annoyed. He was grinning and enjoying himself.

That was the first time I got a taste of who he was as a person: a man who radiated warmth, who had a gift and a sense he was put on earth to share it. Later, I had the privilege of knowing Diego. We worked together as FIFA legends and played on the same side in a Soccer Aid match, and he was a man who, whatever the demands and pressures on him, was a giver. He gave his art to the people.

In the game in Saudi we weren't allowed to tackle him and he displayed all sorts of skills, lobbing me in the first half, then beating our No 2 keeper in the second with an incredible strike where he dribbled through and, from a tight angle, with just a flick, somehow powered the ball into the top corner. We talked about that goal for days. How was it even possible?

In February 1993, Denmark travelled to Mar del Plata to face Argentina in the Artemio Franchi Trophy – a forerunner of the Confederations Cup, played between the European and South American champions. Richard came up with a scheme to man-mark Maradona with Jakob Kjeldbjerg, who had the game of his life. Yet, dropping deep to escape Jakob for one instant, Maradona began a move that led to Argentina's equaliser, from Gabriel Batistuta, and we went to penalties.

I knew Maradona liked to wait for the goalkeeper to move, so for the one and only time in my career, I broke my routine at penalties and did not choose a side in advance. He ran up waiting for me, I stood waiting for him, a battle of wills, and a fraction of a second before he reached the ball, some silly instinct made me move. I regretted it instantly, stopped and moved again but too late – I got a hand on his shot but could not stop it going in. I am *still* annoyed – even to this day. It would have been something else to have saved one from him.

When Maradona died, I found myself trying to explain him to my stepsons, Vitus and Gustav, who were thirteen and eleven at the time. The best way to put it seemed this: take Messi, I said, and imagine Messi at his best. Now think about someone much better. That was Diego.

Euro 96, in England, was the end for Richard. A lot went wrong and I take responsibility for some of it. When we qualified, Richard came to England and we went round potential bases together. Some of the locations were dire, others were nice but too far from the nearest training pitches, and then we saw this place on the northern side of Leeds. It had a lovely pitch you could walk to without even crossing a road and we were offered the whole floor of the hotel to ourselves – unimaginable luxury for the Danish team in those days. The rooms were fine. All three of our group matches were in Sheffield, which would be a little bit of a drive, but on balance this place seemed the best option available.

My God, though, what a mistake. There was nothing to do there, and when there is nothing to do in a camp it kills you, slowly draining everybody of energy. There was not even scenery: this hotel was on a big roundabout. Richard insisted on training at the stadium on the day before games and would not budge, even though after the first match we were more than familiar with Hillsborough. This meant twelve long coach trips, two hours each time, crawling along the M1 to and from Sheffield. Pure monotony. The irony was we went out at the group stage with an identical record – won one, drawn one, lost one, goal difference of zero – to our group performance in '92.

It was after Euro 96 that I made one of two attempts to get Fergie to sign Brian Laudrup. He would have been a fantastic Manchester United player and I think he would have loved the environment: a place that was protective but encouraged flair. Fergie bought Karel Poborský instead. Later, at Manchester City, I persuaded Kevin Keegan to sign Brian. After sustaining a foot injury, Brian had left Ajax in 2000 and retired from playing but had stayed fit, very fit, and come to the conclusion that maybe he wasn't finished with the game after all. I connected him and Kevin up and they went all the way to agreeing a deal, only for Brian to back out at the last moment. Brian was just thirty-three and the type of player Manchester City fans would have adored.

My early negative experiences with the Danish press set the tone for many subsequent dealings with them, I am sad to say. Even at Euro 92 their approach had distasteful elements. One bit of coverage that sticks in my mind involved a Danish weekly magazine, a rag that peddled top rubbish. It published a front cover juxtaposing Bent Christensen, whose wife was pregnant, and Kim Vilfort, who was going through such distress with Line. The headline read, 'BENT'S HAPPINESS, KIM'S DISASTER.'

Could you get more insensitive? Collectively, with the backing of the Danish FA, we threw their journalists out of our camp.

We were at loggerheads with the media again at the 1998 World Cup. When Richard stepped down in 1996, I pushed hard for Morten Olsen to be appointed, but the DBU went with Johansson and I am pleased they did. That is nothing to do with Morten and everything to do with Bo. I didn't know much about this low-key Swede when he arrived – but what a coach and what a personality. I learned so much from him.

I remember the first meeting he called. He told the players, 'You have to accept there is a chance you can lose any game you play.' We were up in arms. *What? This guy thinks losing is okay!* But then Bo explained: 'You have to accept there is a chance you can lose any game you play; only then can you use all your concentration and energy for winning.'

Hmm, I thought. *Yeah. Not bad.*

The criticism from journalists and lack of love that came his way from the DBU and the public ground Richard down in the end, and by Euro 96 he had closed up. Gone were the songs and the trips to McDonald's. We did less as a squad off the pitch and the tactics were cautious on it. When Bo arrived, everything lightened up.

Bo loved golf. Every training camp, he was looking to get us out on the course. His psychology was subtle. With Richard, when you were in camp you were in camp. With Bo you could say, 'Would you mind if, this afternoon, I leave the camp for three hours?' He would say, 'Of course! If it is important, then of course you can!' And you would go away and think, *Mmm, it isn't that important, is it?* And you would stay.

He never told you what to do, he just guided you towards what he wanted. He answered every question with a question and always made you think. Our camp at the World Cup in France was the polar opposite to the one at Euro 96. We were based near Marseilles, in a gorgeous place called Hotel Frégate. A golf resort. It was relaxed and secluded and we had the course to ourselves. Our families came to visit, the weather was sensational, the pool was nice. We played plenty of golf, but not so much we got tired. Bo trusted us to know our limits. We were in complete balance, as a group.

Of course, the media criticised Bo for being loose and lenient. They found a lot to criticise. They criticised our form in the warm-up games – as if warm-up games ever matter. They hammered our performance when we beat Saudi Arabia in Lens in our World Cup opener. In it, we scored, controlled the game and conserved our energy, knowing that three points in your first game at a tournament is always a good result. Yet the press slaughtered us, demanding more sparkle. Then we met South Africa in Toulouse. I have never played in more sweltering conditions. The sun was searing, the air was still and dry and I am convinced to this day the referee, Colombia's John Toro Rendón, had sunstroke.

He gave the worst officiating performance I ever experienced. His decision-making was weird beyond weird. I worked with Lucas Radebe not long ago and the South African players felt the very same way. Random decisions, mad decisions: we made two substitutions and both players, Miklos Molnar and Morten Wieghorst, were red-carded within minutes of coming on. For nothing. Morten would not hurt a fly. A South African, Alfred

238

Phiri, was sent off for a vague offence. Rendón was sent home without refereeing another game in the tournament.

The random Rendón, on top of the stifling weather, rendered a proper football match impossible and both sides were happy enough to draw. South Africa were a talented outfit; even with conditions perfect, a point would have been okay. Of course, our media didn't see any of that. We were a dreadful side, they said. We shouldn't be playing golf; Bo was an awful manager. Bo just shrugged. You couldn't rattle him.

When we met France in Lyon, the situation forbade risk. We needed a draw to guarantee going through, but would almost certainly progress with a narrow defeat. South Africa had to beat Saudi Arabia and effect a three-goal swing in goal difference. France scored, with a Youri Djorkaeff penalty that I nearly got to. We equalised. They scored again. The other game was level and we were content to play out a 2–1 defeat, knowing that would be okay. Now, though, our press became the moral guardians of football, bringing up the so-called fixed match between Austria and Germany in 1982. 'The spirit of the game.' All that rubbish. The fact we were in the World Cup last 16, for only the second time in the nation's history, was ignored.

Our next opponents, Nigeria, had a fantastic team and were even tipped as contenders to be the first African side to win a World Cup. They had Jay-Jay Okocha, Nwankwo Kanu, Finidi George, Sunday Oliseh, Taribo West and were captained by my old friend, Uche. Great players. The game was at Stade de France and at training the night before the game, Bo called Michael and me over. He told us he was considering starting with a certain player. In unison we said no. We suggested he should instead pick Peter Møller, who in every training session since we arrived in France had been banging them in. Bo said, 'Hmm, thanks,' and the next day Peter was in the team. Peter scored three minutes into the match and assisted Brian for our second goal after twelve minutes. Later, Bo told me he had already made his decision, but when he heard what Michael and I had to say he changed it. He had the ability not to need to be the cleverest person in the room.

Our quarter-final against Brazil is still agonising to reflect on. It was a game in which, as a team, we did not understand our opportunity. The build-up was all about Brazil's great players, Ronaldo, Rivaldo, Cafu and the rest, and we were not exactly nervous, but maybe their reputations were at the back of some players' minds. We should have gone for them, smashed them, but we were too respectful. It was only late in the game, too late, that we realised we were actually the better team.

In a funny way, we were not helped by scoring early, because that encouraged us to sit back. They equalised via an exceptional finish by Bebeto, who guided his shot into a tiny space between my fingertips and the post. I was criticised for the third goal and after all these years I should be big enough to accept it . . . but I am not! If you watch the replay, you will see our defenders tracking back as they attack and that there is always at least one defender in my eyeline, so I am contantly having to adjust my position. Rivaldo struck his shot at the precise moment I shifted weight onto my wrong foot.

*　　*　　*

Brazil was my last World Cup game. I could have clung on and continued to Japan and Korea in 2002, but international football began losing its appeal after 1998. It was not her but me, as they say. I was becoming tired by the continual demands on my body and mind, and when Morten Olsen replaced Bo in 2000, it spelt the beginning of the end for me. Morten was one of the most important figures in my career and for so long I had been keen for him to become Denmark manager, but I was too long in the tooth by the time it happened. I knew how hectic and demanding Morten could be from our days at Brøndby, but what I did not expect was that he had not mellowed or changed much over the years. It turned out he was still super-intense. I realised at his first training camp that it wasn't going to be for me.

Let me tell you a little Morten story, from Brøndby. In the winter we sometimes played or trained in Malmö, where there was a nice grass pitch to rent. This was before they built the bridge from Copenhagen to Malmö – yes, from TV, *The Bridge* – so you travelled by ferry. Once, we boarded the boat home and we players piled straight into the cafeteria to have a meal that had been pre-ordered by someone at the club: meat with French fries. This is a public restaurant, we are Brøndby and he is the great, famous, Morten Olsen. Denmark legend and captain. But he didn't care about any of that. The last to arrive at the café, he took one look at the less-than-healthy stuff we were eating and went berserk, screaming at the waiter, 'PUT THIS CRAP AWAY! WHO SERVED THEM THIS?' The fellow passengers watched, disbelieving, but Morten was oblivious. In his world, the word 'compromise' did not exist. In his own career, he compromised on nothing, which was part of what had made him such a great player and, in those days, the right manager to drag Brøndby to where we needed to be.

But by the age of almost thirty-seven, I did not want to be treated like a child any more. I was captain in Morten's first qualifier versus Iceland and then he picked me for Northern Ireland in October. As soon as I saw my name in the squad I just had an instinct. *No thanks.* More travelling, more time away from home, more weeks where mentally and physically I could not rest? I was beginning to feel enough was enough.

I had always wanted to go out on my own terms and not make the mistake of continuing when my heart was no longer in it. So in March 2001, I called Morten and he was seriously disappointed. Fair dos to him. He said I had been a great servant to Denmark and should have a farewell game, suggesting I play in our spring friendly at Parken stadium versus Slovenia. I am not big on goodbyes but it was nice to recognise my career in that way.

So I played. I had sixty-five minutes before being substituted by Peter Kjær and was able to leave the pitch saying thank you and goodbye to the nation. I was embarrassed about the attention but, in truth, enjoyed myself. The reception was lovely. As was the clean sheet.

14

PORTUGAL

Nobody gets the perfect ending, not in life and certainly not in football. Think how Eric left Manchester United, or Roy, or Giggsy, or Becks, Brucey, Gary; the list is long. The dream exit, where the only tears are happy ones – that is not in anyone's script.

You could say I came closest. My last act, as a player, for the club I loved was lifting the European Cup as their captain. My last touch – when the ball skimmed my head in the chaos before Teddy equalised against Bayern – was in the opposition box. For a goalkeeper, that is not bad.

But I don't see it that way. Goodbyes are overrated and, in my view, life is less about what you did and more about what you could do next. In those terms, I look at my Manchester United career and see something incomplete. It should have been added to. I might have won more, done more. Leaving in summer 1999, when I was thirty-five but fit and still at the top of my game, was a big mistake for both me and the club.

My ending should not have been the end – and nearly was not. Not once but twice, Alex Ferguson asked if I would re-sign for the club. It never happened, because I made misjudgements, the first time regarding myself and the second time – sadly – him.

I'll tell you that story in the next chapter, but my first offer to play on for Manchester United came in the Hotel Arts, in

Barcelona, at our victory party after the 1999 Champions League final. I don't remember too much about the party itself, not because of drink but because in the huge release of pressure at the end of that game I kind of went blank. But I do remember, amid the celebrations, the scramble to sign me. Paul Stretford, who had taken over from Rune as my agent, came up and said that Fergie and Martin Edwards wanted a meeting with me, to see if I would stay. They proposed breaking off from the party for a few minutes and having the conversation there and then.

I was tempted, but it was probably the wrong moment for me to be asked. If the message had been that they wanted to schedule a meeting for a couple of days' time, and we had discussed things then, I'm sure the outcome would have been different. But, put on the spot, I said, 'No.' My first thought was *I really want to stay*, but my second was about all the practicalities. The removal people had been in during the run-up to the last few games of the season and I had my house already packed up and our belongings in boxes ready to transport to Copenhagen or wherever. On 12 May, while I was playing at Ewood Park in an evening kick-off, we had suffered a break-in. The children and my ex-wife were not at home, thankfully, but my ex took it badly: she took it as proof England was becoming dangerous and confirmation that we should go back and live in Denmark.

All of that was in my head and so I said, 'No, no, I've made my mind up.' There were other little factors, including the fact that I was about to join up with Denmark to play important Euro 2000 qualifiers against Belarus and Wales and wanted to focus on them rather than think about my future. Over the next few days,

I had no real regrets. I had built myself up for the attractions of a different climate and different experiences from England, as well as a schedule less punishing than that of the non-stop football I had been grinding my way through for years.

For better or worse, I am a decision-maker. Instinctive. Definite. Overall, those attributes have served me well in life, but this was a time when making a spur-of-the-moment call did not work out for me. Hindsight is wonderful, of course, but let's say I had stayed at Manchester United in '99. The manager would have given me a six-week holiday, recognising the burnout I had felt the summer before, and I would have come back completely different mentally, refreshed, better prepared. I would have been fine.

I loved playing with that team. It would have been fantastic trying to emulate '99, trying to win another Champions League, the Club World Cup, more Premier Leagues. In 1998–99, I loved the chase at the end, playing every three or four days, with every game like a cup final. I felt back to my old self. I was playing like my old self too.

Imagine staying, playing rubbish and Fergie dropping you ... When doubts and tiredness overwhelmed me in the early part of that season, thoughts like that were in my head, but they seem silly now. Hindsight is wonderful because without day-to-day issues clouding them, you see situations with clarity. You have spent time analysing them, weighing up the angles, reflecting on the whole picture with maturity. So, of course, from this distance it seems obvious I should have said yes that night in the Hotel Arts when Fergie asked me to stay. But I can talk about it for ever – the fact is, I answered no.

245

My leave-taking was low-key. Back in Manchester, our victory parade on a hot, chaotic day was beautiful, but absolutely draining. It ended, despite protests from me and Roy on behalf of the squad, with a long presentation at the MEN Arena, organised by the council. One by one players went on stage to make a little speech. Twenty seconds. 'Thank you for all your support, thanks for everything, I love Man U, blah blah.' It seemed to take for ever.

We were shattered. I wanted to sleep for weeks. On the team coach taking us back to the airport hotel where we had parked seven days before, all I remember is how quiet it was. Not a single person said a word on the twenty-five-minute drive from central Manchester. Then we stepped off the bus and shuffled to our cars with barely a goodbye. We had been through the journey of our lives together, but suddenly needed time to ourselves.

Denmark's game against Wales was at Anfield on 9 June and while back in the north-west of England I organised a photo session for myself at Old Trafford with the three Treble trophies. Later in the summer, there was a reunion with players and their families when David Beckham married Victoria in Dublin. I have the memories and goodbyes from that, but there were no grand farewells. I had missed my chance to make the big speech thanking everyone after the FA Cup final. I could only get round to a few people individually, like Kath Phipps, Manchester United's remarkable receptionist, who has been there since 1968. Another was Albert Morgan, our kit man, to whom I left a special gift. I used to wear a nice watch and a bracelet and give them to Albert for safekeeping. It became a match-day ritual for me to take them off and clip them on Albert's wrist, so he was wearing them during the game. After the Champions League final, he went to give me them back and I said, 'Albert, leave the watch on your arm, it has brought us both so much luck, long may it continue.'

The Kaths and the Alberts are the hidden heroes of football and I have so much respect for the roles they play. They do more than their jobs. They help create the atmosphere and culture that make a club special. You cannot buy the stuff a good person in your life or workplace will give you, whereas you can always buy another watch. And that is how I have always seen things. I am not someone who is bothered about possessions, nor has money ever been a factor in my big career decisions. Don't get me wrong, I would fight tooth and nail to get the best contract, but as soon as it was signed, I would put it aside and never give the terms a second thought.

Money never motivated any move or football decision. Not maximising your playing earnings is something you can regret, if you want to, sitting there in your fifties and looking back on younger days, but I never played for any reason other than the game, and that is a thought that brings me happiness and pride.

In 1998–99, I was too focused on chasing the Treble to give much thought to where I might go after Manchester United. I didn't tout myself around. However, I felt I had plenty of time. I thought, *Finish the season with Denmark, let the clubs around Europe regroup and the offers will come in.* But none of the big clubs needed a goalkeeper that summer. That is the problem for keepers plotting their careers – teams only need one of you. If you find yourself on the market at a time everyone has an established No 1, it doesn't matter how good you are or how big your name is – your phone is not going to ring.

When the offers did come, they were from a club in Greece, a couple in Turkey – and Portugal. Not the suitors I had imagined. But Portugal did appeal. I was looking for a better climate. That felt important. Three or four months of cold, wet English winter every season is no fun when you're playing with a bad back. I wanted a winter break, which the Portuguese Primeira Liga provided, and I still wanted to play in Europe and compete for championships. Sporting Lisbon were one of the suitors and they offered all of that. Portugal itself was a place I loved going to, whether on holiday or as a player. The first flight I took in my life was to Lisbon; the first European Cup match I played in was at Porto. There felt a nice symmetry to making the country my next destination.

When I arrived in Lisbon on 20 June 1999, it was not necessarily to sign a contract. I travelled with Paul Stretford to check the place out and check Sporting out. We brought an interpreter, a Scottish girl, and got picked up at the airport by a club official and the whole trip started with a massive argument.

The entire board of Sporting Clube de Portugal, Sporting's parent organisation, were assembled in their offices, which are located away from the José Alvalade stadium, waiting for me to come and sign a contract. I wasn't going to sign anything before working out whether this move was right, so I asked to be driven around potential places to live first. The directors wanted me to sign first, *then* do all that. I could hear the poor club rep being berated on his phone and I sat in the car thinking how difficult the language sounded. I couldn't understand a word. I ended up getting my way, but it all got very temperamental. As I would learn, Portugal can be an emotional place.

We drove to Estoril and Cascais and the area was perfect. Precisely the lifestyle I wanted. We ate a late lunch and went to the Sporting Clube offices. Then the circus started. Our interpreter was there to ensure any contract I signed would be, word for word, the same in Portuguese and English. Paul had had a few bad experiences in Portugal. He had moved players and a manager to Benfica and they had been left with money owed to them. He wanted my contract registered with FIFA and for it to stipulate that if I wasn't paid on certain dates – the fifth of every month – then Sporting could be penalised: they would owe me the remainder of my whole deal.

The guy we were dealing with was the sports director of the club's football division, named Carlos Janela. *Janela* means 'window' in Portuguese. So, Carlos the Window. He was so eager to get the transfer done but, seriously, the negotiations took for ever. In the middle of the night – something like 2 a.m. – we finally agreed everything. I signed the contract. I was so tired. All I wanted was to go to my hotel and sleep. Carlos said, 'Okay, but first we go next door.' Next door turned out to be the press room – full of press. In the middle of the night! I was speechless. And Carlos started up.

He made a big speech. Sporting had not won the title for seventeen years. He was part of a new board. They had just sacked their coach, a Croat called Jozić – I inherited his apartment – and employed Giuseppe Materazzi. Carlos said, 'We have an Italian coach because now we want to be professional.'

Now? And continued, 'We've just signed Peter Schmeichel and now we will win the championship – because Peter Schmeichel wins the championship everywhere!' *What the . . .?*

I sat staring at this guy. I was already a bit wary of him, because everything you asked for, he smiled and said, 'Yes! Of course!' but when you tried getting it in the contract, it was a problem. Things like a car. Because of Paul's experience with Benfica, he said I had to be very specific and put down precisely what I wanted: Jeep, unleaded petrol and so on. I also had Sporting commit to provide a full-time language teacher who, along with the Jeep, would be available from the first day of pre-season training. Neither was, of course. Absolutely nothing agreed in that contract ever turned up at the time or in the shape it was supposed to.

There is a mentality of casualness in Portugal. It is lovely most of the time. People take things easy. The first word you learn is *amanhã*, which means 'tomorrow', and it took plenty of *amanhãs* before the car arrived and I could drive it back home. It was low on fuel. I took it to a service station and filled up. Inside the fuel cap was written *gasóleo*, which I assumed meant 'petrol', given I had ordered a petrol car. So I put in petrol. Yet after driving 300 metres, *boomph*, the engine went dead. *Gasóleo* meant 'diesel', even though I had stipulated in my contract an unleaded-petrol Jeep. When I complained, Carlos the Window just laughed.

We got to my first pay date. There was no pay cheque. I knocked on Carlos's door. '*Amanhã*,' he said with a smile.

'No,' I insisted, 'you have to pay me today.'

Carlos said, 'Ah! We can't pay you because you don't have a bank account.'

I said I did, I used a bank in England, and I had already given the club all the details. Carlos replied that I had to use Banco Espírito Santo in Portugal. This was a new one. I had to go and open an account there, providing all sorts of documentation, but still no money came in.

'Aha,' said Carlos, 'it takes two days.'

'I'll go to FIFA,' I replied.

'Two days, Peter,' he beamed.

After three weeks, still no money. I banged on the Window's door. Under duress, he agreed to write a cheque. In Portugal, everything is notarised and you need stamps and countersignatures, so it was a lengthy process. Eventually, he handed the cheque over and we shook hands. Just as I was leaving he said, 'Don't cash it.'

What?

He explained there was no money in the football club's account and begged me to wait another two days. I did and when I cashed it, the cheque miraculously cleared – but every month, on the fifth, it was the same pantomime, me knocking on Carlos's door, or somebody else's, and engaging in some sort of wrangle. Yet I soon realised I was the only player being paid even remotely on time. Some guys in the squad were a year behind in wages. And Sporting was the best-run club in the country.

I adjusted to the Portuguese way of doing things. Harder was getting used to Materazzi. I arrived for pre-season a Treble-winner, still on the highest of football highs, but walked into a morale-sapping prison camp. Materazzi was *very* Italian. Very different from Fergie, Kiddo and Steve McClaren. He wanted to

251

control everything. What you did when you were not training. How much you ate. What you drank. Every detail.

In Portugal, they have great respect for each other – which I loved. When players eat, they arrive on time and eat together. The captain sits at the end of the table, and when he sits down and says 'Bon appétit' everyone can eat. Nobody leaves the table before the last guy is finished. These rituals bonded us together. However, Materazzi wanted every player to eat exactly the same amount. Our full back, Quim Berto, was five foot five and half my size but got the same portions as me. I was permanently starving.

Training was similar. Everyone did the same exercises, same sprints, same knee-ups, same everything. That was okay, but the sessions were long and dreary. We spent a lot of time doing shape work, forty-five-minute drills where you played 11 v 0 and stayed in formation moving the ball around. The boredom was killing me.

We started the season badly. Draw, win, win, draw, draw, win, defeat. All against little teams. Our football was awful. Materazzi made strange selections. Sporting had fifty to sixty players on its books; some were in the squad, some were out on loan and some were out in the cold – including several of our best ones. We drew with Gil Vicente and our fans staged a demonstration, barricading the boardroom and locking everyone in. All the players' wives, including mine, were inside. Eventually, the protesters let the wives go but kept the board incarcerated – until it stepped down. Quite right too. The Window and his cronies were useless.

New directors were appointed, led by Luís Duque. He was a lawyer and an adviser to the president. He was fantastic – the opposite to the Window. You could trust this guy, and the new sporting director, Carlos Freitas. After going out of the UEFA Cup to Viking Stavanger, Duque sacked Materazzi and appointed Augusto Inácio, a former Sporting player. He had also played for Porto and was their left back in my debut for Brøndby, one of those amazing coincidences football throws at you.

I liked Inácio a lot. His training was inspirational and, unlike Materazzi, he thought it was a good idea to pick our best players. He built a strong side, with a midfield of José Luís Vidigal, who went on to play for Napoli, and Aldo Duscher, who went to Deportivo La Coruña. We had a good centre half in Beto and a canny striker, Alberto Acosta, who scored twenty-two goals. Under Materazzi, Acosta, Duscher and Vidigal had been out of the team. Another of our strikers, Kwame Ayew, brother of the great Abedi Pele and uncle to André and Jordan Ayew, became my very good friend. He spoke every language imaginable, plus all the dialects of Ghana, and he filled in as my interpreter because – surprise, surprise – the one promised in my contract never showed.

Inácio was a grown-up. I had only one problem with his training, which was that he would not give us a weekly training plan and only told us when the next practice was when we finished a session. This was no good to me. I knocked on his door and said I had kids at school and needed to know what I was doing. He said the reason he kept players guessing about the schedule was that players might look for when there were later sessions and go out in the afternoon on the day before, drink wine and take it easy.

Every day, Inácio liked to hold a 9 a.m. meeting where he would give us a pep talk, reminding us what we were working towards: 'Remember, guys, our job is to win this league.' So, I said, 'Okay, but every day you tell us we're here to win. You can only win with winners. People who go out in the afternoon and drink wine are not winners. You will find out who you can trust.' He said, 'Yeah, I see your point.' The next day, he had a two-week training timetable pinned up on the board. I liked his humility, that he would listen.

Estoril and Cascais were everything I hoped for. I loved the area and the quality of life it offered. I loved Portuguese food. It is simple – fish and vegetables; meat and vegetables; fish and rice; fish, rice and vegetables – but always tasty. I can't remember a bad meal in Portugal. The most difficult aspect, for me, was cultural: getting used to what appears to be Portuguese irrationality. But it is just a different mode of being. Who was to say that I, with my uptight and logical Scandinavian ways, was right?

Two stories that sum up Portugal. To use their toll roads, you stick a little box on the windscreen of your car which signals when you pass a toll and charges your bank account. First my box wasn't registered properly, then I had the 'wrong windscreen' on my car, then the garage stuck the box on my grille and it worked for two months, then it stopped. I had a home in Portugal for seven years and only ended up paying for those two months. I tried speaking to the roads people about the problem so many times, but it was *Amanhã*. No one cared.

However, there was also a time when Kasper and Cecilie were playing football in the garden. Kasper had this habit of dressing in full uniform for whatever he did. If he was playing doctor, he was head-to-toe in doctor's gear. If he played football, he was in full kit. So he had his football boots on and while kicking about with Cecilie accidentally stepped on her knee, making a huge gash with his studs. I raced her to A&E in Cascais and as soon as the staff saw that a kid was injured they dropped everything – within half an hour she was stitched, given a tetanus shot, bandaged up and we were home again. Half an hour! That is Portugal. You can argue that a lot of the place doesn't work – but when you really need it to work, it works better than anywhere.

My other challenge was the convention for Portuguese teams to spend a lot of time in camp. Mentally, that was tough, given my age and the culture at Manchester United – where you had freedom and free time, so long as you did not abuse the manager's trust. The disparity between Portuguese clubs was difficult too. One week you could be playing a Lisbon derby, in front of 60,000 at a screaming José Alvalade, and the next at a village ground, watched by 1500. Some of the smaller places were like the Danish second-tier venues where I played at the start of my career, and I did sometimes wonder, *What am I doing here?*

But the team was so enjoyable to be a part of in that first season of 1999–2000. From the end of October to the beginning of May we had a twenty-seven-game unbeaten run, winning twenty-two of those matches, to reach the Portuguese cup final and stay ahead of Porto in the title race. It was tight between us and in March we landed an important blow, defeating them 2–0 at a jam-packed José Alvalade. The atmosphere was incredible. With two games to go, we had a chance to clinch the championship at home against Benfica. For Sporting's fans that would have been extra sweet, but Benfica scored with a free kick, in the final seconds, top corner, and beat us 1–0.

Our final match was at Salgueiros, who play in a suburb of Oporto. Porto were playing Gil Vicente. If we failed to take all three points, Porto could overtake us with a victory. All week, we read in the newspapers about Porto promising the Salgueiros players bonuses if they beat us, and when we got to their stadium we found the pitch was like a horse field. The grass had not been cut, and they had watered the goalmouth so much that it had puddles like rock pools. The dressing rooms were tiny and there were just 4500 spectators there. We put it all aside, however, and thrashed them 4–0. Porto lost their match and we were champions by four points.

I could not take much part in the full-time celebrations because I had been selected for a drugs test and got into an argument with the Portuguese FA official, who said my first sample did not have enough 'density' for him to take a measurement. Pardon? I've never heard that one, before or since. I had to gulp down water and wait another forty-five minutes before I could deliver this jobsworth a second sample.

We drove back to Lisbon, three hours by motorway, and it was very late by the time we arrived on the outskirts of the city, but here came another example of Portugal's weird way of thinking. Our coach stopped at a toll – and there was an open-top bus, ready to go on a tour of the city. Some players boarded that. The rest of us stayed on the team bus, which drove to the stadium. All of this, in the middle of the night!

Tears as I lift the European Championship trophy, watched by my great friend John Jensen.

Michael (left) and Brian Laudrup were back in tandem for Denmark at Euro 96.

Inconsolable after our quarter-final exit from the 1998 World Cup.

Brazil's Rivaldo beats me to end a great adventure and our hopes of a place in the last four.

Sporting have won the Portuguese title for the first time in 18 years and I'm off to celebrate.

Somewhere in this joyful green-and-white scrum is a Danish goalie.

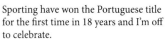

Ruud van Nistelrooy hovers as I face United in Aston Villa's colours in 2001 – I hated playing against the club I love.

Left: An overhead kick in a Villa game – I never minded doing the unorthodox and always trained with the outfield players.

Below: Steeped in United but signed to City – a pre-season chat with manager Kevin Keegan in 2002.

Kasper, Cecilie and a classic Manchester United shirt.

Schmeichel & Son. With Kasper at a Sporting Lisbon training session. Our two years in Portugal were fantastic for his goalkeeping development.

Sven-Göran Eriksson managed Kasper at three clubs – here they are at Notts County.

Kasper vowed he would win the Premier League one day – and did so in Leicester's amazing campaign of 2015–16.

Above: Kasper stops Luka Modrić's extra-time spot-kick, but Croatia advance in the 2018 World Cup.

Left: With Sir Alex Ferguson at the Treble Reunion match in 2019. It was brilliant to hear one last team talk from the gaffer.

Below: Jaap Stam checks I'm still in one piece. After all my injuries over the years, I expected to play for a couple of minutes, but managed to last for half an hour.

Above: Kasper receives the trophy from Prince William in 2021 after captaining Leicester to their first ever victory in an FA Cup final.

Right: Laura, my soulmate. We love the outdoor life and I took this picture when we were out on one of our walks.

Like father, like daughter: Cecilie loves football and Manchester United. Here we are at the Treble Reunion in 2019, with the Premier League, FA Cup and Champions League trophies.

At the José Alvalade, the idea was each player would be introduced and trot to the centre circle, taking applause from the fans. They wanted to do it by shirt number so, as No 1, I was the first out. Our families were there and initially it was great. They called my name, the press officer pointed to the stage, I jogged out and there were my kids, running across the pitch to meet me. Fantastic. Two or three more players were introduced, but the crowd was getting more and more excited and, finally, could not contain itself. There was a pitch invasion. I grabbed Kasper and Cecilie and sprinted with them to a tunnel behind one of the goals, which led to the changing areas. Only the door was locked. With fans clamouring around us, someone from inside opened it and we took sanctuary in the dressing room. We were stuck there until four in the morning. It was crazy.

The title was Sporting's first since 1982 and it justified the move, for me. I had times, standing in the penalty area of some tiny, rural ground, when I asked myself, *Why?* Deep down, I knew I should really be somewhere like Old Trafford, Highbury or Anfield. The strangeness – and sadness – of no longer being a Manchester United player never quite left me. But I did what Sporting signed me for and that was to help deliver them back to the top of the Portuguese game. I had stayed a winner. That said to me that, in football terms, the move was okay. And from a human point of view, it was deeply enriching. After returning to England with Aston Villa in 2001, I kept our home in Cascais until 2006 and Portugal remains a favourite place to holiday and play golf. I'm remembered fondly by Sporting fans and that means a lot to me too.

* * *

Paulinho. Let me tell you about him. Just to have known Paulinho was worth the whole experience. His role at Sporting is indescribable, but I guess you could say he is an adult mascot. He could not even speak when he came to the club (though he does now) and he walks with one stiff leg. During my time, he slept three or four nights a week in the dressing room, despite having his own apartment. At first, you think he is a simpleton and feel sorry for him. Then you come to understand: he is one of the happiest, most magical people in the world.

The story goes that at birth he had some sort of problem and his family put him in a home. He grew up with learning difficulties and physical issues which meant he was bent over, nearly 90 degrees. The only word he could say, or would react to, was 'Sporting'. The football club was the light in his life. A visit was organised where he met the Sporting players and they took to him. 'Come and see us any time,' they said and Paulinho became a fixture around the dressing room. The players loved him but played all sorts of pranks on him. And Sporting eventually gave Paulinho a role.

He became assistant to the assistant-assistant kit man or something. Gradually, his back straightened up – it was probably down to all the stomach muscles he developed having to duck away from all the toy punches players aimed at him. He even took part in little training drills like penalty shoot-outs.

When I arrived, everyone said, 'You've got to meet Paulinho,' and I told him that in English, to say hello, you said, '**** you.' So, every morning he'd come up, bow, shake my hand and say, '**** you.' But he is no fool. His family abandoned him as a kid, but when his association with Sporting made him an institution in Portugal his family approached him, trying to get something out of his fame. He told them . . . well, what he told me every morning by way of a greeting. That showed the substance to him.

I absolutely adore him. Just being with him made me happy – and still does, when I go back to Sporting. He doesn't want money, he doesn't want celebrity, he just loves that football club and wants it to love him back. He works incredibly hard. If you asked him to clean your boots, they would come back as if brand new.

The culture at football clubs comes from beyond whoever the players, manager and board are at any given time. It comes from people. It comes from those who give rather than take – and, in life, true givers are rare. The first question I will ask about anything is why? I did that in football. *Why am I playing this game? Why am I playing for this club?* If Sporting had not taken Paulinho in, perhaps he would not even be alive, and I loved being at a club with a big heart like that. It was something that helped give my stay there meaning.

At Manchester United we did a little bit for everyone. We tried to meet as many requests from fans and the community as possible. New players followed the example of old ones: after training and matches, you spent time signing autographs. A good kit man like Albert and, before him, Norman Davies, plays a big part in setting the dressing-room mood. Kath Phipps has played a bigger role for the club than she could ever imagine. I first met her long before becoming a Manchester United player, in 1986, when I came to Manchester with Denmark Under-21s to face England Under-21s at Maine Road.

We practised at Manchester City's old training ground, Platt Lane, and after a session I persuaded our coach, Richard Møller Nielsen, to take a detour past Old Trafford even though it was nowhere near the route back to our hotel in the city centre. We parked up beside the Munich clock and I went into reception. I felt like a Catholic at the Vatican. Wide-eyed. Tingles.

I introduced myself to the lady behind the desk: it was Kath. I explained who I was and that I was a massive Manchester United fan and asked if I might sneak a peek inside the stadium. She made a call and the groundsman arrived, to take us out to see the pitch. I stood by a corner flag, just gazing at the grass. Wow. Wow. Wow.

It always struck me, from that day, the incredible capacity Kath possesses for tapping into what is important to other people. Throughout my years at United she opened my mail and sorted through the requests. I got into a routine of driving home past Old Trafford most days and sitting next to her for half an hour in reception, chatting through all the letters and composing replies.

When I return to Manchester United now and see Kath on reception, I get more tingles. I'll say, 'Kath – are you still here? You must be about 200 years old.' She'll laugh. On those visits I make a point of going round and saying hello to people, and the continuity is striking. Anne Wylie, the head of player care, has been in her post for more than thirty years. Many of the ground staff remain the same, like Lester, who looks after the dressing room. Tony Sinclair, the head groundsman, was a kid on the staff when I arrived.

When I played, most afternoons I would visit Old Trafford to hang out with the office people for a while. I did the same at Brøndby. It was about connecting – with the club and by extension the fans. I got to know the Kens – Ken Merrett and Ken Ramsden – who both served as club secretary. Then there was the incredible Lyn Laffin, Fergie's late secretary. She was like a person with seven brains and twenty-two arms, and had an amazing capacity for getting things done. Booking flights, finding a plumber, speaking to estate agents – she would do all that for you. All while organising the manager's complicated diary.

These were the people who made Manchester United special, as did the club's history. There was probably a time when the Glazer family's understanding of the institution they own was not up to the level it should have been and certain people were excluded from the directors' box, but all that has been corrected. Richard Arnold, who runs Manchester United on a daily basis, arrived from a commercial background but has grown to understand exactly what United means. You have Matt Busby's family still around on match days and Fergie has his seat in the box. I am one of a number of former players used as a club ambassador and the club has become better at tapping into its own, if you like, family stock.

Ole Gunnar Solskjær played a big role in bringing the meaning of Manchester United into the foreground again. While he was manager, he brought the heart and soul back to the club.

15

HAD BETTER DAYS

My last day at Sporting Lisbon should have been 26 May 2000 – exactly one year on from the dream night in the Nou Camp. A week after winning the league, we drew 1–1 with Porto in the final of the Taça de Portugal (Portuguese Cup). Four days later, on 25 May, at the Estádio Nacional in Lisbon, we lost the replay 2–0. I stormed off the pitch, furious for several reasons, but most were to do with the referee.

The next morning, I called Luís Duque to set up a meeting and went to his offices with Paul Stretford. For some time, Paul had been in dialogue with Fergie, who wanted to bring me back to Manchester United. And over the past three weeks Fergie had been nudging us. *Get yourself out of your contract there* was his message to me. *I can sign you, if you are on a free.*

A return to United was what I desired most. But I had not wanted to upset my club or interfere with our pursuit of trophies, so I decided to wait until the season was over before pulling the trigger. Looking back, that might have been a mistake. Anyway, as Paul and I were en route to see Duque, I called Fergie to update him.

'We're going to do this.'

'Good,' he said. 'Ring me when you're done.'

It promised to be quite a day. I yearned to be back at Old Trafford and Paul had brokered a good deal for me to return.

The contract, wages and all the details were agreed. I had been looking forward to getting things out in the open and making the move happen. In the evening, I was due to fly to Copenhagen to join up with Denmark and was excited about that too. We would be beginning preparations for Euro 2000 where, following our 1998 World Cup performance, we had a chance of doing well.

I felt ready to close my Portuguese chapter. It was nothing to do with Sporting or the country. I liked the club and loved living in Portugal, but I was struggling with the monotony of being a footballer in Portugal, of continually being in camp. I did not like being stuck in a hotel, bored out of my brain, being treated like a little kid – and then going and playing on some horse field in a village, when I had come from the venues of the Premier League and a system at United where a great manager gave a grown-up dressing room freedom and responsibility.

Carlos Freitas was with Duque and the meeting with them was bitter-sweet. They told me I was far too important to let go of, but I laid things out, on a personal level, without mentioning United. I said, 'Listen, if I had come here from Brøndby it would have been different, but it's too late in the day for me to get used to the Portuguese system. I'm thirty-six, I want to live as normal a life as possible and I want to return to England.' They listened and eventually said, 'Okay. We want you to stay. We love you. But we respect that you gave us a championship. You came on a free, so of course you can leave on a free as well.' It was humbling, even beautiful. To annul the contract, we had to sign new documents, get notaries in and everything countersigned, and this took a while – but finally it was done.

Driving away, both Paul and I had mixed feelings. We were happy the meeting had gone the way it did, yet sad because Duque, Freitas and their staff were all so sad. But I knew what I wanted. We rang Fergie from the car to tell him the good news. No reply. We rang again. No reply. We kept ringing and still he did not pick up. Eventually, I called Old Trafford and asked to be put through to Martin Edwards. I could hear straight away that something was wrong. 'Peter, it is out of my control,' Martin said. 'You'll need to speak to the manager.'

It is a forty-minute drive home from Sporting's offices to where I used to live. My house had entry gates and a driveway that sloped to the left to an underground garage. On the right, there was a walkway to the front door along which was the kennel for our two dogs. As I drove down to the garage, one dog jumped out in excitement and went under my wheels. It made a dreadful noise. 'Yowwwwwwwwwww.' I had such a horrible mix of feelings: worry about Fergie not answering and panic because I knew the dog was badly hurt.

It was a funny little dog, the cutest thing, a mix of every breed going and lovely as hell. We called it the circus dog. We got it from a stable and it could jump six feet. It was always full of beans. I called my ex-wife, who came home with the children and took the poor creature to the animal hospital. Everyone was devastated.

The dog went straight into intensive care and the vet gave it a 50–50 chance of surviving. Back at home, sitting talking to Paul, I just felt in shock. Where was Fergie? What was he up to? I just hadn't seen any complications coming.

I needed to pack and head to the airport with Paul. We were sitting in the departure lounge when, at the hundredth time of trying, Fergie finally answered his phone. Paul put him on loudspeaker. He was saying stuff like, 'Yeah, well, I have to do something else, I have to think about the future of the club . . .'

There would be no transfer.

I interrupted. 'What the **** are you on about? How dare you?' I said. 'We spoke to you this morning. If you knew all this, why didn't you stop me then? I've gone in, got my contract annulled and upset all the people at my club – for something you had decided wasn't going to happen.'

One thing with Fergie: when you came up with a good argument against him, he had nothing to say. He would never contest the point and be shown up as wrong. So, he repeated himself: 'Aah. I have to think about the future.' It turned out 'the future' was Fabien Barthez.

We ended the call. I sat there, stunned. I no longer had a contract – anywhere. I had lost a cup final the night before. I had run over my dog.

Soon my flight to Copenhagen would be boarding and this suddenly felt like the very worst afternoon. One of the things that was bothering me most was that I had told my kids we were going back to Manchester and they were happy. I had just said goodbye to them for half of the summer, and now I would have to call home and tell them the bad news.

Paul and I talked and came up with a plan. We would tell Sporting I had made a big mistake. That I had come home and told my family we were going back to England, but they had said, 'Absolutely no way. We love living here.' So Paul called Freitas and he was so happy to hear of my apparent change of heart. He would get the notaries back in and the annulment put in the bin.

I rang home and my ex-wife, having come back from the hospital, said the vets thought the dog was in good shape. They reckoned it would pull through. I made my flight and checked in to the hotel in Copenhagen where the squad was joining up the following morning, then I went out to see some friends who lived just up the road for dinner. After such a stressful day, it was nice to have a couple of drinks and I ended up staying out late, finishing in the nightclub at the hotel. When I woke the next morning, I had twenty, thirty missed calls and messages, all from my ex.

'Where the **** have you been?' she said, when I called. 'The dog is dead.'

At the Euros, Denmark conceded eight goals in three games, and we could have conceded twenty-five. We did not score a single one. We went to the tournament with the wrong squad and it was a complete waste of time. We took several injured players, hoping they would get themselves fit, but they never did. A rubbish tournament, just to round the summer off.

16

THREE BAD ENDINGS

The second season with Sporting was my worst in football, not because of how I played but how other things worked out. The club sold Duscher and Vidigal, our engine room, and acquired a whole gang of players, most of them on free transfers, including Sá Pinto, João Pinto and Dimas. Those three were good, experienced footballers, starters for Portugal, but Sá Pinto got injured and Dimas was a left back. We didn't need a left back. We already had a good one, Rui Jorge.

Selling talent and player trading is Sporting's model. In hindsight, I understand that. But at the time the changes annoyed me. They weakened the team and then the directors went out and said, 'Now we're going to win the Champions League.' We didn't even get out of our group.

After another summer without a rest, thanks to Euro 2000, my body broke down. A pain in my right knee got worse and worse and worse. I needed an operation to shave my patella down and missed a chunk of games because of the rehab. One of those was a disastrous derby with Benfica. They hammered us 3–0 in the Estádio da Luz. Their brash young coach sprinted down the touchline on three occasions – each time a goal went in – milking the acclaim of his fans. That whipped our supporters to a peak of fury.

Sporting sacked Augusto Inácio the next day and the day after that, the Benfica coach quit his job. Rumours flew that he was coming to us. Our fans protested and within hours the car park in front of the José Alvalade was filled with demonstrators. 'We don't want him, we don't want him,' they chanted. Our board, terrified of the media, abandoned plans to recruit the guy.

He was José Mourinho. I had it confirmed, subsequently, that he was lined up and ready to become our manager. So – the last chapter of my career might have involved playing for José and I do wonder how that would have turned out. Just three seasons later he made Porto Champions League winners. What Sporting did after missing out on Mourinho was bring Inácio straight back. Great. I loved Inácio. He took one training session – and the next day they sacked him again.

In came Fernando Mendes, an old guy who had been working with the Under-17s and whose heyday was twenty years in the past, when he had won a championship. He was completely out of touch with modern football. After a month they sacked him too.

Manuel Fernandes took over. He had been top scorer of Sporting's 1982 title-winning team. His coaching experience amounted to stints with little clubs, like Tirsense and Santa Clara, and his biggest claim to fame was scoring four goals in a 7–1 derby rout of Benfica back in the day. On the bus, going to his first away match in charge, he put that game on the TV and sat back to enjoy watching himself. He lost all the players in one go, there and then. As a coach he was clueless: having spent a career battling relegation, he was frightened of every team we played, no matter how small.

I had an option to extend my contract, but I was done with camps and done with how Sporting was being run. Paul sounded out clubs in England. Aston Villa were interested and from the start I liked the idea. Villa was a massive club, always difficult to play against, and Kent Nielsen had played for Villa. I remembered how much my old friend from Brøndby had loved the place. Villa was also a neutral kind of club, where former Manchester United players, like Paul McGrath, had been successful but still accepted by United fans. That was very important to me.

I only had to speak to John Gregory once to know this was a guy I wanted to work with. He looked the part, and in management that does count. He appeared an authoritative figure, sharp and smart, but when he talked you quickly realised there was a human streak in him and a good understanding of human behaviour and human needs. There was just one thing about John I did not like, which was that on the touchline he would whistle all the time. It grated on me.

I looked at Villa's squad. Paul Merson, David Ginola, Dion Dublin, Mustapha Hadji, Steve Staunton, George Boateng, Alpay, Juan Pablo Ángel, Hassan Kachloul: pretty good. Coming through was an incredible crop of young players: Lee Hendrie, Gareth Barry, Mark Delaney, Jlloyd Samuel, Darius Vassell. At first, everything was as I had hoped. I felt John was a top manager. Like Fergie, he clearly liked big, vocal characters in his dressing room and could deal with them well. His team talks were very good. Precise and to the point. You would come in at half-time and he would turn to Paul and say, 'Merse, you take it.' He let the players do a lot of the talking because they were the ones on the pitch, feeling the game. Then at the end he would say a couple of well-chosen words. I felt respected as a human being and that this was a high-performance environment, where the demand to perform as a top professional was there. You were given responsibility.

The next guy was the opposite. We'll get to that.

The dressing room? A really enjoyable place. Merse, I got in a good moment. By that point he had already come out about his addiction problems and what I loved was he wanted to protect the young players, educate them not to make the mistakes he made. He would talk to the group about his experiences. He told us stories about the crazy things he had done. Stuff like, 'Here I was, Paul Merson, playing for England and I found myself in a crack den in shorts . . . by the way, my England shorts.'

We had players from areas of Birmingham where there were big drug problems and he wanted to help them out. He wanted to help everyone. He laid himself bare and I had incredible respect for that. I suspected that while he was out of the bad old situations in a physical sense, he was still there in his head, fighting his issues every day. I thought him very brave, brave enough to ask for help on a daily basis. The help was we listened and let him get his problems out.

Dion Dublin is one of my favourite people in football, just the nicest guy, respectful to everyone. There was a depth to Dion in terms of culture that I loved – it was unusual, being in a dressing room with someone with similar interests to me in jazz music and other arts. Ginola, Kachloul, Hadji and me became a crew. We found ourselves in the same boat: grown-up men, living in Birmingham away from our families (Kasper and Cecilie had stayed in Copenhagen for school), and we met two or three nights a week to eat together. David stayed in a chic boutique hotel with a lovely bar, where we would go for tea. Mustapha took us to Moroccan restaurants in town. It was a long time since I had socialised with anyone from the dressing room and it was nice to have that for a year.

We led the Premier League after ten games. We were still seventh late in January 2002, when John Gregory left after a wrangle with Doug Ellis over transfers. John Deehan and Stuart Gray took temporary charge but I began mulling things over. I phoned Paul and said what do you think, would I be capable of caretaking? He said, 'Oh, by the way, yeah. Oh yeah.' He suggested I call Fergie. I told him I was thinking about throwing my hat in the ring to be Villa's caretaker manager: obviously, I would have to prove I was up to the job. Fergie was highly encouraging. He said he would phone Doug Ellis for me. Soon, he rang back. He said he could not get hold of Doug, but had called Graham Taylor, who was Villa's director of football.

Up to that point, Taylor had been very nice to me. Almost every match day he would come up and say, 'Pete, it's so great to have you, the fans love you, I can see your influence being spread through the squad.' And Fergie told me, 'When I talked to Graham, he said they're already speaking about you for the job. Expect to be approached.' I was very excited. That evening, I went to watch the reserves. I was a regular at their matches. I would sit in the stand talking to the coaches and thinking about the players. Mentally, I was starting the transition into management.

My routine involved getting to the training ground early, breakfasting there while reading the papers, and spending time chatting to staff. The next day I arrived at Bodymoor Heath at

7.30 a.m. Once all the players were in, Doug Ellis appeared and said he wanted everyone to go to the meeting room straight away. He said, 'I want to introduce your new manager.' In walked . . . Graham Taylor.

The temperature in the room dropped. Taylor talked for an hour and finished by saying, 'I want the first team in the dressing room.' There, brandishing a sheaf of papers, he told us, 'I'm not one of them new, modern managers into all this data stuff. I do things by intuition. *But . . .*' The papers were Prozone print-outs and he said we were not running enough in games.

Before his first match, we did set pieces. We had not conceded a single goal from a set piece all season. Taylor wanted to change how we organised when defending them. I said, 'Gaffer, why do you want to do this?'

He didn't like that. 'I am the manager and you will do what I say,' he said, raising his voice.

We began conceding goals from corner kicks, and after we lost to Middlesbrough – whose winner from Ugo Ehiogu came, yes, at a corner – I was at the training ground having my breakfast, looking through the back pages. Deehan tapped me on the shoulder. 'Gaffer wants to see you.'

I went to Taylor's office and he said, 'Listen, I'm not taking up the option to extend your contract another year.'

I replied that I did not want to stay anyway.

'And you're not playing any more,' he added. 'I need to see my options for next season.'

Was he kidding? He then went on about not wanting to be the manager who presided over my decline. 'You've had such a great career. I won't let it happen on my watch,' he said.

Hmm. I had been playing well, keeping clean sheets in one third of my games under Gregory and even scoring with a volley when I came up for a corner at Everton. Look, Taylor achieved a lot with Watford and in his first spell at Villa, and was respected and liked in football and media circles, so my purpose is not to speak ill of him. But I owe it to Villa fans to be honest about my departure: There was so much I enjoyed about the club, but it wasn't the same for me after he took over.

After our meeting, I called Paul Stretford and we talked through my options. I wanted to be a manager. I had learned from Fergie and knew how the master approached the job. But I also wanted to absorb other examples. Inácio had been a great coach, Gregory a superb man-manager, but my time with both had been short and Morten Olsen had been early in my career, before I started thinking too much about how managers did their jobs. I wanted to learn more and was intrigued by Kevin Keegan. He had been such a brilliant manager for Newcastle and done well at Fulham. He was top of the Championship and clearly set to take Manchester City back into the Premier League.

Here was someone I was keen to work for. I wanted to see the magic. What was it about Keegan that made players, everywhere he went, play out of their skins? So when Paul said Manchester City might be interested, I was excited. The rivalry between the Manchester clubs in 2002 was nothing like it is in 2021. Manchester United had conquered Europe and been English champions seven times in the previous ten seasons, whereas Manchester City had spent half that time outside the Premier League. This was six years before Sheikh Mansour and they bore no comparison to the Manchester City of now.

They were part of a good-natured local rivalry, but just not seen as Manchester United's direct competitors. Going there would not be particularly controversial. Plenty of other former Manchester United players had made the same move, but I did want to make doubly sure that everything would be okay with my former club, so I called Fergie. 'City?' he said. 'That's not a bad idea.' He liked the fact I was thinking about management and had started my B Licence at Villa. He gave his blessing and said I could ring any time: he would support me.

I loved the prospect of living near Manchester again and suspected my family would jump at the chance of going back. In the three years we had spent away from the area, Bente had realised it was a great place after all. The kids had grown up in Bramhall and that carried value. As soon as I mentioned Manchester City, they said, 'We're coming.' This move just seemed the right one.

Keegan was not the boss I had hoped he would be. He loved big stars, but was not always successful at managing them. We had Nicolas Anelka, who was always late and never seemed to care. Our biggest talent was Eyal Berkovic and I became a sounding board for Eyal, because he was someone who, if you put your arm round his shoulder, would give a lot back. Yet under Keegan he felt ignored.

Our last pre-season game was at Preston. I leant back to catch a cross and upon landing felt something go in my left knee. Rob Harris, our head physio, came on but could not find anything wrong. I played on and after another minute was in pain again, so went off.

Rob and the doc examined me properly at half-time. They suspected my cruciate had gone and thoughts started running through my head. I would be out for a year – and I was nearly thirty-nine. Imagine the controversy of me signing for Manchester City then not actually playing for them. And was *this* how bad a cruciate felt? I could not believe the pain. It was like I had been shot.

There were eighteen days before our first Premier League game, against Leeds. Well, that was out. At this point, I loved Keegan. He had a long chat with me after the game. This is football, he said, this stuff happens, consider it a challenge: late in your career, can you come back from such a blow?

'You have a fight in front of you and I will help you win that fight,' Keegan concluded. I was appreciative and felt a whole lot happier.

I drove home. My family were still in Denmark making preparations to move back over. I was renting a place by myself, a little townhouse on a farm development. I had to get out of the car to open the gates and it was excruciating. Even after chugging painkillers, I barely slept. The next morning, Rob was coming to take me to get scanned and see a knee specialist, and when the buzzer for the gates went, I tried to get to the entry phone. I took a step from my bed and my knee collapsed. The pain was like nothing I had known. I passed out for a few seconds.

I hauled myself off the floor, let Rob in and went for the scan. It confirmed ligament damage, but not to the ACL: to the posterior cruciate ligament. The doc felt there was no point operating because this was an injury that should only really affect me when I planted my leg, stepping back – something I could avoid in training and not have to do too often in games. Rob started my rehab the next day and when he checked the joint said, 'This is weird. Normally there would be more give, but your knee is unusually stable.'

We realised that, with this stability, I could actually start putting in a bit of physical work and that I might not be out for very long. We settled into a programme. I would come in early and get treatment from Rob first thing, so that I did not take up any time that he needed to spend with the rest of the players. When they came in to get worked on before training, I would go to the gym. When they trained, I had more treatment, then had more again post-lunch, once the other lads had left. After that, I would do a training session by myself. I then went home, rested and had dinner, and then at 9 p.m. Rob and I met again at Total Fitness in Wilmslow for another session. We did this every day for a month.

I missed Leeds but played the next game, versus Newcastle, keeping a clean sheet. Rob created a little extension to my shin pad which absorbed some of the impact when I landed on my left knee. I was finding that my only real issue came when I landed directly on the knee, pushing my lower leg backwards – but how often was that going to happen? No more than two or three times in a game.

Sometimes, there would be a wave of excruciating pain from my joint, but I would carry on through it. I was getting stronger and playing well. Rob, a New Zealander recruited from Wigan rugby league, was the best physio I had ever seen – and I had worked with some brilliant ones – while our fitness coach was also sensationally good: Juan Carlos Osorio, who managed Mexico at the 2018 World Cup. Manchester City had gone out to recruit the best physio and best conditioning guy in the world and, in finding that pair, had done a pretty good job of meeting their target. There was one problem. Rob and Juan Carlos were not Keegan's staff; they were club appointees.

When Keegan found out about our sessions at Total Fitness he was bitterly unhappy. He told Rob it was forbidden to work with players outside of the club and accused him of disloyalty. His behaviour disappointed me. It felt very unfair on Rob and I was trying to recover from injury – I didn't want unnecessary noise around it. When he fell out with Rob for such petty reasons, he lost me. I started to see him differently.

Joey Barton was a rough-edged kid with a bit of talent. He might have avoided the trouble he got into as a younger man, and done more in his career, had Keegan not indulged him, treated him as a playmate, allowed him to walk around talking tough. Every afternoon, I would see them playing head tennis in the gym. I hated that. It seemed a million miles away from how Fergie fostered discipline and respect in young players.

In training one day I got the ball and threw it out quickly to Shaun Goater, aiming to turn defence into attack. Shaun lost the ball. No big deal. Derek Fazackerley, Keegan's assistant, yelled at me. 'Pete, you can't do that.' I was, 'What? I've been doing that my whole career.' We had a heated argument on the pitch.

When the session was over, Keegan called me to his office. He would sit at his desk with Arthur Cox, his old assistant and comfort blanket, in the corner. Arthur never said much, just went around with a *Cough, cough, hey, y'know*. Keegan told me off for challenging Fazackerley. I wasn't having it. I pointed out that quick distribution had always been one of my strengths and, instead of trying to change me, at the age of thirty-eight, maybe he could try and build a pattern of play around that attribute. Keegan said nothing.

Arthur followed me out of the office. *Cough, cough*. 'Pete,' he said in his deep voice, 'you're an experienced player and you can't talk to your manager like that. You have to let things go. Y'know.'

This, I thought, is like a kindergarten. By Christmas I had decided I was not going to play beyond the end of the season. The enthusiasm had been sucked out of me. My body ached in so many places, my back, my shoulders, my knee. I always promised myself that if I woke up one morning and thought, *I don't want to do this any more*, that would be the point I would call it a day. And there I was, driving to work, having to fight to summon the enthusiasm to go through the training-ground gates.

I drew on my experience of 1998–99 when, having announced in November that I was leaving Manchester United at the end of the season, I had to talk about it for the next six months. So, for the moment, I kept my thoughts to myself. I had a column in the *Sunday Times* and decided to use that to announce my retirement when the time was right. In the end, I waited until mid-April before doing so. I still had mixed feelings. John Wardle was the loveliest of guys, a great chairman, and there were some wonderful people at the club.

We had some good players too. Richard Dunne and Steve Howey, Niclas Jensen, Marc-Vivien Foé, Shaun Wright-Phillips, Goater. Eyal and Ali Benarbia. Sylvain Distin, Sun Jihai – what a footballer he was. Darren Huckerby, Paulo Wanchope, Kevin Horlock, Danny Tiatto . . . I could go on. It was a decent squad and, to be fair to Keegan, he knew how to be competitive in the Premier League. He did what he had done throughout his career, which was to buy experienced players who could do the job and not think too much about development.

We were a team, though, which had good days and bad days. We could win 2–0 at Spurs but be beaten 5–0 by Chelsea. When that happened, at Stamford Bridge in March, it underlined how little some players really cared. Half of the lads had transport waiting for them at the filling station on Fulham Road and as soon as we got back to the dressing room someone said to me, 'Hey, if you want to come now, we can catch an earlier flight home.' Feeling humiliated and just wanting to get out of there, I said okay. We had the quickest shower and ten minutes later were running through the crowd of spectators still leaving the stadium to get to these cars. Embarrassing.

My last away game was at Anfield. I look back on the day with pride. Liverpool had a superb team and I made one of my best ever saves, from an El Hadji Diouf shot. He was close in and I was unsighted but got down low to my right and managed to deflect the ball upwards against the bar. I jumped straight back onto my feet and leapt up to catch the rebound too. We won 2–1.

Let me tell you about the Kop in my day. They pulled a trick on away goalkeepers. When you ran out at Anfield, they applauded you. The first time, you applauded back – and they laughed. 'You're shit!' Then the pies, coins and lighters would start raining down. But for my last game there, I was Manchester City captain and chose to defend the Kop End, and when I jogged towards it, the Liverpool fans stood and clapped, with genuine feeling. I waved back – and they amplified their clapping. That was a fine, fine moment for me. You spend your career being hated by a set of fans, who hate the club you love, but at the same time they respect you and respect the game. Rivalry aside, I respect Liverpool and their supporters back.

My final game in professional football was also Maine Road's last match. Two dinosaurs put to bed at the same time, eh? The meaning of the occasion, to the club we played for, should have motivated our players – but a couple appeared not to care, and Maine Road's farewell fell flat. We lost 1–0 to Southampton and that day, for me, reflected the flawed culture Keegan was responsible for. When you lead a group, you have to instil a sense of mission. What do we want from this game, this season? What are we willing to invest? Instead, there was no sense that anything was being developed or built. Most of the players were great, but one or two just seemed to be collecting their money, passing through.

I was ready for the next stage of my life. I have never been a sentimental guy. When I move on, I move on – so there were no tears or regrets about my 748th game in senior club football being my last. I was thinking about positives. About getting control of my life back after putting full-time football first since the age of twenty-three.

At the back of my mind, I also felt that by retiring I would help Kasper. He was sixteen, progressing quickly at Manchester City and moving into that grey area between youth and senior football. I knew I had to give him space, not overshadow him or pile on the pressure by still being around. Already, I had a sixth sense that things were going to be difficult for him on account of his name. I looked at sons of famous players like Paul Dalglish and Jordi Cruyff and the challenges they experienced when trying to establish themselves in their own right. I witnessed Jordi's first-hand. When he joined Manchester United he said he wanted to be known as Jordi and given any number other than 14. The club gave him 'Cruyff 14'.

There was one more reason to be thankful about retirement. I would never have to play against Manchester United again. Those times I did, it amplified a horrible, nagging sense that had lurked at the back of my mind from the day I left United in 1999. That, now, I was . . . *less*. Even in the good times during the last four years of my career, I could never quite shake off that sickening feeling.

In my short spell at Villa, we played Manchester United on three occasions. Each time it lowered my sense of worth. I remember the first match. I would be facing Ruud van Nistelrooy. I did not even know the guy, and yet he was now the big thing at *my* club, *my* Manchester United. That felt so alienating. I hated the whole game, a 1–1 draw at Villa Park. We also played United at home in the FA Cup and I got through that. The match I really struggled with was the one at Old Trafford, in the league. I walked in through the players' entrance . . . and I had to go to the wrong dressing room, the away one. I hated the media attention on me too.

The overriding feeling I had around those matches was of being on the wrong team. It felt like I was only playing for my team because I was not good enough to be on the other side. I had never felt anything like that in my life. Probably part of my talent was that in my own ignorance, or arrogance, I told myself, 'I am the best. Nothing can beat me.' But when you're playing against United, you are not the best. If you were the best, you would be playing for them.

I would look at my old mates on the pitch, Fergie on the side: my team.

Why am I not in that team? *Because you're not good enough, Pete.* God, I really struggled with that.

My worst experience was in the Manchester derby at Maine Road. *Why am I even playing against United in a derby?* Keegan, being Keegan, casually handed me the armband. 'You take it today.' I could have screamed. Didn't he understand? But you cannot refuse an armband. That would be to dishonour the club to which it belongs and give the wrong message to your team-mates.

I was warming up and collected a ball. As I bent down for it this woman, in her sixties or seventies, leaned over and screeched, '******* Schmeichel, let's see where your ******* loyalties are today!' That threw me. She was a *City* fan. To play a game of top-level football, you have to get yourself into a mental bubble and stay there, maintain total focus. But this woman's reaction stayed with me and played with my head.

When we scored I thought, *Right, I am playing for this team, I'm captain, I have to show I care.* So, I celebrated. I should never have celebrated. We won 3–1 and I walked off the pitch hating myself. It was the first and only game in my life that I won and did not enjoy. I was upset and angry when I got home.

I don't know if it was the stress of it, whether it was genuine pain or in my mind, but in training the day before the return game at Old Trafford, my back went again. I told myself I could not duck out of the match, I could not give myself an excuse, so I tried to play. I worked with Rob all afternoon and in the morning felt okay. But when I went out for the warm-up at Old Trafford, the pain returned sharply again. I had to come in and say to Rob, 'I can't play.' To this day, I am not clear whether it was a psychological or physical thing, but I am so happy I took no part in the match. Even if there is a little voice deep inside that tells me maybe I ducked out of it.

It is what it is, but I am sad my time at Manchester City has been used, by some, to detract from my Manchester United career. If I had ever imagined City would one day be United's competitor and that, by being there, I might help them progress towards that, I would never have played for them. I could never have played for Liverpool, Arsenal or Chelsea, and that's why, when I returned to England, Villa was the perfect fit: big ground, fantastic club, but not Manchester United's rival. At the time I joined Manchester City, they were the same.

It annoys me that some people, now, applying the logic of who Manchester City are in 2021 and not what Manchester City were in 2002, try to question my loyalty to Manchester United. It annoyed me that Fergie allowed talk to spread that he was not happy about me playing for City – when in reality he was encouraging when I called to get his opinion on the move. Let's be absolutely clear. I did not betray Manchester United. I played fair with Manchester United. My greatest desire after leaving Manchester United was to go back there and I put myself on the line, in Portugal, to make it happen. If there was betrayal, it was not by me.

But it is all part of my story. It's football. I am the luckiest man in the world because I played for Manchester United and I now work for Manchester United all over again. The final three years of my career probably featured as many bad experiences as positive ones, but I can have no complaints about how good football was to me overall.

If I had to post a status update on my career it would read, 'Happy, really happy.' And in those post-Manchester United years, my biggest goal was to find experiences that would help me learn – and learn I did.

Anticlimaxes and knocks? It's the game. It's life. You pick apples from the tree and you fall off the branch. You get up and climb again. You recover from adversity.

No regrets.

17
LIFE AFTER FOOTBALL

My life after football started while I was still playing, in some ways. In April 2002, I was nearing the end of my time at Aston Villa and one of the FA Cup semi-finals – Fulham v Chelsea – was at Villa Park. The BBC asked me to be on their panel. Until then, I had kind of avoided the media. I did not like interviews and did not view journalists with trust. So I told the Beeb I was not sure about my language skills in English and that maybe it wasn't for me. But they were persuasive. You'll be fine, they said; come give it a go.

They added that I would be on with Gary Lineker, Mark Lawrenson and Alan Hansen and promised those three would look after me. I mulled things over and said okay. I absolutely loved it. The BBC asked me back for the FA Cup final in Cardiff and then to be part of their World Cup coverage and I was involved until the quarter-finals. I discovered television was something I found interesting, something I enjoyed and could imagine doing for a couple of years. After announcing my retirement in 2003, I signed a contract to do *Football Focus* and a few live BBC games.

This meant putting the move into management that I imagined making on the back burner, but I told myself it would only be for a while. The end at Manchester City had been so disillusioning that giving myself some space before jumping back into the game seemed no bad thing. And having a job as soon as I finished made a hell of a difference to me compared to other guys who retire.

It meant that instantly there was something to look forward to. I went to London every Friday, filmed *Football Focus* on Saturday, then travelled home. I had the rest of my week to explore other things. Life was good. Albeit that all the time I was thinking, *This is not what I will do for ever.*

I still envisaged ending up back in football. We lived in Alderley Edge, where I had bought a lovely old house, a former bishop's lodge, 125 years old. It was the best house I ever had. From there, you were a few minutes from the village centre and around there were acres of farmland. Every day, I would go out with the dog and spend hours walking the fields. I had a little loop that would take me all the way round the outside of the village. The time to myself, in the fresh air, was precious because when you quit as a footballer you are on your own for the first time in your adult life. There are years of adrenaline to let go of and a tangle of thoughts and feelings to unravel. People in normal jobs wind down towards retirement, but a footballer makes the transition in the blink of an eye. It tests you to the core.

I used those long walks to talk to myself. I talked about what life was about, what I wanted to do with my time, who I was supposed to be. *How* I wanted to be. Because, retired, you have to go back to being who you really are – if you can remember who that person is. You can no longer claim extra-special treatment. As a player you are looked after, timetabled, monitored, motivated, fed. You are flattered and applauded. There is not much in life you really have to do for yourself. Even in your own home, you are a prince. Your needs and your routine take precedence – because you have to be ready to play. Everything is you, you, you.

Then you quit. Now, you do not have to be ready to play. Or ready for anything, really. You cannot claim so much attention from other people. In your house you are not the most important person any more. You become quite conflicted with yourself. *Wow, I'm not a footballer any more, so I am a . . . What is my identity?*

I had the fittest dog in the world. He was out with me every day I was at home, sunshine, snow and wind. On those walks I pondered, muttered, cleared my head. Some ex-players compare retiring to leaving the army, and I get that. One of the greatest challenges is replacing your old routine. As a player, except for your very brief summer holidays, every day for twenty, twenty-five years you have a strict schedule: training ground first thing, breakfast, treatment, training at 10.30, lunch, more treatment, analysis meeting, gym, home, eat, sleep, do it again.

Try replacing that overnight. I started going to the driving range every day at exactly the same time I would have gone to training, on the dot. I began lining up golf games. Alan McInally lived on the other side of the M6 and we would meet up for rounds that I booked to take place during training time. I think people who have been in the army call themselves 'institutionalised', and I was similar. The bubble you enter as a teenage footballer, and are protected by right up to the start of middle age, really bursts.

Another challenge is to your fitness. Why did I retire? Why do most players retire? Because they can no longer stand going into training. But very quickly you realise that not training is a bad idea. You start blowing up because you eat more than you should. You drink more. After a few months I looked at this big, red-cheeked guy in the mirror and was a bit embarrassed. I tried hitting the gym but I cannot describe anything I would rather do less. I used to go to Total Fitness in Wilmslow, a nice place, but as soon as I walked through the doors, I had no inspiration. I hated it, absolutely hated it. That has been my story with gyms ever since. I am fitter and slimmer at fifty-seven than I was at forty because I either do my exercise outside – on the bike, riding by the waterside or in the forest near my home – or with a personal trainer. Committing to a programme with a good PT works for me. It has confirmed to me that I'm a team player, that I don't train alone.

As you stumble along as a newly retired footballer, what you are doing is searching. You are looking for replacements. How can I replace *that* with this? What would give me these things I loved so much about my old life? You think and think, you experiment, but then it hits you. Nothing will replace being a footballer. *Nothing ever, ever, ever, ever.* You can complain all you like when you are a player, 'This is wrong, that is wrong,' but if you really knew what life is like after playing you would shut your mouth. You would accept every bit of adversity, all the bad times as well as the good.

That's just the honest truth. You see a lot of former players getting depressed, a lot who you know are putting up a front.

The truly happy guys you meet are the guys who have roles in football.

A conclusion I came to while out in those fields was that managing remained what I wanted to do most. As I walked, I tried to formulate what my values were, trying to predict situations I might find myself in as a boss. How would I deal with that, what would I say to the players? You could say I was play-acting, rehearsing. I was trying to prepare myself mentally for what I was sure would come next, to clarify the manager I would be. I was certainly not going to be Alex Ferguson. Nobody can be Alex Ferguson. We all know examples of ex-Fergie players who have gone out and tried to be like him. It does not work.

These conversations under my breath and with the dog went on for years, by the way. I am not talking about a spell of a few months, I am talking about *years*. And then – all of a sudden, it felt – I found that eight of them had passed. By then, immersed in my TV career, I had moved back to Denmark because much of my work was there but found myself still broadcasting, yet still thinking (or was it now fantasising?) I would one day move into management. And, because I had retired at almost forty and then had these few years in television, time had marched on. Suddenly I was approaching fifty. I thought, *Woah*.

What prompted me to take stock was a call from Neil Bailey. Neil had been youth coach at Manchester United and now worked for the PFA as a regional coach educator for north-west England. In 2001, while at Villa, I had started my B Licence. It involved a two-week residential course, after which you completed some work, then went back for another residential stint before more work, and then being assessed for your badge.

You had ten years to book yourself in for the assessment part. When Neil rang he said, 'Listen, Pete, if you don't finish your B Licence this year, you will lose it.'

I did my bits and bobs with him and completed the badge. I thought I might as well do my A Licence and enrolled straight away, but found it completely uninspiring. The format was similar. A residential course, some work, then another ten days' residential: all of it going through the motions, learning what you already knew in the first place. You took a coaching session, for which you were miked up and filmed, and my feedback was a whole page, written in tiny letters that were difficult to read. I didn't go back for the ten further residential days.

Then Neil rang and said, 'Listen, we've changed the course, we understand that for ex-players it has to be different.' The new format involved one-to-one tuition and studying in short blocks rather than long residential spells. He told me Dwight Yorke was doing his badge, so Dwight and I teamed up and enjoyed getting our A Licence together, with Neil assessing.

This encouraged me to do the Pro Licence and I really loved that. It was the first course where I really learned something I could see was of very real value for the type of role that would suit me in football. The coaching element? That is not what enthused me. I know I will never be a particularly good coach. But I do know I could be a very good leader. I can take people with me. I am interested in leadership methods and philosophies. I have ideas about how I would like to lead people.

Fergie was an incredible leader and a very ordinary coach – so it worked for the greatest. On those rare occasions when Fergie had to take training, it was a great source of amusement to the players. I remember him starting one session, getting fifteen minutes in, being all over the place and turning to Brucey and going, 'Ach, you take it.' So, being in charge of a team, with outstanding coaches working under me, was what appealed – and still does.

Maybe it is getting late in the day, but who knows? If the right opportunity was there, I would definitely do it. But it would have to be right. I have a full life, plenty of work, and I am a happy man: I don't sit regretting not being in the game. It has got to the point where the average reign for club managers in top leagues is forty games. If I could be guaranteed three years and the chance to build something properly, I would take it on. But would I risk my health, my sanity, for forty games? No way.

I look at Brucey, my mate. He is a damn good manager, by the way, but how many times has he had to go through being let down by a club, being sacked and having to start again? After the Pro Licence I took another qualification, the FA Level 5 course for technical directors, and that is a role that appeals. For me, the lingering interest in going back into the game is nothing to do with money or an ego trip but about the idea of building, creating. The adventure of taking something from one point to another and making it better.

The challenge I have is that I know precisely what I want. I have strong convictions, I'm certainly not a yes man. I am well aware that for a certain type of owner – I'd say the wrong one – this may be off-putting. Also, I have never ever applied for anything, or touted myself around. I get that mentality from my father. I could apply for a million manager's jobs, get one and get sacked – but be considered 'a manager now', be on the merry-go-round. And the next job would follow. But I don't want that. It's not me.

Outside football, you can replace the routine, reforge an identity, restore the sense of purpose in the end. But can you replicate the excitement? When I look at my working life after playing, the best times have been when there is excitement.

Seventeen years after retiring as a goalkeeper, television is still my main job and it brings me a lot of pleasure, but what I love most are those rare moments when I am truly on the spot, when I have to perform. Briefly, it becomes a half-substitute for playing. Half, because you have still rehearsed and prepared, and TV programmes follow set schedules and formats – whereas in football every game is completely unpredictable.

A life in football takes away your ability to be a normal person. You have been addicted to pressure, even fear. You always long for some of the old nervousness to come back. The closest thing to playing, in TV, is when you are doing live shows with a studio audience. I hosted a charity show in Denmark to raise money for breast cancer research. My co-hosts were two women and one was Camilla Ottesen, a fantastic host who I had worked with before. The first time we met we quickly bonded, finding we were on the same wavelength.

Now, when you are doing a studio show like that, the anecdotes and links have to be delivered with the right timing and right wording, and you move around the stage in a way that is planned in advance. The preparation is considerable and we had a rehearsal earlier in the day and a dress-rehearsal before the audience arrived. It came to the live show and during the countdown to the credits I had an impulse. I looked at the two girls and said, 'Do you know your stuff?' They said, 'Yeah.' I said, 'Okay, let's throw the cue cards away.' Camilla said, 'Yes!' The other said no. Camilla and I did the whole show without prompts or autocue. Knowing that we were on the spot, that we had to be on our game and we had brought the pressure on ourselves, made it feel just a little like playing.

I hosted a Champions League draw from Monaco once when the production company messed up and, as I walked onstage with my co-host, Melanie Winiger, our in-ear communication went down. This meant we were on our own, with no help from the floor. We had to lead everything ourselves and get it right. That was one of the most enjoyable shows of my life.

My first big TV stint was *Match of the Day*. I was cautious about a lot of things, not least my language. I knew I could not be as good as Alan Hansen, because he had done it so long and had the timing. In my contract I wanted to have performance coaching. One challenge you face at the start when you move into punditry is you are still a footballer inside. You do not want to criticise people you still see as your colleagues, to upset them, because you know how infuriating it is when pundits are unfair. So, I was very cautious in how I talked about players on the show, and maybe that made me look bland.

Anyway, I enjoyed *MOTD* and found my feet there, but things did not end tidily. I was called up to Niall Sloane's office one day, the BBC's then head of football, and Niall said, 'Pete, I have to tell you, you're off the show.' He wanted to bring Alan Shearer in, which was fair enough, but his ideas for alternative ways to use me were not appealing, so I said, 'I'm not budging, we made a deal.' I had a three-year contract to do *MOTD* and this was year one. We fell out and Niall said, 'Okay, you're not doing anything for us, then.' The lawyers came in. I left, being told I would never work for the BBC again.

By then I had another very enjoyable gig, hosting Champions League coverage for TV3 in Denmark. It was great. I worked with good people and helped develop the product, while the station grew and grew. I was with them for eight years. Since then, apart from hosting 2014 World Cup coverage for TV2 in Denmark, most of my work has been with English or US broadcasters – and, of course, I did work for the BBC again.

Every year from when the show was launched, I was asked to be on *Strictly Come Dancing* and in year four I eventually said yes. I danced with Erin Boag; it was brilliant. While in the studios, I would go over and chat to all the old *MOTD* guys and everything was forgiven and forgotten. I started doing stuff, once again, on the various *MOTD* shows. I especially love working with Mark Chapman, an incredible host with a rare gift for driving the show without ever trying to make himself the most important person onscreen. You find the bad hosts are the interrupters and the good are those who let you flow.

Most of my punditry now is for CBS, which I love because they work to the very highest values, and PLP, the Premier League's host broadcaster, whose programmes go to rights holders across the world, reaching massive audiences. In those early *MOTD* shows, because of language issues I probably took too much time for their liking to deliver my analysis and was often interrupted before making my point. Something you learn over time is to make your points more sharply and quickly. Delivering criticism also comes with age and experience: you get to understand how far you should go and fair ways in which you can criticise.

I enjoy CBS and PLP because they give you space. Let's say a goalkeeper makes a mistake. In their shows, I can say, 'Yes, that was an error but what you have to know is . . .' and have room to explain the action from the keeper's point of view. That is the pundit's job, after all. You are there to put the viewer on the pitch, not just fill up a few seconds with words. I believe sports broadcasting is moving, in general, towards the quality approach. It is why Sky's *Monday Night Football* is so good: you have experts taking their time to talk about the detail of the game and bringing the layman onto the field of play.

TV work has helped me continue enjoying one of the gifts my playing career gave me: travel. At the 2018 World Cup, I made a show for RT that involved travelling Russia, exploring the cultures and traditions of host cities. I learned how to make gold bars in Ekaterinburg, rode a sleigh pulled by huskies in Sochi and played a few bars of Rachmaninov's Piano Concerto No 2 in St Petersburg, with the great pianist Denis Matsuev.

Seeing the world broadens the person. In 1993 Manchester United toured South Africa. We met Nelson Mandela. I look back and can barely believe I had that privilege. Mandela was softly spoken and a big fan of Ryan Giggs, who he was keen to talk to. We did a soccer clinic in Soweto and, driving to the training pitch, watching barefoot kids running, laughing, in the streets, experiencing the joy when we arrived was . . . wow. Something that will never leave me.

I have had similar experiences in Asia, elsewhere in Africa and in Brazil. Soweto was the first time I think I understood how the world truly works, that our European way of living is not necessarily the correct way or the best way, it is just our way. That people who have less than you can be a lot happier.

I came to England from Denmark with a conviction that Danes knew best. It does not take long to understand that other people do not see it that way. The more I travel, the more I realise my values do not count for much, in fact. That in this world it is all about how people get through the day. Are they struggling? Are they happy? In a poor country you might see fifteen people living in a small space but leading happy lives. Their values and relationships may well be better than yours.

I guess what I want to get across most is that as a footballer you have to have something different in your world besides the game. The ages from eighteen to thirty are your key career years but also your biggest period of evolution as a human being. In that period, you have to have something to stimulate your personality that is not football.

If I was a club owner, I would definitely have a school in my football club. I would make sure that when we took kids on full-time at the age of sixteen they continued some kind of education, something that would get them doing stuff other than playing football and going on Instagram. A stimulated brain will come up with solutions in tricky moments, whereas a stagnant brain will not, and I believe this applies on the pitch. A stimulated footballer is a better footballer.

At my club I would tap into every aspect of the player. Who the parents are, what they liked doing as a kid. If they liked to draw, I would give them art classes. I would have a music room at the training ground. I would provide something that would make these guys a little different from ordinary players because, at the end of the day, the difference between winning and losing the Champions League is that guy. The guy who understands something nobody else does in a situation.

Why was Ole there, in that spot at the back post in 1999, at precisely that moment, to score? He always had a special mind, one that allowed him to analyse games so brilliantly while he sat on the bench, before coming on to make a difference. He is an intelligent person who always thought a little differently. He grew up in an unusual place. Like me, he came late to the full-time professional game, having experienced a world beyond football.

Outside interests allow a player to survive the pressures of a career. Having family and looking after your kids, that's great, that takes you away from football, for sure – but your kids will grow up and leave, so what are you going to do then? What are your life skills? Your survival skills? One of the biggest players I played with always talked about the watches he collected, the houses he was building, but never anything of human value. Now his coaching career is over, I often wonder how he is. When I meet him, he seems lost.

For me, music was always the world outside the game. I played the piano, the drums. I learned the guitar. I had a recording studio at home. I never recorded anything, by the way: all the gear and no idea, as they say. But it took me away; it gave me an insight into something else and inspired me to think in other ways.

There is something else about life after football that you need to know. It can be . . . *sore.*

The point of telling you the following is not to pretend a footballer's life is terrible, or a bid for sympathy. I just want you to know the facts. You get out of a football career what you are prepared to put in – and part of your investment has to be physical.

At the age of fifty-seven, I have two permanently painful shoulders, worn-out ankles and feet and, most serious of all, a chronic back condition about which the specialist's report makes grim reading. It is complete wear and tear, years of diving around and a big body crashing to the ground. The disc between the L4 and L5 vertebrae has worn away and now there is just bone grinding against bone, nipping one of the major nerves. Medically, there is something that could be done, but it is not worth the risk.

Then there are my hands. Where to start? The finger I dislocated, twice, at Charlton in 1999 is very sore down at the base. The joint is completely gone. I see a hand specialist in Manchester and we keep an eye on the latest joint replacements available, but none are strong enough yet to be worthwhile. My fingers have been broken and battered, several times over, and it is remarkable they are still relatively strong and flexible. It is probably down to keeping them agile through playing the piano and guitar.

With my back, I'm okay day-to-day – until the moment I try and carry something. With my shoulders, I have to keep training or they seize up. I'm nothing special, just average – most ex-footballers who had long careers are similar. There are bumps and aches, cracks and strains that we just have to carry around. And, personally, if you had told me at the start of my career that this would be the price, I would take it all over again.

I could tell you twenty-five stories of playing through serious knocks. In autumn 1987, in pre-season at Brøndby, I fractured my finger in two places but got a call the next day from Richard Møller Nielsen. He was then in charge of the Olympic team and we had started our campaign on fire. He needed me for the next game, ten days away, but he said if I didn't play for my club at the weekend, he couldn't select me. I played with strapping round the fingers and just hoped nothing would happen to make the injury more serious. It was agony – but I got through the games. In football, that's just how it is.

At Sporting I suffered an embarrassing injury before a trip to Madeira to play Marítimo. We were mucking about at the training ground. I was chasing a guy and as he was running in front of me his elbow swung back and hit my left hand as it went forward. I heard the crack. I didn't tell anyone except the physio. We tried making a splint and all sorts of stuff, but ultimately I just had to get strapped up again and play. I had to make two saves in the game, both – Sod's Law – with the left hand. So painful. After the game I had it X-rayed and there were two broken metatarsals.

There was a time, warming up before a game at Tottenham, when I strained my calf. Fergie really wanted me to play, so I tried, but it was impossible and Kevin Pilkington had to replace me at half-time. That was the William Prunier game, by the way. Spurs won 4–1. Then there was a match against Blackburn when I had fallen badly on my left foot a few days before and twisted my ankle. It blew up really badly. The gaffer was desperate for me to be involved and the doc and Dave Fevre tried to come up with some solutions. I was sent home with a cryo cuff – a compress which clamps round your joint and flushes iced water around your foot every two hours. I stayed up until 1 a.m. to get in one more flush, then was up very early to start the process again. I could sleep on the physio table later in the day, I figured.

At 8 a.m. on match day, we were trying everything, experimenting with strappings and supports. I never got to more than 60 per cent okay – but that was enough for Fergie to pick me. Blackburn won 2–0, with Alan Shearer scoring twice, and though both were good goals, I fancy that if I had been able to move properly I might have saved one and prevented the other.

As for 1998–99, I played through a groin injury for the entire season. It was very painful kicking the ball. If you go through footage of the FA Cup semi-final replay with Arsenal, you'll find a moment when I save from Dennis Bergkamp, then drop to the ground. I wasn't injured. I was just in so much pain from the groin that I needed a minute or two to rest and for Dave to come on.

When I left the Danish league in 1991 I took with me a bad shoulder problem that didn't clear for the rest of my career. It happened in my last month of playing for Brøndby. I jumped for the ball and somebody grabbed my foot. Because my instinct was to hold on to the ball, when I fell I took all of my weight on my shoulder. I could hear it go: *kerrunch*. It was my right shoulder, as well, my throwing arm. So literally every time I threw a ball for my last twelve years as a professional it felt like my arm was coming off. The damage, which is an issue to this day, is to the tendon that keeps the collarbone in place. It kind of snapped and another tendon got damaged. As long as I keep exercising it and having treatment, it's okay. Leave it for a week or two and it's a disaster.

I could go on. I've already told you about playing through ruptured knee ligaments at Manchester City. My last big football injury came in 2006, playing in Soccer Aid. The deal was I would do the first forty-five minutes. Gareth Thomas, the rugby player, was on my team. Twenty seconds before half-time, I parried a cross down into the ground and went to pick it up when Gareth arrived and tried to smash the ball into Row Z. He booted my right hand and smashed up the index finger. Broken in three places – my hand specialist, Michael Hayden, operated the next day and screwed it back together. I did rehab with a hand therapist in Wigan, who worked wonders.

These are just the war wounds you accept as a player. At the draw for the World Cup in Russia, in December 2017, there was a reception for FIFA legends and we were all ushered into a room because Putin wanted to meet us. Gordon Banks was there and in came Pelé, in a wheelchair. The two of them went straight to each other and began talking. It was a magic moment. I had to get a picture but I didn't want to intrude, so I waited near them until they were finished talking. I could hear their conversation.

'Oh, what about that ——? I had an operation on it last year.'

'And how's your knee?'

'Do you get trouble with ——? Me too.'

Two of the very, very greatest – exchanging information on injuries.

I guess that brings me to David Busst. The date is 8 April 1996. Manchester United are going for the title. Coventry come to Old Trafford and win a corner after a couple of minutes. Noel Whelan meets it at the front post and I stretch and make a one-handed save. I push the ball to my right and keep moving with it. I see a Coventry player charging in at the back post, getting ahead of Brian McClair. All he has to do is touch the ball and it's in, but he seems to sit on his own leg, right in front of my eyes. He screams. He really screams.

It was Busst. His injury, which involved compound fractures to the tibia and fibula of his right leg, was indescribably horrific. I had to walk away. I could not take it. The poor guy was on the floor in the most terrible pain. That was the day I fell in love with Dion Dublin. While the rest of us shrank away, Dion sat with Busst and held his hand, calming him down. It takes some person to do that. The referee, Dermot Gallagher, handled the situation superbly too.

The game stopped for nine minutes while Busst received treatment. There was a pool of blood in my goalmouth, in front of the post. Busst left on a stretcher to a standing ovation and Gallagher was about to restart when I looked at the blood on the grass. I waved. 'Ref, I can't play with that.' He understood.

They brought on someone with sand and cleared the blood away. The rest of the game was flat; nobody wanted to be on that pitch any more. We won 1–0 but did not feel in the slightest bit like celebrating. The mood in the dressing room was bleak.

Word came through that Busst had been taken to Booth Hall Hospital in Irlam. The next day I called Eric. We both wanted to check on Busst, to see him and give him our best wishes. We arrived at Booth Hall but at reception they told us that, sorry, they had no patient of that name. I said, 'Listen, we were involved in that game yesterday, we know he's here.' They said okay and that we could not tell anyone but Busst had been transported to a special unit, so severe were his problems. Eric and I felt even worse after that. Busst was on our minds for a long time and when we played a testimonial for him, it was poignant to see him come on, limping.

But my story involves something else. Whenever I had visitors over from Scandinavia, they would want to see Old Trafford, walk on the pitch, see the tunnel and all that. I was showing some visitors round the stadium one day and I was about to knock on the door to the tunnel – there is always a guard inside – when it swung open. Out stepped David Busst.

I was, *Wow*. And he looked happy. He said, 'Hey, I know you and Eric came to the hospital that day. You don't know how much that meant to me. Thank you very much.' I asked what he was doing at Old Trafford, and he said he now worked with kids and had taken a group of them on a special trip to the stadium. I thought, *Wow*, again.

It was a small moment of closure. What happened to him has never left me. It was the worst thing I ever witnessed on a pitch, and so close up that it almost felt part of me, if that makes sense. It might seem odd to say, but it sort of bonded me with David Busst. We have a relationship now and will be forever linked. I always knew he would never kick a football again, but that meeting went a long way in helping me . . . heal, I guess. There was David, moving on with his life after football and doing something great.

18

SO, I TRIED TO BUY BRØNDBY

So, I tried to buy Brøndby. I even looked into buying Manchester United.

Before telling you *how*, I want to start with the *why*.

Always start with the *why*.

It was August 1999, and I was at the start of my stint with Sporting Lisbon when I took a call from an old friend. Hvidovre were in financial trouble and he represented a group of fans who were trying to help the club survive. He just came out with it. 'Fancy buying Hvidovre?' From there the proposition grew.

It was kind of bad timing, but what really appealed was the chance to create something in football, to build, to utilise ideas and insights I had developed during my career. Plus, I could see an opportunity – both in sporting and business terms. On 29 December, I bought the club from Niels Erik Madsen, the guy who had given me a job selling ads for his newspaper all those years before.

The opportunity? It lay in the fact that, unique among Danish clubs, Hvidovre A/S owned its playing licence. Others' licences belonged to mother clubs that ran the professional outfit while overseeing associated amateur and junior teams. But Hvidovre A/S was independent from Hvidovre IF, its mother club.

The licence would offer scope to create a completely new football team, and at the time Copenhagen was expanding along a big strip of land all the way out towards Kastrup airport, called Ørestad. I had this idea of creating an alternative to Brøndby and FC Copenhagen there. I had meetings with the mayor and land was earmarked for us to build facilities and a multi-sports stadium. Major construction companies were on board. All I had to do was get the project financed.

My biggest problem was I lived in Portugal and could only run the show remotely. I trusted people to do it for me and that was a mistake. Within ten months, all the money was gone. I am not blaming anyone, because if you want to run something your way, you have to be there to do it in person, whereas I could only attend board meetings in Copenhagen every three months or so. I was not ready to retire from playing and take charge of things because, as I understood only too well, nothing is better than being on the pitch.

Hvidovre was a lesson learned. An expensive lesson, for to keep the club afloat I paid everyone's wages out of my own pocket and footed all Hvidovre's bills for eighteen months. Eventually, in 2002, I had to get out, giving the football club back to Hvidovre IF for free, after settling all its debts. My hope had been to keep things going until I could return to Denmark full-time. The timing was a pity, because twelve months after I relinquished ownership, there was a credit boom and it would have been much easier, in the changed market, to find money to finance the new complex in Ørestad and sustain and grow the club.

Ownership was not something I had ever planned on, but Hvidovre unleashed a flood of ideas. I wanted to try again sometime. Why own a club? Why not stay on the golf course and in the TV studio after retiring? For the same reasons I was also looking at going into football management. When you have knowledge and feel like you have something to offer and can put it into the world, then you want to find a vehicle. You want to do it. You get an urge – call it a creative itch. I wanted a say in how football was developing. I wanted to make people better. I had seen all the good stuff and all the bad stuff in the game and craved an opportunity to lead a club on the right path.

At Brøndby, I had been part of a set-up that pioneered professional football in Denmark and scaled heights unknown to any Danish club. At Manchester United, I had been part of a journey where my club became the biggest in the world commercially and the best in Europe on the pitch, and seen the new Premier League transform football as a business. At Sporting, I witnessed how to do it the Portuguese way. Then how *not* to do it. Aston Villa and Manchester City were full of lessons, good and bad. And Hvidovre had taught me some of the hard realities of running a football club.

I felt I had a unique package of experiences and insights that should be put to use. And I started eyeing Brøndby, who were drifting, in slow decline.

Brøndby had won a title in 2004–05 under Michael Laudrup, but immediately sold the best players in their squad and, a year later, Michael left. FC Copenhagen were now indisputably Denmark's dominant club. Commercially Brøndby were also slipping. I could see people in the hierarchy clinging to power, their credibility based on what they had done twenty years previously rather than any recent successes. There had been a time these people were trailblazers and risk-takers, and now they were the opposite: time-servers, protecting their positions.

Had I returned as player-manager in 2001, I would have implemented new ideas. I felt, very strongly, that Brøndby's future lay in investing in facilities and especially its academy, because there was a pool of talent in Denmark, but the best local players were no longer staying in the country to start their careers, as my generation had. Instead, they were being attracted by clubs from Germany, Holland and beyond, a pattern that continues to this day. Look at Pierre-Emile Højbjerg. He was at Brøndby until he was seventeen but went to Bayern Munich, and could you blame him? When you're a talented kid just out of school, with a choice between Brøndby's ill-equipped academy or Bayern – or Ajax, the Premier League or wherever – what are you going to do?

And where Brøndby were once able to recruit the Danish league's best by offering professionalism and better pay, now other clubs were professional and paid well too. For Brøndby to be what the club should be – Denmark's No 1 and a credible European force – it needed to think a different way. The key to attracting good players of any age is providing the best facilities, best coaching, best environment, best chance of developing, best chance of winning. That is what Brøndby should offer. The best chance, if you like, of becoming a super-pro.

In 2007, I joined up with an acquaintance, Aldo Petersen, to explore buying the club. Petersen was not Denmark's most popular guy. He was a phenomenon in the financial world, part of a so-called 'Billionaires Club' of five Danish stock-market investors who had made a fortune through aggressive trading, but he was prepared to put up 250 million kroner. His group would fund a takeover of Brøndby and I would front it. After the purchase, I'd be sporting director, looking after the club's football strategy.

However, Brøndby's directors, still led by Bjerregaard, had no intention of ceding power. It would have to be a hostile bid. In Danish law, if you want to buy a public company listed on the stock market, every member of its board has to receive your offer, hand-delivered. In September 2007, there was a reception for someone at Brøndby stadium and we used that event to present each of the club's directors with our proposal in writing. They were completely taken by surprise.

We sat back, waiting for a stock-market announcement informing Brøndby's shareholders of our offer. Danish law suggested the board were obliged to recommend our bid: their responsibility as directors was to make money for their shareholders and we were offering the chance to do this. We thought we had the club.

It was then I learned another lesson – in how to play politics. It was dished out by Bjerregaard. By nature, I am more of a straightforward type. I say what is on my mind and I'm no good at playing games – whereas he is a master. I had prepared everything in terms of what we would do after we took over, but I had not prepared a game plan for the actual takeover process, because I didn't imagine it was necessary. I called a press conference, thinking I needed to communicate with the fans – a big mistake.

I gave the media a few hours' notice and that gave Bjerregaard time. When the press conference began, one particular journalist piped up, armed with all sorts of questions, questions that would drag me off topic and make the whole thing look like it was about personalities and not the serious ideas I had for the club. I am convinced Bjerregaard prepped him. This guy kept asking about individuals and about Bjerregaard in particular: was I ousting him, why did I want rid of the man who had built everything?

I should have given a politician's answer: 'The executive of the club will be reviewed in due course, blah blah.' And I should have kept reiterating my key messages. However, after being pressed, I opted for honesty and said, yes, Bjerregaard would no longer be in charge. The press conference ended up a disaster. The reporting was all 'Schmeichel versus Bjerregaard'. The next day one newspaper carried a giant headline about me: 'THE KILLER OF THE KING.'

I was shocked. We had played by takeover rules and offered to bring fresh finance and energy to the club, and, perhaps naively, I thought people would be excited by my involvement. Brøndby's stock-market announcement, when it did come, was pathetic, a two-page document of which the first page was all about Peter Schmeichel and borderline libellous. The second page contained just two lines – two lines that summed up precisely why Brøndby needed to change. They were something like 'Oh, by the way, Codan is discontinuing its sponsorship of the club.' Codan were the club's long-term main sponsor and this was actually significant and disastrous news. The board buried it under all the rubbish they piled on me.

Two days later, I met Bjerregaard and two other board members, hoping to talk them round to accepting our plans. Despite what the press said, I didn't want a war. But they would not budge.

The desire to take a football club and build something special still burned in me and the bid for Brøndby prompted quite a chapter in my life. Now it was known that I was interested in getting back into ownership, I was presented with all sorts of options: clubs on the market, clubs in different countries that were ripe for a buyout.

However, I did not want to be an owner just for the sake of it. The project would have to have meaning and be special. At one point I was involved in a consortium that had the opportunity to buy a significant chunk of Manchester United. It was a time when the Glazers were under pressure because of debts left over from their 2005 takeover, especially hedge-fund loans – called payment-in-kind notes, or PIK – for which they were person-ally liable. These stood at £232m in early 2010 and were rolling upwards at an eye-watering interest rate of 16.25 per cent. They would spiral to £600m by 2017 if not addressed. They were on top of the £500m-plus United owed to banks from conventional loans.

Fans were protesting and the feeling in the City of London was that, if the deal was right, the Glazers might sell some or all of the club. My group held negotiations to buy out the PIK in return for 30 per cent of United and a seat on the board. Deep down, I never really believed we would succeed, but I enjoyed the process: learning about the corporate world, discussing with experts where the sports industry and broadcasting was heading – especially in terms of digital – and making valuable connections. When the Glazers resolved their financials through a £500m bond issue and then floating United on the New York Stock Exchange, any chance of taking a serious stake in the club disappeared.

My interest was twofold. I wanted to release United from suffocating borrowing and I had a vision of a club owned by supporters and run along the lines of Bayern Munich, where elite people – some drawn from its stock of former players – run the club but answer to ordinary shareholders, the fans. Buying in would also have been an opportunity for me to go into the club and drive development. Something I was very serious about was that United needed to start planning for the future – to secure Fergie's services for as long as possible, while working on a proper succession plan through which he could groom and, after retiring, mentor the next guy. Also, to place the academy again at the centre of the club.

In 2013, Aldo Petersen returned with another bid for Brøndby and this time succeeded in buying the club. I could have been part of the takeover. Petersen and I had remained in dialogue and he wanted me to come in as his director of football. An hour before I was due to fly out to Jakarta from Copenhagen, for an event as a Manchester United ambassador, he called to say his new takeover attempt was on and we had a long conversation, where I set out the conditions for me joining forces with him again.

These involved, among other things, how Brøndby's board should be comprised. Some of the directors were just fans and I felt that needed to change. While fan ownership is wonderful, fans running the day-to-day business of a club almost never works, and I thought Brøndby needed a fully professional board, made up of high-quality people with specialist expertise in areas relevant to the business. 'Sure, sure,' Aldo said. My itinerary was crazy. I flew via Bangkok to Jakarta and went straight from the airport to the event, which was a mass viewing for fans of a Manchester derby. There was a meet-and-greet, a press conference, the game and then a dash back to the airport to catch my return flights. I did not make a phone call until I arrived back in Denmark, forty-eight hours after I left.

Petersen had completed his takeover and already installed a new board. It consisted of seven directors: four of his guys, a club rep and . . . two fans. I rang him. 'Ah, Peter, what does it matter?' he said. 'We have four votes and they only have three.' I told him that was not the point.

He asked if I was still in and I said I needed to think about it, and when I reflected on how things had gone down I could see Petersen was not really interested in change or in shaping Brøndby the right way. He just wanted to do what it took to own the club; to him, it was just another investment, something with which he could take a share price from A to B, then cash in and move on. Fair enough in terms of his world, but it wasn't for me, so I declined. Brøndby's value did increase from A to B and within eleven months, Petersen took his profit and sailed off.

One of Petersen's investors, Jan Bech Andersen, bought more and more shares until he had control. Andersen is a Brøndby supporter who has been very successful in business, but this seems to have created a cultural problem at the club. There is no consequence for underperformance. If Brøndby lose 40m kroner in a season, everyone knows good old Jan Bech will cover it. On the pitch, the story of the last fifteen years has been one of mediocrity. The team lags far behind Midtjylland and FC Copenhagen, not enough players are being developed, not a lot is being built. It really pains me to see where Brøndby are now.

At one point, I had discussions with Andersen about how to take Brøndby forward, but I think he was more interested in cherry-picking ideas and tapping into my contacts. I looked into joining another takeover attempt, but walked away because all the money going in would have been used to buy shares rather than develop the club. For me, it would only be worth doing something if the investment was on the football side.

I still believe in the dream of Brøndby that was created in the 1980s and which my generation lived as players. Brøndby should be about family, about identity, about excellence, about local talent and its development. It could be the Ajax of Scandinavia. One thing that struck me back in 2007 when I made my takeover bid was how many quality people from the Premier League were willing to come and help me bring the standards and expertise of English football to the Danish scene. Now, when I talk about my visions for Brøndby, people who have coached, played or worked in the Premier League are still interested. The idea of Brøndby appeals – as does the idea, in this otherwise short-termist football world, of going somewhere and having three, four, five years to build something.

I have all the respect in the world for Bjerregaard. He was a guy who looked into the future, stuck his neck out and made big things happen for a small Danish football club. It was he who gave me the opportunity to be a pro. We are still on friendly terms. The world needs people like him, who have ideas, and what he did, he did for Brøndby – he never took any money out of the club. It was never about ego; in his heart was the club.

Those times he turned me and others over in order to keep control was because he genuinely thought that him keeping control was best for Brøndby. Had I owned the club, I would have asked him to help me in certain ways, and mentor me at certain points.

For me, the *why* is still there, the itch has not gone away. The desire to take a club and create something new and different and good in football continues to burn. When I look at the game in 2021, I see a need for change. I see a sport that is now too focused on the elite, on money and on individual personalities. It is in danger of forgetting its essence: the people. Communities and ordinary fans.

I want football to be wide and fantastic. Not narrow and plastic. I love the English tradition of professional teams supported by passionate locals all the way from the Premier League into the fifth and sixth divisions. I spent a year following Notts County in League Two when Kasper played for them and I don't think I've watched football in a more enjoyable environment. No glitz, no hyped-up stars, no £1,200 season tickets – just the people and their team and honest players giving everything to both.

If I were a manager, I would only want to work for a good owner, who understands football is about the long term. That it is about development and identity and community and communicating with the fans – and that investing in all those things requires patience and time.

Those good owners are hard to find, but maybe I could be the good owner myself someday. Maybe soon. With me, you just never know.

19

GOALKEEPING IS NOT ABOUT SAVING

My leaving present from Manchester United was a statuette. Cast in bronze, 30 centimetres high and 40 centimetres from boot to fingertip, the figurine is of a fully stretched goalkeeper flying to his left like a superhero to make a perfect, one-handed grab of the ball.

Me.

I was presented with this beautiful memento at a party at the Royal Lancaster after the FA Cup final in 1999 and knew instantly which save this carving commemorates. It is a save that, in fact, embarrasses me. It came against Tottenham in 1994. They played a cross into my box from the left, but not a threatening one. The ball was almost at the 18-yard line when Steve Sedgley met it, looping a header towards my goal. His effort presented no danger; floating up in the air, it was clearly destined to land two or three yards wide of my posts. I could have left it to go out for a goal kick.

However, me being me, I was keen to restart play quickly and send us off on the attack. So I dived high to my left to scoop the ball out of the air. I was horizontal when I reached out and took it cleanly in my left hand. Visually, it looked amazing but, actually, it was a 'save' of zero significance. Just a bit of showboating.

And I was never a showboater. So, as a representation of good goalkeeping, I don't like it.

As a piece of art, it is beautiful, though, and that is the first point I would like to make in this chapter. When it comes to the job of a keeper, what looks good and what *is* good are not the same things. If there is one position on the pitch that tends to be misunderstood, misdescribed and badly analysed by non-practitioners, I believe it is that of the goalie. Even the greats get goalkeeping wrong. For example, Fergie was no expert, let me tell you.

That stop against Spurs was in January of the 1993–94 campaign. At the end of that season, I drove with the family back to Denmark, for our summer holiday. Our route took us through Holland and we decided to break the journey with a night in Amsterdam. We went out for a walk there, and in a marquee in a square near our hotel there was an international photography exhibition: 'Photos of the Year'. The very first picture on show, two metres high and three metres wide, was of me, frozen in time, flying horizontally and catching that Sedgley header. Its title was *The Best Save in the World*, and in that one moment which the photographer so skilfully captured, I guess it *does* look like the best save in the world. But, of course, it is not.

The Best Save in the World was sports photo of the year and the image has followed me ever since. How do I regard it? Well, it looks good, seriously good, and there is no harm in looking good . . . In fact, the image is my screensaver and logo, and while most of my medals and mementos are in the museum at Old Trafford, I have the statuette in my house. It is nice to look at. But if you ever see the photo, do *not* take its title literally. The greatest save in the world? A non-event. Absolute proof that the camera can lie.

The biggest misunderstanding about goalkeeping is that it is about saving the ball. It is not. Of course, saves are an important part of the job, but to be a good goalie it is not necessary that you are someone who makes a lot of them. How does that make sense? Well, it really all depends on what team you play for and what that team needs from its keeper. Let's start by thinking of the keepers who, as I write this in 2021, are the established No 1s of the Manchester clubs, David de Gea and Ederson.

Manchester United think De Gea is the best in the world and Manchester City believe Ederson to be the ideal goalkeeper. De Gea makes incredible saves, but is a reactive rather than proactive player. He does not stand behind his defensive line, pushing them up and claiming balls over the top. He is not preventative, nor is he involved in build-up play. But on the line, there are very few better. His style is a big reason why, for the past several seasons, Manchester United have adopted a habit of sitting back and defending deep.

Then you look at Ederson. What are his strengths? His distribution is rightly celebrated. He is an incredible passer of the ball. As for saves, it is hard to remember many spectacular ones he has made. As a shot-stopper he is okay, his basics are good enough, but he is not called on to make a lot of stops because he prevents things from happening by pushing his defence out and keeping the opposition away from goal, and by roaming far from his line to deal early with their attacks.

Those contrasting styles tell you that goalkeeping is not one thing. It is a role played differently according to the needs of different teams – like any position on the field, in fact. Stereotypical thinking would be to rank the 'best' twenty-five goalkeepers in the world and say they could play for any side, but that assumption is false. I do not believe De Gea would be of much use to Pep Guardiola's game plan at Manchester City, and if Manchester United signed Ederson he would change the way they played.

Because of rule changes and the ascent of coaches like Guardiola who preach an 'eleven-man game', goalkeeping has undergone more evolution than any other playing role in the last twenty years. For me, it is without doubt the hardest position to play. Yes, I would say that, wouldn't I? But the fact is the toolbox you need to do the job has become enormous.

Break it down. You still need all the old-fashioned skills. You have to be able to handle the ball, catch, dive, move sideways, be good on your feet, be quick at moving forward and back. On top of those, nowadays you have to be an outfield player too. You should be able to distribute to colleagues, which means reading the play, deciding which passes to make and executing those, and have feet good enough to manipulate the ball under the pressure of high pressing.

An outfield player is right in the mix of a game and a lot of what they do is instinctive, a reaction to what is going on around them. Whereas, apart from saves, everything a goalkeeper does is premeditated. *Where do I position myself? Do I come for the cross or stay? When this ball comes back to me, who do I play it to?* It is about staying with the game, all the time concentrating, concentrating, analysing, analysing. There are decisions, decisions, decisions.

Concentration is a skill. The fitter you are, the better you concentrate, so you can improve your concentration by improving your conditioning. There are also cognitive exercises you can do to sharpen up, but most of all concentration comes down to innate ability and using strategies to stay in the game. I liked to come outside or to the edge of my box and be as close as I could to my team when we were in possession. I would direct team-mates – 'Left!', 'Right!', 'Scholesy's on!' – that kind of stuff. This was knowing very well that they could not hear me: I was doing it for me, to make me feel I was part of what was going on.

When you play for a big side who dominate possession, it is easy to lose concentration because you spend a long time with the ball far away. You can get suckered into other thoughts. *What am I doing tomorrow? Shall I paint the carport?* If you let your mind wander for a second, you will make mistakes.

Then there is resilience. When a striker misses a chance, there is acceptance that scoring is hard. *At least he was in the right position. He'll score the next one.* Yet missing a chance has the same 'cost' as letting in a goal. When a goalie concedes as the result of a mistake, it stays out there. *What a rick. Dodgy keeper.* Everyone thinks about it. You are humiliated. If you play for a big club, your error will be spoken about for weeks and weeks.

So, mental strength is vital. It may well be the most important tool in a good keeper's box. The moment you make a mistake you know exactly what the reaction will be, yet you have to put this out of your mind, get straight back to your job and make sure you deal with the next situation. When Basler's free kick beat me early in the Champions League final I knew for sure I would be blamed – while also knowing there was nothing I could do about the goal. I had to take those thoughts and chuck them away. Feeling sorry for myself would have been fatal. I was in the biggest game in my club's history and I could not dwell on what had been and gone and I could no longer do anything about.

In my mind, I never had a bad game. Never messed up. Every season, in the league table, there was a number in our 'goals against' column which suggested that, yes, I had in fact conceded a few times – but these were not events I elected to remember. When I went into 'risk mode' I needed that feeling of invincibility. Of course I analysed my performances; analysis and reflection make you better. But I did not do so thinking in terms of 'mistakes'; it was more with the question in mind of *Could I have done something differently there?* If I made a direct error that led to a goal, I did not dwell on it. *One of those things. I was poor in that moment. Move on.* The goals where I did not make an obvious mistake were probably the ones I thought about more, because then I could ask, *Why did that happen? Did I cover my angles enough? What was my starting position like? Should I have shouted at my centre halves to show the guy wide?* Every scenario on the pitch is one you can learn from, but none are worth beating yourself up about.

I have to be honest. With the exception of my performance against Sheffield Wednesday in 1998–99, where the context was a worrying one of feeling vulnerable in general, I did not care one jot when I dropped a clanger. If I chucked the ball in the net, so what? One of those things. This was my version of Bo Johansson's philosophy. Bo came into my life in 1996, at a point relatively late in my career, and put words to something I had always felt inside. *Accept that the worst happens, sometimes, and concentrate on doing your best.*

What goalkeeping *is* about is preventing. Preventing the ball going in the net, ultimately, but also preventing scenarios where conceding might happen. Calling the right thing to a defender can be preventative and therefore a good piece of goalkeeping. Banging the ball into Row Z to buy your team time to reorganise – that might be a good piece of goalkeeping too.

It does not matter how you keep the ball out of the net. It hits you in the face, on the shin, the shoulder and does not go in: fine. There is a massive set of stereotypes about how things are supposed to be, and when pundits come out with them – 'Oh, he used his legs there,' 'Dear me, he went with his wrong hand,' 'Hmm, that was an unconventional save' – I cringe.

I have never had the desire to be a goalkeeping coach. But if I was one, I would start with the individual. What kind of goalkeeper are you? What kind of goalkeeper do you want to be? What kind of keeper does the team need you to be? What is your identity? Yes, there are fundamentals: basic skills all keepers must have, which require exercises all keepers should do. But that is training, not coaching, and I despair at all the conveyor-belt sessions I see keepers having to undergo.

A goalkeeping coach might have a group of six or seven keepers in their charge, all with different heights, weights, strengths, mental make-ups, backgrounds. The coach should make space to treat them like the different individuals they are and work in a bespoke way, one on one. Obviously it helps if the keepers in the group are suited to their team's style of play. That is the responsibility of the recruitment department and (for the younger ones) the academy. Too often, clubs end up with a collection of disparate goalies with not enough in common. Their clubs have acquired them or developed them without thinking about the type of keeper they actually require.

I have told you about my mentor, Jørgen Henriksen, and his idea that goalkeepers should do their technical work in their own time and during training sessions do all the same stuff as the outfield players. I believe such an approach is essential. Think, also, about what I said regarding the injuries a keeper picks up over a career. Specific goalkeeping training is physically hard and should be minimised, because you don't want to add to the stresses on a keeper's body.

I have pulled Kasper up on it. By specific training I mean all those routines where you're diving after balls: the more of that you do, the quicker retirement comes. Even a quick drill of saving twenty shots to your left then twenty to your right means forty dives, forty big impacts to the body, and if you do that every session you might end up with 160 such impacts per week, which adds up to 6,000 to 7,000 over the course of a year. We keepers are big guys and every one of those impacts is severe, so unless they are necessary – i.e. in games – then I do not see the point.

As I have said, fitness helps concentration – so a keeper will benefit from all the conditioning work outfielders do. Decisions require game understanding – so a keeper will also benefit from the outfielders' tactical drills. Being good with your feet has never been more important, so there is an obvious upside to taking part in possession exercises and small-sided games. If the attackers are practising step-overs, great, why not join in? The changes of direction and honing of footwork – they will help you too. Communication? Again, that grows the more time you spend with the group.

Jørgen coached me precisely the way I should be coached from day one. It took a year and a half, but I brought him with me from Hvidovre to Brøndby and later fought tooth and nail to get him a position with the Danish national team. Our work together involved two or three sessions a week, working both on the Richard Møller Nielsen stuff like catching and throwing – those rudiments that you just need to repeat over and over – and on the fine technical details. There were never any long drills of diving about. Think of top golfers. You do not see them on the range smashing five hours of drives. They spend their time on putting and chipping, on practising fades, draws and spin. They work on their short games and groove their technique.

A lot of what made me came from Jørgen. The 'I am the best' mindset. The mind games of projecting arrogance to discourage the opposition. Jørgen worked on an essential question: 'What do you know?' We would move around the penalty area, him with the ball, me covering my goal. If I could get it off him, great – but more important was ensuring he could not score. If he could manoeuvre himself half a foot of space to shoot, he would put the ball in the net. Move, move. Cover, cover, cover. Then he would put his foot on the ball and I had to tell him precisely where my goalposts were, without looking round. I would touch a spot on the grass, 'Here's my right post,' then go and touch another, 'and here's my left post.' He would say, 'Correct!' or 'You're off.' I learned to always know where my posts were that way.

We had another exercise which he called 'Prolonger-arm'. It was just punching. Punching – but with the so-called wrong arm. Actually, there is no such thing as a 'wrong arm' to punch (or, for that matter, save) with. A conventional view is that you should go with the arm nearest the ball, when in fact using the other arm can extend your reach. Try it. Extend your left arm horizontally and imagine reaching for a ball. Then bring your other arm over and reach with that. You should find your body naturally allows it to get a little further. Through Jørgen, I learned about this – and that getting distance on a punch is almost zero to do with power. It is about using the ball's momentum and helping it on its way. With the right timing and technique you can punch a ball 30 yards without effort.

Psychology? A goalkeeper's is most similar to that of a striker. We do the same jobs, basically, in reverse. We are the players who make the difference. Whether goals get scored comes down to us. Many ingredients are the same: the waiting, the sense of being separate from the action yet part of it, the need to come alive in key moments. Patience, concentration, mental sharpness are essentials. Just as the striker has to keep making the right runs and taking up the right positions until the ball finally comes their way in front of goal, so the keeper has to cover, cover, move, move, wait, wait, wait – until it is time to make the save.

If you play midfield or defence and are having a bad game, one way out of it is to simply try harder. Run further, tackle more, win some headers. But if you are a goalkeeper or striker you cannot just 'try harder', you cannot force yourself into the game. That would make you worse, too manic; you would unsettle your team. You are in a position where you set the tone: ask any defender if they would rather have the best goalkeeper behind them or the best midfielder in front of them and they will choose the goalkeeper. And ask if they would rather have someone who is vocally crazy or quiet in the goal – they will pick the loud one.

Another detail of mentality: at training I hated people messing about with my area. Putting balls in my net as a joke, mucking about with the goal, leaving bibs around near the posts. I hated all that. What is your job as a keeper? It is to keep your sacred goal area clear. It was a mental thing, a visual thing – I never wanted the sight of a ball in my net. Psychologically, I wanted it always to be pristine. On match day I was no different. I put nothing in my goal. I brought a towel with me but always chucked it on the grass behind the net. Never *in* the net, as I see some keepers do. I would have hated that, visually. You keep your goal clear to show the world who you are. Your opponents too: *Nothing gets in here today*.

*   *   *

It must have been nice being David Seaman, having David's calmness, but you can wish for a million things; I am happy being me. When a career is over, you have to look back at it in total, at what overall output you had. In that respect, I have no complaints.

I never assessed myself while I was playing and think that, in general, whatever you did yesterday is worth far less of your focus than what you are going to do tomorrow and today. But sometimes what I achieved hits home unexpectedly. I listened to a conversation between Laura and her daughter, Lola, recently. Laura was telling Lola to avoid men who are whiny and dependent and that the best partners are guys who don't make a song and dance, who handle their own stuff and are comfortable in their own skin. Lola said, 'Yeah, but it's okay for Peter – he has been the best in the world at something.' It was the first time I really digested being 'the best' on a personal level.

For years and years people have told me, 'You are the best,' 'You were the best,' and it was always, 'Yeah, yeah, thanks.' But hearing it like that from Lola made me think about it in human terms for the first time. The person who was voted 'best ever Premier League goalkeeper' by *Match of the Day* viewers (an accolade that really meant something, by the way) or gets billed as a 'FIFA legend' – that was and is not just Peter Schmeichel the player but Peter the person. It is . . . *me*.

One reason for writing this book is to try and answer the question why? Why me? Why not someone else? I was talented, but many people are talented; talent alone does not make the difference.

I think one ingredient common to all people who reach the very top of something is that they have a different way of thinking. It's eighteen years since I played and that is a long period of 'civilian life'. You socialise, go to dinner parties and hear the things people complain about, and very often I find myself thinking, *I just don't get it.* Having a different set of priorities, a different way of thinking, sets a person apart. And goalkeepers are different to start with. Difference, in the position, can be a power source.

After I left Manchester United they said I was irreplaceable. Of course, that was not true. I was perfectly replaceable – it is just that Fergie took far longer than he should have to recruit Edwin van der Sar. When he eventually did, I played a role in it.

Fergie had considered signing Edwin in 1999 but went for Mark Bosnich instead. Edwin went to Juventus and by the time he came to English football in 2001, Manchester United had Barthez, and Edwin signed for Fulham. In 2005 I found myself sitting with Fergie at a dinner in his honour to raise money for Nordoff–Robbins, the music therapy charity. Tim Howard was his keeper at the time and it was not working. Wrong style. Howard was superb for Everton and a USA legend, but he was in the category of reactive goalkeepers. He preferred to stay on his line. I said to Fergie, 'I don't understand why you haven't changed the goalkeeper,' and mentioned Van der Sar. Sign him, I said, and the whole defence would be able to push up. Fergie said, 'Ahh, but he is too old.'

True, Edwin was approaching thirty-five, but he was in excellent shape and I said to Fergie, 'Listen, if you sign him, Edwin will give you two to three years to find the next one.' Fergie said, 'Hmm, I never saw it like that.'

Edwin was the perfect keeper for Manchester United. We have contrasting personalities but had similar styles. We commanded the whole 18-yard area and turned the game quickly, distributing the ball 30, 40, 50 yards to get the team up the pitch. Those are the keepers Manchester United need. Fergie looked at Oli Kahn for a time but, in my opinion, Oli would not have been a 'fit'. Oli had exceptional reactions and remarkable bravery and was a goalkeeper of the very highest quality – but in a different style. He did not catch the ball but punched everything away; he did not come for crosses; he did not push his defenders out; he stayed on his line.

Gigi Buffon is one of the all-time greats, but another whose style would not work for the way I believe Manchester United should play: Buffon makes incredible saves and has a tremendous mentality but is also a reactive keeper. If you want to play like Manchester United did between 1991 and 1999, or from 2005 to 2011, then hire someone like me, or Edwin, or Ederson, or Manuel Neuer. If you want to play the José Mourinho way, then I'm not your guy; Edwin and Ederson are not your guys. Then, you should go for De Gea or Buffon or Jan Oblak.

My first goalkeeping hero was Sepp Maier. When I was growing up, the amount of football on Danish TV was limited and the 1974 World Cup, shown extensively, seemed an incredible treat. I had seen Bayern Munich in the European Cup final, where my eyes fixed on their keeper, this big guy with his big shorts and unflappable manner. I thought he was really cool. I started to support Germany, because Denmark were never in tournaments, and in 1974 I loved their team: Franz Beckenbauer, Gerd Müller, Paul Breitner – and Maier, of course. I also cheered for Sweden because we got the Swedish sports news bulletins on our TVs. Ronnie Hellström, Sweden's goalie in '74, was another hero.

As the football content on Danish channels grew, we got to see more matches from England and I loved the British goalkeepers. Peter Shilton stood out. It seemed impossible to get the ball past him. He won the European Cup and First Division with Nottingham Forest – who does that? Manchester United had Gary Bailey, and it seemed fitting: the blond shock of hair, the imposing physique. My team had a keeper who looked like me! I idolised Bailey.

Later, my favourites included Jean-Marie Pfaff, because he played for Bayern Munich, and I liked Bayern a lot. I thought Dino Zoff was out of this world. I admired Jan Tomaszewski – a favourite of my dad, of course – and lapped up his exploits against England in 1973. I loved Toni Schumacher. My God, I thought he was brilliant. I didn't wear goalkeeping gloves until I was seventeen or eighteen and already playing senior football, by the way, but when I was at Brøndby I signed up with Reusch, the legendary German manufacturer of goalie gloves. It was one of my first small victories in terms of breaking free of Per Bjerregaard's control, because he wanted me to wear Uhlsport, with whom Brøndby had a deal. But Reusch were the best and Schumacher had worn Reusch, as had Maier.

During the 1988 European Championship, Gebhard Reusch, who owned the company, turned up at Denmark's team hotel to see me. He brought Schumacher with him and Toni was saying things to me like 'We know you are one of the upcoming goal-keepers in Europe, we are keeping an eye on you.' I got to know him and was proud of the fact.

Growing up, Kasper really admired Iker Casillas and used him as an inspiration, and there was a nice symmetry, because Casillas said he grew up modelling himself on me. One keeper I wish I had seen was Lev Yashin. He had an incredible personal story, having lived a hard early life, working in a factory at the age of twelve. He was tough as nails and, apparently, way ahead of his time. But there is very little footage of his career in the Soviet Union. I wish I had watched him play.

As a No 1 keeper it should not matter who your No 2 is. You should be strong enough to look after yourself, whoever is behind you, and I was never a fan of group goalkeeper sessions where the No 1, No 2, No 3 and youth keepers work together. It was another mentality thing. When I was on the pitch, playing, I was alone, it was all about me. So when I did specialist keeper training, I wanted it to be all about me as well. But there is an art to being (and recruiting) a good No 2. Raimond van der Gouw was the perfect No 2. He wanted to play, of course – but he was happy supporting me. He knew Fergie would give him enough games in a season, and he made sure he was ready and performed well in those games. In the dressing room he was sociable and positive and he was one of the best trainers, fittest guys, I have ever seen.

Briefly, I was No 2 for Denmark. I utterly hated it. At certain places – never United – I had one of the bad No 2s, the ones who create an atmosphere around the place, who moan and complain about how they should be playing. Les Sealey was another great No 2 at United, but when Tony Coton arrived I was not sure. *How can he do it,* I wondered. He was such a good goalkeeper himself and I thought, *How can a guy like that take a back seat?* But then you got to know Tony, to appreciate his personality: he is a real man of the world, who understands football, is good to be around and can handle human situations. Those qualities later made him a brilliant goalkeeper coach.

My advice to young keepers is: you have to find your identity. Who are you? What do you bring to the world, the game? Then work on that. And keep working and working and working. Because keepers are the guys on teams who work the hardest, who need to be the most flawless in their techniques and acquire the most complicated array of attributes.

Having my son going into the same line of business has been very useful in helping answer the *why me* question. While seeing Kasper go through his journey, I have reflected on mine. Of course Kasper observed me from an early age and took a few things from my game, but he is also a child of the YouTube age, who was always watching clips of different keepers growing up, so he drew inspiration from others too – and from all that forged an identity which is very much his own.

He has a different mentality from me. I think he is one of the toughest Premier League players in history, mentally. How many mistakes has he ever made? Not many. He has an incredible ability to concentrate, which is why he was able to play in that 2015–16 team, with a deep block and the stakes super-high, and deal with the ball coming into his box all the time. He has created a platform where he can perform at the very highest level, all while overcoming the biggest obstacle you could face as a young player: having a famous dad who did the very same job as him.

From the start, I have hated people comparing us. When they do, it makes me feel powerless, like he is having to endure something just because I am his father. One time when we were playing golf – something we cherish because we don't often get to do so together – we were on the tee box when this man, this very nice older man, came up to us and said to me, 'Mr Schmeichel, I've been watching you all my life and you are the best goalkeeper I've ever seen. I am a big Manchester United fan. Thank you, very, very much.'

That was pretty nice.

And then he looked at Kasper. 'And you, young man. You're not bad either. In fact, you're very good. But you will never be as good as your dad.'

Seriously?!

What a thing to say. This guy had been very polite, but I could not help myself.

'What the **** are you saying? Why are you talking like that? How's that going to help?' I yelled.

There were two reasons to do so. One, I was really hurt personally. It was such an offensive thing to say to my son that this guy needed to be told. And two, I deliberately went big on him, because I needed to show Kasper something: *I've got your back, I don't buy into all this.* Because I certainly don't.

He has had to live with that nonsense. He wins the league, people mention me. He gets into the Champions League and the questions are about me and 1999. At the World Cup in Russia he was exceptional, helping Denmark to the second round and saving three penalties as they went out to Croatia after a shoot-out. Had Denmark got through, they might have gone all the way to the final and he would have been accepted as one of the best in the world.

For that is what he is. Regardless of being his dad, I would tell you that he is one of the strongest keepers I have ever seen.

20
KASPER AND CECILIE

Let me tell you a story about Kasper. I flew over from Denmark, with a friend, to watch a game at Old Trafford and invited my son along. We had seats in one of the boxes and before the match they brought round the Premier League trophy, so that VIP and corporate guests had the chance to be photographed with it.

When the trophy came to our box, we duly took our pictures. Then Kasper said to everyone present, 'The next time I hold this trophy it will be because I've won it. Next time you see my picture with it will be when it is mine.' This was March 2014, when he was playing for Leicester City in the Championship. Two years and two months later he had it in his hands again, as a Premier League winner.

How many people would bet on themselves in that way, at a time their club was not even in the Premier League, never mind a 5000–1 shot to win it? And not just bet on themselves – but go and back it up?

That is Kasper, a footballer who has had to dig deeper into his own reserves of resilience than nearly any. There is famous footage of him wearing a mini version of my green 'Schmeichel 1' shirt, playing outside the Old Trafford home dressing room with Alex Bruce, Tom Ince and Mark Hughes's son Alex. Every day after school in our cul-de-sac, Kasper and Alex Bruce would bring a small set of goals out and play football with each other. Kasper was always the goalie.

Those were the innocent days. He did not set out from the beginning to be a professional goalkeeper. He went through phases when he wanted to be a policeman, a doctor and a fireman. But he was always interested in football and goalkeeping. His issues started when he began playing for his school. My God, the cruelty, the petty-mindedness of some parents of boys from opposition teams. They stood shouting at this little boy: 'Hah, you think you're as good as your dad . . . but you're shit!' That kind of stuff. He was a child, but they did not care.

I stopped going, because I came to the conclusion that my presence on the touchline was not beneficial to him. I felt in a Catch 22. You want to go and support your son but know that being there will work against him. Opposition kids abused him too. People are people, you cannot change it; some will always be vindictive and stupid. Some people, when they are around a famous person, change their personality. They become somehow bold. They march over and interrupt your conversation. 'Oh, I've never done this before, but can I have your autograph?' They think they own you. All of that was part of the territory for me, but here it was getting twisted and turned upon my child. Kasper, quite naturally, grew discouraged.

I would say to any adult who stands on the sides yelling at players in a kids' game: grab hold of yourself. Remember the obvious. THESE ARE KIDS. These are little, vulnerable human beings with underdeveloped emotions who are learning about life. Cruelty and aggression will stop them in their tracks, make them insecure, sad. Support them. And if you don't have anything supportive to say, shut up. If you really have a need to go and scream at footballers, then buy a ticket to a match and go scream at the professionals, because they are equipped to take it. If I ran a country's football, I would have zero tolerance – anyone raising their voice at kids on a football pitch would be banned from attending junior games and never welcomed back.

I saw what being barracked did to my son. He came home very sad sometimes. And my remedy of not going to watch him any more – that was sad for us too. He even stopped playing for a while and went to a gymnastics club. He was fantastic at gymnastics, by the way. He worked one-to-one with a tutor, a former GB Olympian called Paul Bowler, and he was good enough to compete. It is one of the reasons he is so agile. Instead of football, I started going to his gymnastics, to watch him train and offer my support there.

When he was getting yelled at in those school games I said something which, looking back, was wrong. I told him, 'This is part of it. If you want to play football, you have to take this stuff.' In hindsight, I can see he might have thought, *Okay, if this is football, I want no part of it.*

Then again, what else could I have said? I also told him that what he was having to go through was out of order. I tried to say the right things, but maybe I would have been better just listening and sympathising. If you cut to the chase, I was probably not the best parent. I was in the thick of my own career and did not have a lot of extra capacity. I lacked the bandwidth to deal with stuff that was outside of my own needs and pressures as a player. I never watched football on TV, for example. In my Manchester United days, I avoided the newspapers. I had enough on my plate with the demands of playing for United and Denmark. From the start, when Kasper began playing, I had to dig deep: *My son has a game, I had better go and watch it.* To then witness the behaviour my presence provoked was very difficult. But, if I am being truly honest, I think that also gave me a bit of a cheap excuse to stay away. Probably, it was a bit of both.

Now let me tell you a story about Cecilie. Being the child of Peter Schmeichel presented challenges to her too. When your dad is a famous footballer, of course there are benefits, but there can also be issues and life, for my daughter, was not always straightforward at school.

Cecilie must have been thirteen, maybe fourteen – an age when girls, especially, are emotionally vulnerable. We were living in Alderley Edge and she found herself being picked on at school, basically because of me. 'Your dad's this . . .' 'You think you're that . . .' The jealousy was ridiculous, but I get it: kids don't know any better.

There was this one girl, the self-styled 'it girl', who dominated the peer group. She would hold court and when she said 'jump', other girls jumped; so when she said 'tease Cecilie', that's what all the other girls did.

This went on for quite some time. Often, Cecilie would come home from school crying. One day, I sat her down and said, 'Enough is enough. I cannot stop this for you. Your teachers cannot stop this for you. There is only one person in this life who can do that – and it is you.'

We talked. I told her that the best way to fight back was to confront this girl. Talk to her. Tell her directly what the teasing is doing, how it is making you feel, what your experience of school is like as a result. Then tell her that despite all that, she does not matter. That in the bigger picture of your life, she is an unimportant speck. That you will happily continue being who you are, whatever she does. Cecilie had been trying to solve the problem by getting in with this girl and her cronies, and I said you have to do the opposite – walk away.

Well, Cecilie was brilliant. She phoned the girl up. She said, 'Do you know what you're doing to me?' and, calmly, she laid the whole thing out. The next day at school, her tormentor miscalculated. The girl told all the others about the conversation, thinking she could use it to provoke even more teasing of my daughter, but it had the opposite effect. Knowing that somebody had at last stood up to the bully was the catalyst for others to do the same, and now she had everyone telling her they didn't like her behaviour – and she lost her status and had to change her ways.

For Cecilie, the tables also turned. Among all the girls and, indeed, boys in her circle she had new-found respect and life at the school was good for her from then on. I like the story because it sums my 'other child' up: a girl who might not be as famous as her brother, but is just as mentally tough, just as special. My daughter, she fights her own battles – and, being Cecilie, she wins.

For the children of footballers, the attention it brings is not the only difficult thing. Players move about in their careers, taking their families with them, and Cecilie likes to joke, 'I grew up on a plane.' The timing of my moves meant her having to change countries at a few tricky points in her upbringing. The first was when I joined Manchester United, not long before her first birthday. The period when we were settling into life in England coincided with the stage in her development when she should have been learning to talk, so when her speech was a little slow to come, we simply put it down to her being in a new country and suddenly surrounded by a different language. In fact, she had a hearing problem that affects a lot of little children and as soon as she had grommets put in she was okay and everything changed – but it took us some time to work out the issue.

Another example is that she has always been into cars and could not wait to get her driving licence. She applied herself to passing the test and gained her licence at seventeen, when we were still in England. But no sooner had she done that than we moved to Denmark – where you have to be eighteen to drive a car. She was also the one who had it hardest when we moved to Portugal. Nearly 50 per cent of the Portuguese population are Benfica supporters, so at school there was a lot of teasing about me playing for Sporting, especially when we had a bad result. She was only nine years old and it was not easy for her to put up with.

We left Manchester when Kasper was twelve, and Portugal was important for Kasper's football development. There, he joined his first proper club – Estoril – and the environment was better for him, no silly parents, far more enjoyable. Their boys' section had practice sessions in the evenings, sometimes on the beach, sometimes in Parede, which was thirty minutes from our home. It was different. He really progressed, although when he arrived back in Denmark two years later, it was still not clear whether he wanted to be a footballer.

He went to a school called Oure Efterskole. It was not a boarding school in the English sense, but pupils do board and it follows the Danish system of 'after schools' where, once you have done the equivalent of GCSEs, you can spend a year focusing on a specialty. That could be sport, music, art, agriculture, whatever. From there, you might go to college, into an apprenticeship or full-time work.

Oure Efterskole was renowned for sport and performing arts and Kasper specialised in football. It was his coach there, Bo Pedersen, who inspired him to try and become a pro. 'Have you any idea how talented you are?' the guy told him. Of course he did not, because he was my son. He was the son of a Manchester United goalkeeper and not a goalkeeper in his own right. Unfortunately, that was to become a theme for the next ten years, but this coach cut through all that and saw it.

He switched Kasper's ambition and enthusiasm to maximum setting. In 2002, when I signed for Manchester City and the family came over to live with me again in Cheshire, Kasper joined Manchester City – but it could have been Manchester United, had they been willing to give him a chance. He had a trial which was supposed to last a week, but on the first day, going for a ball, he was kicked in the face and a tooth came loose. He went to hospital, where the doctors advised a couple of days' rest. Dave Bushell, United's development officer, told him not to bother coming back.

So, Kasper went to Manchester City. Jim Cassell, their academy head, something of a legend in youth coaching, loved him and Alex Gibson, his coach when he joined City's Under-15s, was terrific. I started watching his games again. I saw as many as I could. When he played at home, I watched from Jim's office, which looked out onto the youth pitches at Platt Lane.

One Saturday morning they were playing Blackburn. I arrived two minutes late. As I turned the corner from the training-ground building I got my first view of the game. At that very moment, Blackburn took a corner and their centre half was unmarked. It was just him versus Kasper and he headed it over. Time froze. The player was Alex Bruce and my mind's eye saw two little boys in our old cul-de-sac. I looked again and on the touchline of this academy game, there were Steve and Janet Bruce. We stood together watching our sons play, having watched them from our windows for hours upon hours as little kids. Wow.

A couple of years later, Kasper had just signed for Leeds. I got a call from Janet. Like Steve, she is from the north-east and you know how, in that Geordie accent, sometimes you don't know if they are happy or sad? She said, 'Oooh, Peter, have you heard about Alex?' I was like, 'Oh no – what's happened?' She said, 'Ah, no, Alex has also just signed for Leeds!' So our two boys even got to play together, one of those magical coincidences football sometimes throws into the mix.

One of the things about Kasper of which I'm most proud is his willingness to educate himself, and in his early football career that involved going to extremes to get game time. He went to Darlington on loan, then Bury, for two spells, then Falkirk and the tough school of the Scottish Premier League. Instead of sitting in the reserves, playing nice, fluffy, academy games, he went out and played for teams and managers whose existence depended on his performances, with team-mates who needed results to earn the bonuses that paid their mortgages. Darlington, for example, had a 25,000-seat stadium that was five-sixths empty, an owner in prison and financial pressure to get out of League Two. It was rough. People were scraping to get by. I travelled the country, watching as many of those loan games as I could.

In August 2007, I was in Russia shooting a series for the Discovery Channel – a European version of the American series *Dirty Jobs*. Kasper called to say there was a chance he could be starting the season as Manchester City's first-team keeper. City's first game was West Ham away and he might be playing. I rescheduled as much of the filming as I could and made arrangements to get to London. It was not easy. I was in Yaroslavl, 250 kilometres north of Moscow, and organised a car to take me to the airport. I said to them, 'You must get me a good, safe vehicle with a good driver.' I came out of my hotel at 5 a.m. and was met by the oldest car I have seen in my life. And the driver was the grandad of the guy who built it!

I had the choice: do I risk my life in this broken-down wreck, driven by a pensioner, and see my son – or stay here? Of course, it was no dilemma, really. I got in the car. The old man proved every bit as bad a driver as he looked. He was going fast and slow. We were on country roads with other crazy drivers, people overtaking and undertaking, the speed limit completely irrelevant to everyone. I just closed my eyes and accepted things. *If we crash and I die, I'm going to die in the knowledge my son was playing today and I tried to get there.*

The journey went on for ever. I was booked on British Airways and of Moscow's three airports, the flight of course departed from the airport furthest away. We hit an eight-lane motorway, jam-packed with traffic. We slowed to about half a mile an hour. I kept checking my watch, in panic. My ancient driver started nodding off and rolled into the car in front of us. Its driver got out, in a rage.

To describe him, he was wearing shorts and a vest. His face was purple with fury and he kind of looked like Putin. Reaching in through the window, he grabbed my old chauffeur and hauled him out of the car and then went to fetch something from his car. *Shit, he's going to get a gun.* Miraculously and thankfully, at that very moment the traffic started moving again and my guy jumped back in our car and hit the accelerator. The vest guy came running after us and managed to get hold of the taxi sign on top of our car and rip it off before running back to his car, making do with that as revenge.

My driver was trembling but was able to complete the rest of the journey and get me to the airport just in time for the flight. In London, I went straight to Upton Park. West Ham were lovely, they looked after me. I even had time for some food. Then I took my seat in the stand. The teams came out.

My son is playing in the Premier League.

It suddenly hit me.

My son is playing in the Premier League!

I have watched him play a million times, but here he is now, nineteen years old and playing in the Premier League. I stared at Kasper and could not stop thinking that in comparison to everyone else he looked like a child. *My son is still a child!* And I got really nervous. I felt terrified. My boy – there he is, exposed to the whole world, and there is nothing I can do. I cannot protect him. The lions are coming.

Five minutes in, Kasper had dealt with a cross, caught a shot and made a good pass. *This is all right.* On he went, doing all his jobs well. *He can deal with this!* And there was a point when the nerves left me and I just sat back and enjoyed it. That has been the story ever since. Watching Kasper is a treat. For the first time since joining Manchester United all those years ago, I actually enjoy watching football.

Cecilie was – still is – a real tomboy and football is one of her passions as well. She loved playing. She was always out with Kasper in the garden, with the ball. Later, when she played with a girls' team in Denmark, she was a goalkeeper too. When I was playing, she always came to my games and after I stopped, she usually wanted to tag along whenever I was going to watch a match. For obvious reasons, her team is Leicester – and, deep down, Manchester United.

On our cul-de-sac in Bramhall, her playmate was Amy Bruce, Alex's little sister. Amy wasn't much into football, so they didn't join the boys for kickabouts: it was all dolls and imaginary games. In those days, the opportunities in England for girls to play football were limited, which was a pity for Cecilie because if she was growing up in Manchester now, I'm sure she would have had great fun playing for girls' teams. Yet football did end up serving her well.

She was keen to finish her schooling at Oure, as Kasper had done, and one of the main reasons we moved back to Denmark in 2007 was to support her there. But initially she took the brave step of going over to Copenhagen by herself and boarding at Oure, where she got in by being accepted via its dancing programme. But she found most of the other girls on it were ballet-trained and extremely good and quickly realised it wasn't going to be for her, so she talked to the teachers and persuaded them to let her switch – to the football programme.

Oure was incredible for her. There, she met her future husband, Joakim. They were in the same dormitory. To this day she has a large social circle made up of friends she made during her year at the school. After Oure, I was keen for her to go to a local college, but nobody makes up Cecilie's mind for her – she chose a different institution and I spent three years worrying that, because she had moved countries and schools so often, and her education had been unsettled, she might struggle to pass her degree course. But she kept saying to me, 'Dad – relax, I've got this, I'll be fine,' and she came out with a really good mark.

I'll never forget the feeling when she got her results. It was very similar to that experience of sitting at Upton Park watching Kasper and being hit by the sudden realisation: *Your kid's going to be okay . . . more than okay.* Cecilie is my little girl and my urge had always been to protect her, maybe even – if I'm honest – to be controlling sometimes. Well, that was the moment I knew she'd be all right, that she doesn't need me, doesn't need her dad for anything other than to be her friend.

And what a sweet feeling that is, when you realise your children are truly strong and independent. When kids are younger, you try to warn them about everything, to shield them from the pitfalls of life and manage their decisions for them. But it is so much better when you get to the point where you don't need to play that role any more. Then you can just relax, enjoy their company, take pride in what they're doing and – if you are lucky – watch them bring up their own kids.

Cecilie's degree is in sales. It was a three-year college diploma plus a two-year apprenticeship and towards the end of it she became interested in working in TV, so she took further training in make-up artistry. Then the career plans went on hold when she had her two children, Noah and Sofie.

She is like me. She will try stuff, do stuff, commit to it, but then be prepared to cut her losses and move on if it is obvious that something else might work better. Which is what she did. When she returned to the working world, she began doing projects for a company that specialises in creating display stands in supermarkets and shopping malls, marketing things like cinemas and entertainment events. She realised that she had found her path: at the end of the day, she is one of life's organisers, a creative person who organises, and the role that is perfect for all her interests and skills is as an event coordinator. She wants to be fully qualified and so she is back in education again, completing a three-year event-management degree.

As well as studying, she is carving a growing niche as an influencer on Instagram. When she was expecting Sofie, her second child, she developed weight problems during the pregnancy, leading to issues and a few home truths being delivered by the doctors at the hospital when Sofie was born. After that she made massive changes to her life and, via blogging and social media, has become an inspiration for a lot of young girls who find themselves trapped in the same situation, who don't have anyone to talk to or know how to change their lifestyle and diet. Cecilie, who lost 30 kilos, posted before and after pictures on Instagram and wrote powerfully about her journey, striking a chord with many women. Now, she has a very active lifestyle, eats well and trains every day. She appears on TV programmes and does newspaper articles talking about eating disorders to try and help others. Last year she was on Denmark's version of *Come Dine With Me*.

Including his debut, Kasper excelled in a run of seven games for City, winning Man of the Match against Arsenal and keeping clean sheets against Manchester United, Aston Villa, Derby and West Ham, that day. Sven-Göran Eriksson, his manager, loved him but came under pressure to play Joe Hart – the English kid – and Kasper ended up on loan again, first at Cardiff, then Coventry. Chris Coleman was Coventry manager and I remember sitting in his office and him saying, 'Your boy is seriously talented, Pete.' Cookie wanted to sign him permanently. The deal fell through, for reasons unclear, and that was the first time I truly became wary of agents and advisers. Wary in general.

I could see, suddenly, how many people were hanging around football with intentions that were not honourable, with an interest only in themselves. In my own playing career I had been fortunate to have good representatives and I had not given too much thought to the problem of how many chancers were in the game. Now, with my son's future on the line, and me trying not to advise him, I could see it: the cynicism, the shortage of those who had players' best interests at heart. I realised something else: that I was a problem. I intimidated people. Some were paranoid that I was pushing my son to do this or that. Nothing could have been further from the truth. I had no desire to be Kasper's agent or manager and I deliberately stepped back from any active role when he made moves and career decisions.

We only spoke about that stuff when Kasper came to me, seeking advice. I never touted him around clubs or tried using my influence to get him ahead in some way. The one and only time I ever spoke to a manager about him was when, to help save the club financially, he left Notts County in 2010, giving up any claim to the six-figure sum still owed from his contract. Kasper became a free agent and I called Fergie and said, 'Take him, he won't cost you a penny.' Edwin was thirty-nine and entering his last year at Old Trafford: for Manchester United, getting Kasper on a free would have been some steal. But Fergie was not interested. I suspect he didn't want any of his former players' sons at his club. He probably did not want their dads phoning him up and offering opinions.

That is not something I would ever have done. We made an agreement right at the start of his journey in the professional game, when he was signing for Manchester City's academy. The deal was this. If he ever wanted advice, he would have to come to me – I would never go to him. I was not going to be his coach, I was not going to be his agent, I would not be interfering. My role was to be his father, his dad.

It made sense from a footballing point of view. One of my strengths as a player was having a clear mind. I always did my own thing. I made my own decisions on the pitch. It would not have done Kasper any good to have my voice in his head saying, *Do this, do that*, when he was playing. But our deal had nothing to do with that. It had everything to do with our family life. We could not be sitting round the breakfast table, me saying he should be doing one thing on the field and him saying another.

There is a trend towards footballers being represented by family members, but imagine being your son's agent, imagine being the player. If you have bad advisers you sack them – but if your bad adviser is your father, what do you do? Sack Dad? I could name a couple of examples where talented players did not fulfil their potential because their fathers were in charge of their careers and pushed them the wrong way. I went through a long career and know there is another life to be lived. You have to be able to come home, leave football behind and be an ordinary person, but if you have lost your ordinary family relationships because your dad or mum or brother or partner or uncle advised you, then what do you have left?

Just once did I ever seek to influence Kasper's development. It was the day after Leicester clinched the Championship title in 2014. I went to their training the next day. Everyone was happy, the atmosphere was loose and Kasper was doing a session with coach Mike Stowell. I said to Stowelly, 'I think you and Kasper have done brilliantly, but there is one thing I wish I could see

Kasper adding to his game. I would love him to be just a bit more brave with his starting position. If only he could start a couple of feet further forward, he would be able to prevent this and that.' This was something Kasper had already discussed and I said it to put something in Stowelly's head. And he took it in; he is a fantastic goalkeeping coach, by the way. Over the years Kasper has really improved on his starting position.

Otherwise, I have not interfered with a thing. If Kasper Schmeichel is one of the world's top goalkeepers, then that is entirely his work, not mine. What I have tried to help with is the stuff around playing. From the start, I wanted to put in his mind that his road was not going to be easy, that he only had to look at examples of other players with famous fathers to know that there would be pressure and there would be comparisons, which would be relentless and unjustified.

The other thing I try and do is demystify football for Kasper. From the start I have gone out of my way to tell him that footballers are not special. Players are just young people with a talent, who have worked hard to develop it and get paid extremely well as a result. But that does not make them special human beings. They are just people. A lot of footballers understand that, but even more of them do not, and it has been a lifetime's assignment for me to put Kasper in the first category. I never wanted to see him caked in tattoos with a different hairstyle every week. When I see that, I see a person spending time and energy on irrelevant things. Someone who thinks, *I'm playing Saturday, so I'm going to get a red stripe in my hair because people will love it.* Instead of, *I'm playing Saturday, I am going to spend every available second preparing for the game.*

There can only be performance. There cannot be an alternative way of projecting who you are.

I understand the younger generation are different. They want to express themselves, put everything on display. Social media has changed humanity. There are seven billion people in the world and that means seven billion worlds are right there in your hand: seven billion lives and opinions being tweeted, TikTokked and Instagrammed on your phone. I want players to ignore the noise and concentrate on the game, and my son is of the new generation, so, in some ways, that means expecting him to go against what is automatic for his peers.

We've had situations where something has troubled him and, as one of the leaders at Leicester and in the Denmark team, he feels he should comment. He might write a statement and ask me to read it before he puts it out. I nearly always tell him to sleep on it and I draw on my own history of communication (or miscommunication!) with the press. I know a few pitfalls. For example, I could use the expression 'training regime' in an interview with English papers, in England a perfectly harmless phrase. But if a word like 'regime' gets picked up in Denmark, you are in trouble. There, 'regime' means 'dictatorship'. So, now, you have just called your coach a dictator.

My point is always that, whatever you say, you have to think about every phrase, and before you speak, you have to consider, 'What am I trying to achieve?' Having a go at someone in an interview is like pissing in your pants. You get a nice warm feeling to begin with, but it very quickly gets uncomfortable. I think Kasper has pretty much succeeded, over his career, in projecting himself in the right way, and while I cannot claim credit for any of his goalkeeping, I would like to think I have had input into that.

The most important thing of all? Our greatest achievement? We still have a father–son relationship. More than anything, these days, we are friends. That is important. My father died last year. I only have to walk out of my house, 200 yards, and there is the cemetery. I go there to water the flowers on his grave. I am fifty-seven and still have a need to show him something, to make him proud. Very often, Kasper FaceTimes me when he is cooking. He likes to show me the dish he is making; like all sons, he wants his father to be proud of him. Believe me, oh, I am. My biggest pride in life is not my football career, but my kids.

Kasper's wife is Stine, a qualified midwife and they have three beautiful children: Max, Isabella and Nanna Sofia, the newest Schmeichel, born in May 2021. Cecilie's husband, Joakim, a trained car mechanic, is moving into the management side of his company and works very hard, often on the other side of Denmark, leaving Cecilie with a lot of time to look after Noah and Sofie by herself.

She's a brilliant mother and the other day I picked her kids up from school. We were going out for ice-cream. The first thing little Noah, who is six, did, was run to his room and put on his Manchester United shirt. Fantastic. Except, as well as United, he is also a big FC Copenhagen fan. This means that, as a Brøndby supporter, I have to tease him – but he teases me back, and not in a kiddie way, but in a really sharp, funny manner. Still with respect for his grandad – but it is almost proper banter.

That reflects on Cecilie. She has this incredible mixture of the good bits of both English and Danish character in her personality and has passed it on to her kids, who are cheeky and wild, emotional and strong. They want to be hugged, they want to be carried – but they are also independent-minded, clever, wanting to do things for themselves.

What is Kasper and Cecilie's dynamic? Well, the old roles will always be there somewhere in the background. Kasper will always be the big brother and Cecilie the kid sister, but the more time passes, the more they are just friends: two equals, two grown-ups with their own kids and lives, who share a wonderful bond. Kasper might be the famous one, but Cecilie is just as important to the Schmeichel dynasty. For her, family is at the heart of everything. She is our organiser, the one who looks after the clan, who makes sure we look after each other and have get-togethers.

When Kasper is on the pitch, I don't see him as a child any more. I don't see my son. I see an incredible goalkeeper in whose abilities you can trust. Footage went viral of me losing it in the stand in Nizhny Novgorod as I witnessed his extraordinary feats against Croatia at the 2018 World Cup. He saved a penalty from Luka Modrić in extra time and saved two more when it went to a shoot-out, yet Denmark still lost the round-of-16 tie. Normally, I mask what I'm feeling when I watch him, but that game brought a rollercoaster of emotions.

Another story. Remember Leicester 5 Manchester United 3, that unbelievable Premier League match from 2014–15? I had to miss being at the King Power stadium because I was committed to playing a golf event in Denmark. The organiser was Dan

Sørensen, a massive Man U fan, and he came driving down the fairway in a buggy yelling, 'Heey, United 3–1 up, this is brilliant!' I suddenly got angry. 'That's so insensitive. That's my son!' We came in to find Leicester had turned it around and won. I was so happy and proud, and that evening I reflected on it: *I am happy that Manchester United lost a game.* I had never expected to feel that in my whole life – and, in all honesty, I found it a little hard to deal with.

My feelings confused me until I was doing a show with Jamie Redknapp and he was asked which team he supported. Which of the clubs he had played for: Liverpool? Tottenham? West Ham? Jamie replied, 'No, wherever my dad is managing.' Suddenly things made sense. I thought, *I can live with this now.* It was okay to support more than Manchester United. It is okay that I want my son to win first, then United. Blood is thicker than water, as they say.

Now, I have incredible feelings for Leicester. I am so in awe of what the club has achieved. I might be the only one on the planet to think this . . . but I didn't see them winning the league in 2015–16 as a 5000–1 shot; it was not a surprise to me. I had seen them build, brick by brick, the right culture, the right squad of players. They got to that golden point where as a group of footballers they knew exactly what they needed to do, both in games and in preparation during the week. All over the pitch they had winners who could change the course of a game in one moment. They got to the point where they could even win the league with Claudio Ranieri in charge.

My intention is not to be cruel to Claudio, but 2015–16 was a players' triumph, not one of management. Initially, Ranieri was against the way Leicester played; that game of long, fast coun-terattacks based around Jamie Vardy's strengths. Nor did he fancy N'Golo Kanté. He inherited a battle-hardened team, one with competitive knowledge built on the experiences of two play-off defeats, a dominant Championship season, then the 'Great Escape' of 2014–15. During that season, though they fought relegation, they were close in every single game; nobody beat them lightly. I would watch Kasper and see a team that was going to start winning. I thought, *The only thing holding you back is that you don't know how good you are.*

I am on record during the Great Escape as saying that Leicester could finish in the top six the next season. I could see it. No one could handle their way of playing. At that point most Premier League teams wanted to be possession-based: but how do you deal with a team that just sits there and launches lethal weapons – Vardy, Riyad Mahrez, Marc Albrighton – that come at you with such pace?

Nigel Pearson created an environment in which the bond between players was unbreakable and their idea of how they should play was 100 per cent clear. On the pitch, the players took control. They played the way they felt. They took control of the tactics. I feel sorry for Nigel, because he left the club before he could finish the job: I am convinced, had he stayed, he would have won the league too. Dilly dong? I never bought that stuff.

In 2015–16, I came over to be at every Leicester game I could and watched all the other ones on TV. When you have been in title-winning sides yourself, you see the signs. Leicester had a way of playing and a belief in themselves they never deviated from. They won big games, like Liverpool and Chelsea at home and Tottenham and Manchester City away. After going down 2–1 at Arsenal with twelve matches to go they simply stopped conceding goals. Other sides were not catching up. Tottenham seemed likely to run out of legs because, historically, that almost always happened with Mauricio Pochettino teams. You saw, in every game, Spurs using up so much energy, whereas Leicester hung back and conserved it.

The day it really hit home that they were going to be title-winners was when they beat Manchester City 3–1 at the Etihad stadium. I looked at the fixture list. Manchester United v Leicester, 1 May, Old Trafford. *That's where they're going to clinch the title*, I thought. Of course I was going to be there. May 1 is Laura's birthday and it was to be the first time I had taken her to Old Trafford, but on the day she got sick. She was so brave. We had been invited to lunch before the match with Richard Arnold, Eric Cantona and the CEO of Aeroflot. Laura was determined that nothing would spoil my day. She struggled through the first part of lunch until she felt too ill to sit there any longer and Richard arranged for her to go and lie on the couch in his office for the whole match.

In a way, Leicester did clinch the title that day, because by the next time they played they were already champions. We left on the morning of the following Monday, when Chelsea's 2–2 draw with Spurs at Stamford Bridge ensured that Leicester could not be caught. We immediately booked another trip: to be at the

King Power on the Saturday, to see Leicester receive the trophy after playing Everton.

Leicester went 3–0 up and, fifteen minutes before full time, players' friends and families were called to go down to the pitch. Each player was allowed four guests, so our group would be me, Kasper's wife, Stine, and Max and Isabella, my grandchildren. Kasper went into the game just one clean sheet from winning the Golden Glove. For the entire presentation I thought the match had finished 3–0, but when we finally got to speak the first thing Kasper said to me was '******* hell, that goal we conceded!'

While we had been making our way down to the field, Kevin Mirallas had scored for Everton, with Leicester easing off. Kasper's annoyance was typical of him – and something that pleased me very much.

Players should never chase individual awards. The moment they do that, they stop putting the team first. But the fact is you want to clean the stable, you want to take every prize going, and greed is good for a sportsman in terms of ambition. I liked Kasper's annoyance. Because it said to me that he was already thinking, *Yeah, I've won the Premier League, but I want to win other things.* The way he continues to improve, excel and drive himself on demonstrates that attitude in action.

And so here is the scene. It is just past 5 p.m. on a windy May day in the Midlands. I am in the centre circle of the King Power, standing with my lovely daughter-in-law and beautiful grand-kids. We are 20 yards from the podium, watching Andrea Bocelli sing 'Nessun dorma', amid golden tickertape and fire-works. And then . . . my son goes and lifts the Premier League trophy. *The next time I hold this, it will be because I've won it.*

This man, who not long ago was a little boy kicking a ball in our cul-de-sac with Alex Bruce.

The simple way of explaining my feelings is this. I won eleven trophies with Manchester United, five with Brøndby, two with Sporting Lisbon and the European Championship with my country. Every trophy felt unbelievable, especially the league titles. You have met expectations, you have fulfilled your responsibilities; the pride you feel for your team-mates, the coaching staff, the fans, your family, is incredible. You are on top of the world. You do not think the feeling could ever be beaten. Nothing in your life is going to top it.

But then your son goes and does it, and it feels twice as good. Kasper winning the Premier League was so much better than winning it myself. I am looking at my boy and he is lifting a trophy that he has seen so many times, in my hands. A trophy he has been photographed with from an early age on Manchester United title parades and laps of honour, when all the families join the squad.

My son, a Premier League champion – believe me, oh, I am proud of him.

But the thing about Kasper is he was never going to stop there, and the same is true of Leicester. The following season, they did not just go into the Champions League like happy tourists, but played like a side with serious ambitions, and Kasper was outstanding as they reached the quarter-finals, where they pushed Atlético Madrid to the limit. And since Brendan Rodgers arrived, competing at the top end of the Premier League has been a familiar experience for Leicester, not a novel one.

Throughout that journey, Kasper has continued to get better. He always wants more. And in May 2021, he lifted – as Leicester's captain – another trophy he had coveted since seeing it in my arms as a kid: the FA Cup. Covid travel restrictions stopped me from getting to Wembley to see him doing it, but as I watched at home in Denmark, I marvelled all over again at my son and his team. Their victory over a Chelsea side who went on to be Champions League winners was a masterpiece of togetherness, determination and quality play, not least an extraordinary save Kasper pulled off from Mason Mount in the final moments of the game, to preserve Leicester's 1–0 advantage.

I smiled, because against the same player, in the same stadium, he had made a similarly brilliant stop when Denmark defeated England in October 2020. Wembley and the Schmeichels continues to be a wonderful story.

It was the first FA Cup win in Leicester's history and as the players showed off the trophy, Kasper ran to the stands and brought Khun Top, the owner, onto the pitch to join the celebrations. It was a beautiful scene, one which said so much about a club whose special power comes from relationships: between players, between players and staff, between players, staff and ownership, and between all of those with the supporters. It is a club of unsung heroes who stay in the background, not least Susan Whelan, the remarkable chief executive, whose empathy and abilities were especially important in the aftermath of Khun Vichai's traumatic death.

There is just something about that Leicester story. Vichai would have turned sixty-three a few weeks before the final and his favourite number was eight. At Wembley, Leicester's winning goal came in the sixty-third minute, scored by Youri Tielemans, their No 8.

And here's something else. When Kasper became a Premier League winner in 2015–16 it was on exactly the same day (2 May), and in exactly the same manner (sitting at home while the team's closest rivals slipped up), that I won my first title in 1992–93. And he won the FA Cup on the same weekend that I won my first FA Cup, twenty-seven years previously – against the same opponents, Chelsea.

21
LEGACY

I opened the front door of my house in Cascais and there he was on the porch, my father. I had come armed with a torch, which I raised to his face. I shone its bright, white light in his eyes.

'What do you want here?' I said.

My dad smiled. 'Ah, my family, my family.'

I raised my voice. 'What the hell do you want? You're not welcome here.'

We held each other's gaze. He tried again. I yelled back. This went on for ten minutes. 'Go to the airport,' I told him. 'No one wants to see you here. We don't want you here. Go back. Go back.'

I shut the door on him in the end. Just shut the door. My sister was waiting in the hall and my mother was in the kitchen. My heart was in my guts. I felt sick with a mix of anger and pain.

I have never had to do anything worse in my life.

My dad reckoned he was in the grip of alcoholism for thirty to thirty-five years. So we are talking about from when I was about six, Kathrine was eight, Margrethe was four and before Hanne was born. Not until the last year or two did we realise he had a problem. He was very self-disciplined in a way, careful to never drink at home.

But it was his work. His job was to be among drinkers, playing his piano through the evening and long into the night. He was around alcohol all the time, could not avoid it.

And he had demons. What happened to his father, all his questions about his mother. He carried a lot of hurt in his backpack.

When I was at Manchester United and he visited us in England, I started to notice a few little things that, in hindsight, were signs of an issue. But I never really paid too much attention. Everyone liked a bit of a drink, didn't they? It was during 1998–99 that things started to develop – and quickly. By the autumn of 1999, my father was drinking himself into terrible danger. Over a period of several months, we had tried interventions and to persuade him to go down the rehab route, but without success. He came to that point where an alcoholic either goes into treatment or might die.

He was resistant when my mother, sisters and I made attempts to get him to accept treatment. In denial, he became nasty. Someone explained to me that alcoholism is an illness, that the person you love is still there but is maybe only five per cent of what you see. Ninety-five per cent is the alcohol. But that five per cent – that is your hope.

We read books on alcoholism and tried to learn from specialists. The advice was: isolate, isolate, isolate. That when all else fails, when your loved one refuses treatment and does not want to change, you have to cut them off. You must show them that you will no longer take any part in their destructive lifestyle. By shocking them, you might just be able to reach through their fog of booze and pain, grasp that little five per cent and haul it out.

Kathrine and Margrethe completely isolated themselves from him. He was becoming so manipulative that Hanne escaped Denmark and came to live with us in Portugal, and my mother joined us there too. It was heartbreaking. The Danish national team doctor, Mogens Kreutzfeldt, such a nice guy, went round to my parents' apartment to keep an eye on my father. Mogens called me up one day and said, 'Listen, it's really serious now. He has days left if he carries on like this.'

We were all in the house in Cascais, Hanne and my mother, me and the family. My father seemed to have no way of finding us. He did not have any phone numbers and he did not have an address. All he knew was I had moved to a club in Lisbon. I had gone out into the garden, walking my dog after dark, when my mobile rang.

'Your dad is here.'

I said I was coming straight back and told them not to let him in; on no account allow him in through the security gates.

'We already have.'

He was waiting on the porch to be let into the house and I went through our back door, took a deep breath and opened the front door, torch in hand. That is when, scarcely believing what I was having to say, I yelled at my own dad until he went away.

When our stand-off was over and he had stumbled off into the night, I confronted my mother and sister. I was angry beyond belief.

Why was I the one who had to confront these things? Do the horrible stuff?

Why didn't they support me? Why had they let him in?

An hour later, someone came to the house and said they had found this guy, a guy who was lost and confused but who claimed to be my father. Hanne took Dad to a hotel in Lisbon and got him on a plane back to Copenhagen the following day. He went straight into treatment.

And never touched a drink again.

The whole family was filled with joy. Except my father and me. My mother stayed with us for four months, then when she was sure Dad had straightened himself out, she went home to live with him again and both were so happy – except he would not talk to me. One day I called Mum up and said, 'I don't understand this situation. I don't understand why I am not part of this so-called happiness. Why all of you are carrying on and everything is brilliant for you. Except for me – because I no longer speak to my father.'

She said, 'Ah, but he's not happy with you. He didn't like the way you spoke to him on the doorstep, the way you shone the torch in his face . . .'

For the first and only time in my life, I spoke in real anger to my mother.

'Do you not realise,' I said, 'that he went to rehab because of what I did? You didn't have to do it. My sisters didn't have to do it. *I* had to do it. I did it. Me. And it was the worst thing I've ever had to do. Tell him that torch saved his life – and he should think about that.'

Two hours later, Dad phoned me. He said he had been thinking about everything. 'Thank you, Peter.' We became the best of friends after that.

I still shudder when I think of him on the doorstep, but I guess I helped save my father's life and, in terms of the various things a person can do during their short time on this planet, that's not bad. Dad got twenty more years, twenty pretty good years. Right at the end, he was not so well – but he lived to nearly eighty-six and was so contented in his final two decades.

He tried the twelve steps, but gave up the programme after a year, announcing, 'It's not for me – but don't worry, I am not going to touch alcohol again.' And he didn't. He was brilliant with alcohol after that. He would take your glass of wine and smell it. 'Ah, that is a good year.' But the glass never went to his lips.

I wanted to go with my dad back to Toruń and all the other places in Poland that were important in his life. But we never quite got round to the trip. By the time I began planning one, his health was fading and soon he became too infirm to travel.

He adored Laura. My dad was a real charmer, by the way, and seemed to like several of Laura's friends too . . . When they get together, they compare notes on how he used to flirt with them: in his mid-eighties! Being dapper and well groomed was always important to him, even in his final year, when he was in and out of hospital and was suffering some form of memory loss, he never forgot to groom himself. He kept a little soap bag with nail clippers, razors and all sorts by his bed on the ward.

He was very happy that Laura and I had found each other. I proposed to Laura in the Maldives at New Year 2019 and FaceTimed him. He was in hospital and things were pretty miserable for him by that stage; he kept improving but then deteriorating. Mentally, sometimes he seemed there, sometimes not, and my mother was providing constant care. However, when I told Dad that I planned on asking Laura to marry me, there was the biggest smile facing me on my screen.

'Oh, I love Laura,' he said.

'Well, you are going to be at the wedding,' I replied.

'Oh, yes.'

We began organising and brought it forward to early summer in the hope he could be there. But he did not make it. My father died on 7 May 2019, five weeks before we were married in Egebæksvang Church in Espergærde. We did not want a traditional reception, with a sit-down meal and long, boring speeches. What we wanted was an enormous party. There was a marquee in our garden, a band, a stage, lounge chairs and a champagne bar. We told people that if they had something to express, they could get up and sing a song or whatever.

The guests embraced this. They blew us away. There were songs and small performances; incredible thought went into them. Laura's brother, Theo, was master of ceremonies and did an unbelievable job. First to come up to the mic was Laura and I had no idea she had anything special planned. She made a speech and at the end said to me, 'You are the bravest person I ever met and I want to be as brave, so I am going to sing for you.'

Her friend and friend's husband, a good guitarist, got up and joined her; so, too, a trumpet player she had hired. They performed this most beautiful song, by a Swedish artist, Lisa

Ekdahl, called 'Vem vet'. It means 'Who knows'. I was speech-less. Wow. It was one of *the* moments of my life. It also presented me with a problem: how on earth could I follow that?

Theo called Laura's father, Jens, to the stage and then a couple of others did turns. Then I stepped up, with a guitar. I began by saying how happy and honoured Laura and I were that all those we invited had been able to come to our big day and then I said, 'There is only one person who cannot be here – and that is my dad.' I told the story of FaceTiming him from the Maldives, and of how he had fought like hell to be present but had not quite made it. I then turned to my friend Carsten and apologised.

There is a song that reminds Carsten of his father and I said I was sorry, but now he would have to share it – because the song describes my dad too. It is by a famous Danish musician, Kim Larsen, and it is 'Pianomand' – Piano Man. That was Tolek Schmeichel: the piano man.

Kasper has a wonderful voice, much better than mine, and he was very close to his grandad; they had a connection. When I played for United, my parents would come over, stay with us for long periods and spend a lot of time with the children. I had said to Kasper that, if he wanted, he should join me in singing 'Pianomand', but he wasn't sure. He is a person of strong emotions and I think he wondered whether, if he got up there, he would hold it together.

Emotions were now getting the better of me. It was difficult to even introduce the song without choking up. It was very weird: a lifetime of performing under pressure has given me mental toughness and an ability to control what is going on inside, but for the first time in my life I felt I was losing my grip.

All my feelings about my father were flooding through me like storm water. I had to stop talking at points and turn away; all those things I was used to seeing other people go through.

I managed to start strumming and singing and got through the first verse. Then, Kasper was by my side. He took over for the second verse.

'Is there music and song in the land of the dead, are they swinging there, Piano Man?'

People were crying. The room was hushed and full of emotion. My mum was sitting to one side and I could not see her face, but I know from my sisters that she was very, very happy. Singing that song meant that for the rest of the day people talked about my father. I had wanted to give him a presence. And now he was there.

When we finished, I lingered on stage. 'There is, of course, someone else I need to talk about,' I said, and I began speaking about Laura. I took my jacket off and put the guitar down because I didn't want her to guess what was coming next.

I had written a song. For years, I have been writing songs, but this one was the first that had ever come completely naturally. I had just got it in my head and called it 'The One and Only'. When I had proposed in the Maldives, our hotel was the One & Only Reethi Rah. I had led Laura down by the ocean. There was just us, the waves, a bottle of champagne and a music player on which I played Michael Jackson and Paul McCartney's 'The Girl is Mine'. Laura was blown away. Almost literally, because it was incredibly windy.

So, my song was about all of that. For two months, I had been secretly rehearsing and on the morning of our wedding I had sneaked to the marquee to check the sound system and give it another run-through. I had organised some special accompaniment: my vocal coach runs a choir, who agreed to come and be part of the performance. Had it not been for that, I might not have sung at all – Laura's performance had been so beautiful, I considered just leaving it there to speak for the both of us.

But the choir had arrived, so I picked up the guitar again. I said, 'Look, I can't really say in this speech what I want to express about Laura, so I'm going to do it through music.' I played my song and pretended I was at the end, then the members of the choir, who had stolen unnoticed into the back of the marquee, started singing and from different corners came up to join me on the stage. The mood after 'Pianomand' had been reflective, but the choir brought the gathering back to celebration mode.

That day was everything I hoped for and more, way more. The other person at the heart of it was Cecilie, who planned, organised and helped design the event and did the most sensitive, professional job. I can be a control freak, but every time I looked at the plans for our big occasion, I realised she was on top of every detail and making better calls than her dad ever could. All this, while dealing with her grandfather's passing. In some ways, Cecilie was closest to my father out of us all. She visited him in hospital every day; at the same time as planning our happy occasion, dealing with seeing her beloved grandfather slip away.

I am a brand ambassador for Manchester United. The work has taken me to different corners of the world and places that could be anywhere on the scale from outright poverty to unimaginable wealth. The interesting thing is that when you arrive representing Manchester United, rich/poor, old/young, male/female and all the other distinctions fall away. People express the same common sentiments and experiences. They ask the same questions, want the same selfies. Their basic needs are the same.

No club on the planet possesses Manchester United's reach. There is tragedy and beauty in the club's history and a tradition of special, inspirational players, giving United a unique emotional pull. The role has taken me to exquisite lunches at the Hong Kong Jockey Club, opulent dinners in the Middle East, jam-packed events in South Asia and one memorable – shambolic but wonderful – gala dinner in Ghana. There, I shared a top table with my old friend Kwame Ayew and old foe Sammy Kuffour.

The work has even taken me to the World Economic Forum in Davos. Every major leader on the planet was there, but only one football club had a presence: us. I travelled with Nemanja Vidić, to represent the sports side of the business and speak at a UNICEF event broadcast worldwide. CEOs from all the blue-chip companies came to see us.

Yet the trip with the most powerful memories was Belgrade. Our partner there was a bank. You do the usual stuff, meet executives, speak to the media, and all that was fine. Then they took us out to a shelter for children, run by an incredible woman. Kids there had been abandoned by their parents, abused and left homeless. Their situations broke your heart. But these kids were also happy and bright and well behaved. It was one of the most beautiful experiences of my life.

We were there to hand out Christmas presents – it was December. These kids had no idea who I was – I had played my last game long before they were born – but whenever you get to a place like that there is always someone who catches your eye and you connect with. And there was this little lad, he was so sad, it oozed out of him. He was following the others, but you could see it, the unhappiness.

So I took special care of him and when the visit was nearly over, he grabbed my hand. He wanted to show me where he slept. It was a room with bunk beds, a little table and a drawer. He wanted to show me his few possessions, invite me into his world. He spoke no English and I was emotional. I asked the interpreter, 'What's his story?'

She told me his brother was also in the shelter and their mother was in prison. The previous week she had been caught on the border to Bulgaria, trying to sell the two boys. Oh God.

We were at a big reception that evening, attended by the minister for sport, attended by the minister for sport, the mayor of Belgrade, the head of the FA. The TV cameras were there. Most of the VIPs were there for the media attention, you know the types – those care-about-nothing-but-me guys you see in important positions everywhere.

The chairman of the bank spoke. Then the FA chairman, the sports minister, the mayor. After that, I was invited to the mic. I had nothing prepared, so I looked at all the VIPs and thought, *Right.* I started talking about the shelter. I thanked the bank for taking me there and said, 'You have incredible people in your country, people who take care of your least fortunate kids. You must all be very proud to have a place like this shelter in your town.'

Only at the end did I talk about Manchester United. I said that at our football club we take our social responsibility very seriously, that we are in this world to help people, to give people experiences, and visiting the shelter had been one of my most special experiences working for the club. I painted it on. I wanted to pile on pressure for these people to ensure the shelter was supported and survived.

I believe all that, by the way: that Manchester United's purpose is to bring joy and connection to people's lives.

I have told you that I am not one for nostalgia. But on my travels, I am always asked to talk about the same thing, and I never mind. Wherever you are in the world, everybody has their own little story about the last three minutes at the Nou Camp. What they were doing when we were in risk mode, during those incredible 180 seconds when we pulled off our comeback. Many elements of the stories you hear are similar, but there is always a slight variation, some little detail which made the experience unique to the individual. It is magic, hearing all that.

What I do mind is when people get nosy. 'What was X like?' 'Did Y really . . .?' My shutters come down when people want me to open up the dressing room. I will never do it. 'Oh, Eric? Yes, he was a fantastic player,' I will say and leave it at that.

More than anything, I think being a footballer involves acting in a certain way within a close, controlled environment – the playing group, the club – in order to thrive in a pressured situation. Most likely, you will be one person while doing that and a completely different guy away from it. So, who are any of us to start spilling secrets about each other's personalities?

After the kung fu kick on Matthew Simmons, we had Eric not playing for nine months and you can imagine the media interest during that time. 'How is Eric?' 'What did Eric say?' 'What do you feel about what he did?' But how many stories did you ever read along those lines? None. Because that is Manchester United. We don't trash-talk each other, we don't tell anyone else's secrets.

I hope, therefore, that people reading this book realise there are a few things I have not gone into, for those very reasons. Rows, arguments, fights, personal dislikes. What was said by me, the manager and other players at various times. None of these things matter. We lived that pressure situation, we let off our steam, we got on with things. End of story.

Who, in 2021, is Peter Boleslaw Schmeichel? Perhaps the answer begins with Laura. When my first marriage ended in 2013, I went from living the lifestyle – big cars, nice houses – to renting a tiny loft apartment in Copenhagen. It had one bedroom, an upstairs toilet and you opened a cupboard: there was the shower. I remember looking around this crappy little place and saying to myself, 'I don't think I've been so happy in a long time.'

I was ready to take stock, to process and figure out who I really wanted to be, and even if this place had limited square footage, it represented space. Most of all, I was itching to move on into the next part of my life. This little apartment looked okay. None of the other stuff – the trappings – matters. I was never one for cars anyway, and shopping for clothes I was always a disaster. Possessions have never meant much to me.

I met Laura. I got a call, one day, from my friend Thomas who said our pal, Morten, was in town, and did I want to have dinner? Morten was Morten Andersen, known in NFL as the 'Great Dane' – a guy from Denmark who became one of American Football's finest ever placekickers. We met in a restaurant called Pluto and decided not to have wine because its cocktails are legendary. A few of those left us merry and we started talking to a group of girls on another table. They had been on the cocktails too.

One of those girls was hard to forget. We sparked. For a while, every time I was out in town, I bumped into her and that led to us setting up a date. This was Laura. Like me, she had just gone through a divorce, but two of her kids were much younger than mine, still little boys. She was not in the right place for a serious relationship and nor was I, so we kept it fun.

She was gorgeous. When we went out, I quickly realised most of the male population of Copenhagen thought so too. Another thing I liked was she did not have a clue about football or my career. Sport had never been part of her life – her dad had been into academia – and this I liked. She was somebody who judged me on who I was, not as the public figure.

We decided to celebrate New Year together and rented a house on an island called Bornholm, just us and two cases of champagne. We really clicked and agreed to give a proper relationship a go, though taking things slow.

I had been planning to move back to the UK. All my work was there and it is where I have always felt I belonged. I was looking at places in Chiswick and fancied trying the lifestyle in London. But the way it was going with Laura put all these plans on hold.

I moved out of my little apartment into a great place in Nyhavn and then back to the house I have owned for years, in a village half an hour from Copenhagen. The original idea was to renovate it and sell, but I started to enjoy the house again so much and all the fantastic friends I have in the village. Laura loved being there too. After a couple of years, she said, 'I think it's time I moved in.' I have to be honest, I was not sure I was ready for a big commitment, but the problem was I had met the dream woman. If I had to write an advert for my ideal partner, it would end up describing Laura. So, in the end, what did timing matter?

Laura is independent. She has always made her own way in life and works as a teacher in a state school. She gets me. If I need to do something, she gives me space and lets me do it and I do the same for her. Vitus and Gustav, her boys, live with us, while Lola is grown up and has her own place. They are lovely kids.

In life, you learn not to complicate things. This will sound so clichéd, but we like to wake up in the morning at half six and go straight in the ocean and if the weather is nice, have breakfast by the sea. We enjoy our conversations. We go mountain biking together. We read a lot. We like to save up quizzes from the newspaper and have a big session of doing them, for fun.

Do you believe in coincidence? Early in my relationship with Laura, I went with Hanne to a medical appointment for moral support. Her doctor was delayed and we had an hour to wait and I said, 'Listen, I've met this girl and I think you know her.' I said the name, Laura von Lindholm, and Hanne, who had been in a sombre mood, leapt to her feet and started celebrating like she had scored a goal. 'I LOVE her!' she said. One of Hanne's friends from college was Laura's sister Anna.

Then, when Hanne stopped jumping about, she told me the most mind-blowing thing.

It was about our big sister, Kathrine. When Kathrine was fourteen, she became attracted to the idea of free spirit and living in nature. Her best friend was a girl who lived across our landing. They cooked up a plan to go to a tiny island called Anholt for the summer. Anholt is in the Kattegat sea, between Sweden and Denmark, and was famous for its natural beauty. They wanted to be there, peace out and live among the birds and sheep, but my mum said she was too young. There were huge arguments in the house – which I remembered only too well. The next year, when Kathrine was fifteen, it was kind of never in question – she just upped with her friend and went to Anholt.

On the island, which out of season has a population of about 150, they had stayed with a family. The parents were lovely people, Jens and Sissan, and they had three little girls, Sophie . . . and Anna . . . and Laura. Yes, my Laura. Kathrine had babysat her for a summer and for a while stayed in touch with Jens and Sissan, a couple who had given up the rat race to move to Anholt and live the simple life.

Maybe some things are meant to be.

Finding Laura was a lucky break and we all need lucky breaks. You get a lucky goal, a lucky break of the ball. You meet the right person at the right time. But I do not believe luck is the difference in life. I was blessed with a talent that let me live my dream and I have seen my son live his dream, but I would not say I am a 'lucky man'.

Luck throws up casual things, casual results. Consistent outcomes are only achieved by hard work and ambition, by clarity and having a goal. I have been lucky in the sense I have had opportunities – but I have met and played with loads of people who had opportunities and did not take them. Who was it – Gary Player? – that said the more I practise, the luckier I get? I will stay right behind those words. I will second that.

There are a few sayings I always repeat to my kids: *You only get what you put in. The people you meet on the way up are the same you'll meet on the way down.* There is a Danish saying that you find the right shelf. That is what it is. In this life there is a shelf for you and you need to know what it is. Everyone has something distinctive to offer this world. You do not have to become the best in the world at it; you just have to find out what it is.

In the future I want to be better. Be less commanding, give Laura more room, all that stuff. I want to keep developing as a broadcaster, continue educating myself, be there for my kids and for their kids. In football, I believe there is still more to come: that I could offer something substantial in a leadership role, whether that be in a boardroom, running a club's sporting department or even as a manager.

If it never happens, I will have no regrets. Regrets have no value, they don't move anything, don't help in any way. When you look back on your life, you have to accept that the decisions you made were made using the knowledge you had at that time. Faced by the same situation thirty years later, you might well make a different call, but that is because you have different knowledge, more knowledge, and you have grown.

Although this book has involved reliving my yesterdays, today and tomorrow are what count for me. Laura and I had a misunderstanding recently. We are thinking of moving to a smaller house and were talking about what it might look like. She said, 'You want a museum in your house, don't you, space for all your memorabilia to go on the walls.' I said, 'NO!' What I had told her, in a conversation once, was the exact opposite. 'I *don't* want to live in a museum,' and she had misheard.

What I want is all my stuff to remain where it has been for the last fifteen years: in the museum at Old Trafford. Not at home. I don't want to be reminded every day of who I *was*. Every day I wake up, I want to remember who I *am*.

What is my legacy? Difficult one. I would like to be remembered as one of the best ever to play in goal. I would like to be remembered for having given football something that it didn't have at the time when I played. I would like to be remembered as someone who took my sport seriously and worked hard. And I would like to be remembered as someone who wanted to win. I think that is projected in certain circles as something shameful, wanting to win. But I would like to be remembered as someone greedy, who wanted to win everything.

I played for a manager, maybe the greatest of managers, who was totally wired that way. With team-mates exactly the same. And in Manchester United terms, I would like to be remembered as not just a winner but a survivor: only me, Denis Irwin and Ryan Giggs were part of the teams that won the Premier League in 1992–93 and the Champions League in '99. To stay the course for that whole period, to remain of value under the most demanding boss at a time when our club and football itself evolved so rapidly, is something of which to be proud.

And I would like to be remembered by people who knew me and cared about me, for them to have thought I was okay. That is more important than anything, I do not need to be remembered as any more than that.

So . . . my legacy? That I was one of the best. That I meant something to football. Without being arrogant – I know I did. I travel the world and know I made a difference to the game and that makes me happy. If I mattered to football and mattered to the people in my life, that is all I could want. Deep down that is all that people really want. To matter. Just to matter.

Did I answer the *why*? I don't know. There are many things in this book that I have never stopped to relive before. Now I have done so, I will probably put them aside. And get on with the future. For although you understand by looking backwards, you have to move forwards.

And there is something else that Kierkegaard said: life is a mystery to be lived, not a problem to be solved.

Epilogue
ONE GOOD ENDING

On the golf course, I am a buggy man these days. I avoid running too. For fitness I will go for a ride by the water and in the forest on my mountain bike, or work with my personal trainer. I have mentioned my injuries and the toll that a long professional football career takes on anyone's body. Today, I get pain in my spine, shoulders and sometimes fingers and knee. You live with it. It's part of it.

On 26 May 2019, exactly twenty years after the Nou Camp, I played football one last time. The game was to mark two decades since winning the Treble and raise money for good causes. It was Manchester United Legends v Bayern Munich Legends at Old Trafford. Fergie, twelve months on from suffering a brain haemorrhage, was strong enough to be manager on the day, but it was left to Bryan Robson to organise the team.

So, Robbo called me. 'PEEETE,' he said, in that basso voice. 'Do you want to play?' I said I would love to, but just did not know if I could. It had been a few years since I had strapped on the gloves and I very much doubted my body would be up to a game. 'Just come and lead the teams out, then go off after ten seconds,' said Robbo, persuasively.

That was the plan. Andy Cole and I would make the ceremonial pretence of walking out in our kits and starting the match but be substituted immediately. Coley, following a kidney transplant, cannot play any more and is someone who has not quite had the recognition he deserves in terms of what he did for Manchester United and what a superb player he was. He deserved his own moment and, after mulling things over, I spoke to Robbo again. 'Let Coley come off first and enjoy his ovation. I'll stay on for a few minutes longer.'

It was a really good day. Our XI was almost exactly the same as started the Champions League final. The one difference was that Paul Scholes took the place of Giggsy, who was away managing Wales. In the dressing room, the joking stopped when the gaffer began his team talk. He was still frail, conducting the whole talk sitting down, but my God when he spoke . . .

He began talking about how we had worked so hard to enjoy the careers we did, how lucky we were to have had the opportunity to be footballers, how much we should value the occasion and being remembered fondly at a club like Manchester United. And he built it up and built it up into suddenly telling us we *needed* to win this game. At the beginning, you were kind of like 'mmm', but by the end the hairs were standing up on your arms. We all found ourselves clapping our hands and rolling our shoulders. Saying, 'YEAH, LET'S WIN!'

It was so brilliant. I loved listening to the gaffer one last time. It made you tingle. It was a reminder of how exceptional a motivator he was. Also, that even though I don't like living in the past, maybe it is okay to relive the odd moment now and then. So, I went through my normal routine. I went out to warm up before everyone else. I tried to take things slow but found myself diving after a few practice shots. So stupid. But I felt all right. I said to Robbo, 'Okay, maybe more than a few minutes – let's see.'

Bayern had a few 'young' players. Guys who played long after '99, like Zé Roberto. He was a spring chicken: only forty-five! These guys still looked fit and pretty handy, and as we kicked off, I was thinking, 'Don't let them shoot.' But then we went into their box, the passing and movement good, boom, boom, boom, and Ole – on as a substitute, of course – scored, and I was in the groove.

I made two saves, collected a couple of crosses, had a couple of throw-outs. I thought to myself, *This is good.* I looked at the electric stadium clock. Fifteen minutes. *Okay. Respectable.* I played, I looked again. Twenty minutes. *Let's go!* Twenty-five minutes. *Brilliant.* At thirty minutes, from the dugout, Robbo and the rest started shouting at me to come off. 'Pete! Come on. You okay, Pete?'

I ignored them. But then, with thirty-two minutes gone, my back just went stiff. Seized up. Yet I was still thinking, *Can I get to half-time?* By thirty-five minutes, however, I was in sheer agony. It was too bad. I signalled to Robbo and off I went.

Thirty-five minutes! I am so happy. I went into that game not thinking I could play a single second, yet got more than half an hour again, at Old Trafford, in front of 61,000 United fans, with the gaffer's words in my ear, with Denis, Jaap, Ronny, Gary, Scholesy, Butty, Jesper, Becks, Coley, Ole, Yorkey, Teddy – one more time. It was the first time Laura had ever seen me play; her kids too. There was an event afterwards for the players at which we had an amazing time. We saw each other's friends and families again, we laughed with each other. It felt like something we should have done more of and something I hope we will do more of in the years to come.

Yes, reunions are not always my thing, but there is a balance to be struck.

And one of the messages I would want to give people is that if you have something to celebrate, celebrate it. Because life doesn't offer you much in that respect.

I kept a clean sheet, by the way. When I came off, the score was Manchester United 2 Bayern Munich 0. Zé Roberto and all the 'young' pups did not get past me. A clean sheet. That was nice. But it won't be happening again. That was my last game, and when I say last game, I mean *last* game. Absolutely no way will you ever see me on the pitch again. Another legends match? That would be madness.

How do I feel about that? You know, I don't feel too sad. It is weird, but I have to be honest: since I retired, I have never really had the urge to be on the field. I lost my enthusiasm for playing, I just don't miss it. In the eighteen years since my last game as a professional, there was only one time when I felt a pang.

I was at the Cliff, there to do a session for one of my coaching badges with Neil Bailey, and Neil was late. While I was waiting for him, I took a walk on the pitch.

The grass was soft, the air was fresh and I felt a sudden, incredible urge: to have a training session. And I have never had it since.

ACKNOWLEDGEMENTS

One is the child of one hundred: 100 hours of conversations with Jonathan Northcroft about my life and career, which began at the end of March 2020. The book became our lockdown project. It brought enjoyment and shape to those very strange weeks when life as the world had known it stopped in the first wave of the coronavirus pandemic. Jonathan and I spoke almost daily during that period: me from my house in Denmark and he from his home in Leicester. So the first person to thank, I guess, is the guy who invented Zoom.

From those many chats, we were able to shape the outline of this book and we continued to flesh it out and refine the story over the ensuing twelve months. Jonathan's patience, empathy, research skills and quality writing made him the ideal collaborator. I remember being at a Pink concert when she introduced the director of music and said, 'He makes all this **** sound good.' As I said to Jonathan – 'that's you.'

Thanks, Jonathan, not only for *One*, but for two decades of great friendship and working relationship. Thanks to Roddy Bloomfield, for his masterful editing, assisted by Tim Waller, Phil Shaw and Morgan Springett. Thank you to Jamie Hodder-Williams, for believing in this project so passionately, and to Kim Hundevadt and his team at JP/Politikens Forlag, for their work on the Danish version of my story.

To Melissa Chappell – none of this would have been possible without you. With your energy, wisdom, sharp humour and patience you keep me pointing in the right direction and organised. Thanks for that and for pushing me to stop talking about this book and finally write it. I've had some pretty good managers in my time, and Mel is one. Thank you also to Ross Connolly, Kerr MacRae, Cliff Butler, Walter Di Gregorio and Andreas Houmann – for the time you spent, help you offered and parts you played in getting *One* to this stage.

I am indebted to Eric Cantona, for nearly thirty years of friendship, for helping us all realise our dreams on the pitch at Manchester United – and for so generously taking time out from the many passions and activities in his life to write an inimitable Foreword. Thank you to my mother, for having to undergo my interrogations and my insistence on ripping up the past, if I can put it that way. And, of course, to Kasper and Cecilie.

Finally, to Laura: thank you. Thank you for your patience and your proofreading, for your advice, for listening and – for everything.

PICTURE ACKNOWLEDGEMENTS

The author and publisher would like to thank the following for permission to reproduce photographs:

Section One: Ben Radford/Getty Images; PA Images/Alamy Stock Photo; Paul Popper/Popperfoto via Getty Images/Getty Images; Colorsport/Shutterstock; Jim Hutchison/ANL/Shutterstock; Shaun Botterill/Allsport/Getty Images; Andy Hooper/Daily Mail/Shutterstock; Lee Thompson/Shutterstock; Action Images/John Sibley/ Reuters; Pierre Minier/Onze/Icon Sport/Getty Images; Colorsport/Shutterstock; Phil Cole/Allsport/Getty Images; Colorsport/Shutterstock; John Peters/Manchester United via Getty Images.

Section Two: Juha Tamminen; Colorsport/Shutterstock; Juha Tamminen; Colorsport/Shutterstock; Mark Thompson/Allsport/Getty Images; Marcus Brandt/Bongarts/Getty Images; Allsport UK/Getty Images; Enrique Shore/Reuters; Alex Livesey/ALLSPORT/Getty images; Action Images/Michael Regan/Reuters; Action Images/Andrew Budd/Reuters; PA Images/Alamy Stock Photo; Colorsport/Shutterstock; Julian Finney/Getty Images; Simon Stacpoole/Offside/Getty Images; Magi Haroun/Shutterstock; Matthew Childs/Pool/AFP via Getty Images.

All other photographs are from private collections.

INDEX